FOR *L*OVE & MONEY

FOR *Love* & MONEY

HOW TO SHARE THE SAME CHECKBOOK AND STILL LOVE EACH OTHER

BERNARD E. PODUSKA

DESERET BOOK COMPANY
SALT LAKE CITY, UTAH

Library of Congress Cataloging-in-Publication Data

Poduska, Bernard.
    For love and money : how to share the same checkbook and
still love each other / Bernard E. Poduska.
        p.   cm.
    Includes bibliographical references (p.) and index.
    ISBN 0-87579-969-8 (pbk.)
    1. Mormons—Finance, Personal. 2. Church of Jesus Christ of
Latter-day Saints.   I. Title.
    HG179.P555423   1995
    332.024'0283—dc20   95-21449
                                                            CIP

Printed in the United States of America

10   9   8   7   6   5   4   3   2   1

To all those whose work
is tangible evidence
of their love for others

Contents

Preface

The saying "Married for better or worse, or until *debt* do us part" seems to reflect today's marital realities more accurately than does the traditional vow. And for Latter-day Saint couples, the phrase "Married for time and eternity, or until *debt* do us part" has even greater implications. One of the most familiar puzzles facing LDS couples and individuals alike is how to successfully combine their *finances, interpersonal relationships,* and *spirituality.*

Traditionally, couples have viewed finances separately from relationships and have managed them with pencils, checkbooks, and calculators. But "number crunching" can tell you only where the money has gone; it cannot tell you why. For instance, the numbers may tell you that you went in the hole $200 last month; they don't tell you that you spent the extra $200 because you were depressed. Numbers can't tell you that you are heading for bankruptcy because your spouse is trying to get revenge, or because you feel inadequate and are trying to keep up with the spending patterns of the nonmember "Joneses," or because you feel guilty about the divorce and don't want the kids to suffer.

Likewise, the most practical computer-generated budget in the world won't last a month if the person who created it failed to consider the needs and feelings of those who are asked to live with it. Frustrations are voiced in such statements as "Was I supposed to go barefoot the rest of the month? I needed a new pair of shoes, and I was tired of doing without just so you can balance your budget," or "It's my money. I worked hard for it, and I've got the right to spend it any way I please."

Clearly finances and relationships are interrelated, and only by looking at these two factors from a spiritual perspective can a family establish a successful financial management program. To help families meet this challenge, this book—organized into three parts—explores financial principles, personality characteristics, and gospel tenets.

Part One looks at the way various elements, such as families of origin and personality characteristics, affect the way you view spiritual issues and manage your finances and your relationships. Part Two teaches you how to cope effectively with issues, such as debt management and goal setting, that influence your financial past, present, and future. Part Three will help you integrate information from Part One and Part Two in dealing with specific family types and stages in life.

Ten principles depicting the connection between finances, relationships, and spirituality show how these three factors make a difference in the quality of your life. For example, with the understanding that *most financial problems are not money problems but behavior problems,* you will be able to (1) see better why finances play such a crucial role in almost all relationships, (2) reduce or eliminate many financial management problems, and (3) establish a functional financial management program that provides for your own temporal and spiritual needs and for those of your loved ones.

A guide to finances and relationships must not only provide sound principles but also show how these principles can be applied. Numerous exercises, case illustrations, examples, and worksheets throughout the book provide practical means of applying principles to everyday situations.

Most people are quite capable of putting their lives in order if they prayerfully approach the Lord for guidance, gain enough insight into what's causing their problems, and are given the skills to make the necessary changes. This book is written for ward members and bishops as well as a variety of Church leaders, such as Relief Society presidents, elders quorum presidencies, and high priests group leaders. It will be helpful for those just starting out in marriage, or for those who have been struggling due to long-time problems with personal finances. But most of all, this book is designed to help those who want to manage their finances more effectively while enhancing the quality of their personal and spiritual relationships.

PART 1

Finances, Relationships, and Spirituality

Most families have difficulty managing finances because they focus on *numbers* rather than on *people*. Budgets are seen as a means of accumulating *things* rather than as a means of experiencing *feelings*, enhancing *relationships*, and encouraging *spiritual growth*. Regarding the relationship between temporal and spiritual things, Brigham Young admonished:

> All who would understand the things of God must understand them by the spirit of God. We cannot talk about the spiritual things without connecting them with temporal things, neither can we talk about temporal things without connecting spiritual things with them. Whether we are raising cattle, planting, gathering, building, or inhabiting, we are in the Lord, and all we do is within the pale of his kingdom upon the earth, consequently it is all spiritual and all temporal, no matter what we are laboring to accomplish.[1]

Finances, relationships, and spirituality are *all* essential elements in a successful financial program. Realizing this, and giving each element equal consideration, are the first steps toward creating a family financial management plan that focuses on people as well as on numbers.

Note

1. Young, 1864, p. 329.

CHAPTER 1

Financial Principles and Values

*M*ost people involved with marriage counseling, such as family therapists, social workers, and bishops, are well aware of the interplay between a couple's finances and satisfaction with their personal and family life.[1] For Latter-day Saints especially, a third component—the spiritual aspect of marriage—comes into play. As President Joseph F. Smith stated, "You must continue to bear in mind that the temporal and the spiritual are blended. They are not separate. One cannot be carried on without the other, so long as we are here in mortality."[2]

Yet it appears that most couples are ill prepared to cope effectively with both the temporal *and* the spiritual/emotional stresses of marriage. Arguments in marriage center more often on financial problems than on just about any other area of contention.[3] In four surveys examining some of the causes of marital conflict, finances were consistently ranked as either the first or second most frequent cause.[4] In a survey of couples married for only six months, handling money ranked second among fourteen areas of disagreement.[5] Financial problems are among the top four reasons leading to divorce in first marriages and the biggest problem in remarriages.[6] One study indicated that 89 percent of all divorces can be linked to quarrels and accusations over money.[7]

Recent social transitions have added a new dimension to the challenge. Changes in society's attitudes regarding married women in the work force, and the subsequent advent of dual-income families, have changed the family's financial organization and functions, and greatly affected man/woman relationships.

During the 1950s only 25 percent of American mothers were working outside of the home. Now, almost 69 percent of mothers with children of school age are in the paid labor force and, of these, 76 percent are working full-time.[8] (In 1994, approximately 60 percent of all adult women were in the paid labor force. This figure increases to almost 75 percent among women between 25 and 54 years of age.)[9]

One consequence of this transition in social values is that women are no longer as dependent on men for their financial well-being as in the past. Work availability for women has not only increased the degree of independence experienced within marriage, but has also increased the freedom to decide not to be married.

So, because the women of today's world are quite capable of supporting themselves, the *financial* reasons for getting or staying married have altered. In addition, *social* reasons for getting married have also changed. A woman's status in the community is no longer dependent on her husband's success, and her identity, as well as her credit ratings, can be distinct from and independent of her husband's.[10]

President Joseph F. Smith voiced his concern about the trend toward viewing marriage as a civil rather than a spiritual matter:

> Today a flood of iniquity is overwhelming the civilized world. One great reason therefor is the neglect of marriage; it has lost its sanctity in the eyes of the great majority. It is at best a civil contract, but more often an accident or a whim, or a means of gratifying the passions. And when the sacredness of the covenant is ignored or lost sight of, then a disregard of the marriage vows, under the present moral training of the masses, is a mere triviality, a trifling indiscretion.[11]

As Latter-day Saints, we realize that financial and social reasons for marriage are transcended by *spiritual* reasons. The Lord has ordained marriage for the spiritual progression of the marital partners and the ultimate fulfillment of his plan of salvation—glorious reasons which will remain unchanged.

> In the celestial glory there are three heavens or degrees; And in order to obtain the highest, a man must enter into this order of the priesthood [meaning the new and everlasting covenant of marriage]; And if he does not, he cannot obtain it. He may enter into the other, but that is the end of his kingdom; he cannot have an increase. (D&C 131:1–4.)

Even though families in the Church recognize the sanctity of home and marriage, because of circumstances in the world around us an ever-increasing number of LDS women are joining others in the work force. For many, this has created stress in relationships due to a number of factors: conflicts with traditional roles; internal pressure to be the "perfect" wife, mother, and employee; and the dilemma between wanting to comply with President Ezra Taft Benson's admonition for women to return to their homes and the need to find personal fulfillment and to help provide for the family.

As the complexity of familial relationships increases (due to divorce, becoming the single head of a household, remarriage, dual incomes, etc.), in the Church as well as in the world, the complexity of interactions between money, relationships, and spirituality also increases.[12]

Latter-day Saint couples today, if they are to preserve their marriages, must be able to effectively blend these three essential elements. They must not only be able to meet their financial and relationship responsibilities; they must also be able to prayerfully consider ways of resolving misunderstandings and disagreements over marital roles and religious expectations. This interaction is illustrated by Figure 1.1.

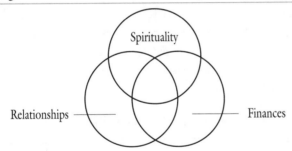

Figure 1.1. *The interaction between finances, relationships, and spirituality.*

Three Essential Elements

Finding satisfaction in the way finances, relationships, and spirituality work together in your partnership depends a great deal on how your expectations about each component match your actual circumstances.

Finances

How much income you expect each partner to provide and how each of you expects the income to be spent is the basis for all ensuing discussions about financial matters. And while dollar amounts alone look good on paper, a mutually satisfying financial management plan must also consider the feelings associated with the dollar amounts.

We seldom spend money just to obtain things. Rather, we spend to experience the feelings associated with the things. Therefore, merely having more money does not necessarily guarantee having more happiness. It is how effectively we *exchange* the money we have that determines whether or not we are happy. Regardless of how much money we have to spend on a car, for example, if the car turns out to be a "lemon," we are not going to feel very happy. Brigham Young pointed out:

> There is no happiness in gold, not in the least. It is very convenient as an article of exchange, in purchasing what we need; and instead of finding comfort and happiness in gold, you exchange it to obtain happiness, or that which may conduce to it. There is no real wealth in gold. People talk about being wealthy—about being rich; but place the richest banking company in the world upon a barren rock, with their gold piled around them, with no possible chance of exchanging it, and destitute of the creature comforts, and they would be poor indeed. Where then is their joy, their comfort, their great wealth? They have none.[13]

Most money is exchanged in an attempt to experience happiness, love, security, power, pride, and so on. Feelings are the emotional overtones associated with a thought, event, or item, and are more related to what something represents *to you* than with how it might be defined in a dictionary. For instance, the dollar amount you owe to a relative may be smaller than many of your other bills, but the feelings associated with *that* particular debt may make you disregard the practicality of paying off the larger, higher interest loans before paying off your relative.

While the actual cost of a single rose may not be high, what the rose represents and the feelings associated with it can be priceless. And if a purchase creates distance and feelings of resentment in the relationship, you may derive little happiness from the purchase. ("No," your spouse says, "I do not want to see your hang glider. Nor do I want to watch you hang glide, or talk to your friends about hang gliding, or have anything else to do with hang gliding. That money was supposed to be used for a family vacation this summer, not to satisfy your need to fly with condors.")

As an equal partner in a relationship that involves finances, you have the right to expect your feelings to be considered in the decision-making process. The final decision may not always be the one you hoped for, but if you believe that your feelings were taken into consideration, you can more easily support the decision, and the relationship is more easily preserved.

Relationships

These words of Brigham Young remind us of the importance of our marital stewardships:

> Let every man in the land over eighteen years of age take a wife, and then go to work with your hands and cultivate the earth, or labor at some mechanical business, or some honest trade to provide an honest living for yourselves and those who depend upon you for their subsistence; then would the woman be cared for, be nourished, honored and blest, becoming honorable mothers of a race of men and women farther advanced in physical and mental perfection than their fathers. This would create a revolution in our country, and would produce results that would be of incalculable good.[14]

Your relationships reflect (1) the degree of commitment you have to another, (2) the degree of understanding you have about another's needs, (3) the amount of flexibility you are willing to exercise to satisfy those needs, and (4) the relative importance, or priority, the welfare of another person has in your life. In a meaningful relationship, you have the obligation to dedicate yourself to these responsibilities and the right to expect the highest level of reciprocity and devotion from your partner.

Spirituality

The spiritual connection with finances can be found throughout the scriptures, such as in the parable of the talents (Matthew 25:14–30); the rich man asked by Jesus to "sell whatsoever thou hast, and give to the poor, and thou shalt have treasure in heaven: and come, take up thy cross, and follow me" (Mark 10:21); and the law of tithing, in which we are asked, "Will a man rob God? Yet ye have robbed me. But ye say, Wherein have we robbed thee? In tithes and offerings" (Malachi 3:8).

Similarly, the spiritual aspects of relationships can also be supported by scriptures: "What

therefore God hath joined together, let not man put asunder" (Matthew 19:6); "Husbands, love
your wives, even as Christ also loved the church, and gave himself for it" (Ephesians 5:25).
Temple marriages provide a sacred opportunity to develop such Christlike love by faithfully keeping the covenants and stewardships we assume when we marry for time and eternity.

To illustrate the importance of the stewardship responsibilities associated with a temple marriage, imagine being in the celestial room of a temple and having Jesus Christ not only spiritually
but physically present in the room with you. Imagine watching him place his arm around the shoulders of your bride-to-be and escorting her over to where you are standing. He then looks at you
and says, "This is my beloved sister, [he calls her by name]. I want you to love her as I have." Now
imagine the Savior taking your hand and placing it in hers. Turning to her, he says, "This is my
beloved brother, [he calls you by name]. I want you to love him as I have." Then, before departing,
he places his arms around both of you and says, "Love one another, as I have loved you."

Accountability for such a stewardship rests heavily on the shoulders of the priesthood holder.
Priesthood implies both accountability and service. In June 1965, President David O. McKay,
while conversing with priesthood holders, admonished:

> Let me assure you, Brethren, that some day you will have a personal Priesthood
> Interview with the Savior, Himself. If you are interested, I will tell you the order in which
> He will ask you to account for your earthly responsibilities.
>
> First, He will request an accountability report about *your relationship with your wife*.
> Have you actively been engaged in *making her happy* and ensuring that *her needs* have been
> met as an individual?
>
> Second, He will want an accountability report about *each of your children* individually. . . .
>
> Third, He will want to know what you personally have done with the *talents* you were
> given in the pre-existence.
>
> Fourth, He will want a *summary of your activity in your Church assignment*. . . .
>
> Fifth, He will have *no* interest in how you earned your living, but if you were honest in
> all your dealings.
>
> Sixth, He will ask for an accountability on what you have done to contribute in a pos-
> itive manner to your community.[15]

As can be seen from President David O. McKay's statement, our relationships are our most
important stewardships. And a crucial interdependence exists between the financial, relationship,

and spiritual aspects of our lives. This interdependency is confirmed in countless everyday incidents that alternate between caring thoughtfulness and misunderstandings, between give-and-take and hurt feelings. It shows up in situations as complex as getting remarried or as simple as buying Christmas gifts ("How come you spent only $23 on *my* mother's gift and over $120 on *your* mother's gift?"), paying bills ("Didn't we agree to use the credit cards only for emergencies? Then what's this Visa bill for $89.43?"), maintaining a car ("You can take the bus, ride a bicycle, or even walk for all I care, but I'm not going to put another penny into that car of yours. Didn't I tell you not to buy it in the first place? When will you start listening to me?"), or meeting our spiritual obligations ("I know things are awfully tight this month, but I also know that if we pay our tithing, we'll be blessed and things will work out.").

Our stewardships in this life include (1) temporal resources, (2) interactions with other children of God, and (3) our own particular earthly missions and eternal progression. Recognizing the way each of these stewardships influences the others—and learning to use that influence in the best possible way—is fundamental to establishing an effective financial management plan.

Ten Financial Principles

To help you develop a financial management plan that will work for you, here are ten principles that provide a broad guide to financial thinking and behavior. By giving these principles thoughtful consideration, you may gain some insight into why you have managed to remain relatively free of financial difficulties or why you have been plagued with them.

Many financial principles can be understood only through years of study and experience, yet some are founded on simple common sense and are easy to understand. These can be expressed in the form of *maxims*—short, popular sayings that embody some familiar truth or useful thought; for example, "You should risk no more than you can afford to lose." Founded on practical life experiences, maxims serve as rules of conduct; the following ten can stimulate thinking about basic financial management decisions.

Principle 1: Financial problems are usually behavior problems rather than money problems.

> For the kingdom of heaven is as a man travelling into a far country, who called his own
> servants, and delivered unto them his goods. And unto one he gave five talents, to another

two, and to another one; to every man according to his several ability; and straightway took his journey. Then he that had received the five talents went and traded with the same, and made them other five talents. And likewise he that had received two, he gained other two. But he that had received one went and digged in the earth, and hid his lord's money. (Matthew 25:14–18.)

Many people believe that they *deserve* a particular standard of living just because they are "being good" and living the commandments, and that any additional efforts on their part should not be necessary. They believe that if they could just make more money, they wouldn't have any financial problems. But in most cases, making more money just adds zeroes to old deficits—instead of owing $1,000, you owe $10,000 or $100,000. Family A, for example, earns $40,000 a year but spends $45,000. Family B also earns $40,000 a year but spends only $35,000. Family A is going into debt at the rate of $5,000 a year, while family B is relatively rich with $5,000 a year to save. The difference between the families may be due to the fact that Family A is a beginning family trying to accumulate needed assets (washer and dryer, furniture, and so on), while Family B is more established and has already acquired many of the basic items considered to be indispensable. However, when two families are essentially equal, then such differences in their financial status are due to behavior.

Similarly, it is not enough to merely calculate how much you owe to determine what steps you must take to rectify your current financial difficulties; you must also examine the kinds of behavior that created your debt problems.

CASE ILLUSTRATION

Manuel and Marta earned $29,000 last year and owe $12,000. Stan and Kristi also earned $29,000 last year and also owe $12,000. Although these two couples appear to be quite similar, there are major differences in the behaviors that led to their indebtedness. Manuel and Marta's debt was the result of a medical emergency and a lack of adequate insurance. Stan and Kristi's debt, however, was the result of Stan's impulsive purchase of a powerboat that caught his interest at a sports show. Marta is now worried about Manuel working a second job to pay off the hospital bill; and Kristi is worried about having to sell one of their cars to pay off the boat contract that was sold to the Sink or Swim Loan Company.

Principle 2: *If you continue doing what you have been doing, you will continue getting what you have been getting.*

> For whatsoever a man soweth, that shall he also reap. (Galatians 6:7.)

If you continue to spend instead of save, you will continue to live from paycheck to paycheck. If you continue to borrow money to get out of debt, you will continue to go deeper into debt. If you continue to use your credit cards impulsively, you will continue to pay high interest rates.

CASE ILLUSTRATION

Mr. Anderson explained to his wife how fortunate they were that the new credit card had arrived in the mail. "Look, we can use the $2,000 cash advance on the credit card we received in the mail today to make the back payments on the mortgage. Then we can refinance the car to make the payments on our other credit cards—they're all at their limits, you know. Then we would only have the consolidated loan payments to worry about, and I think I'll be able to borrow enough from your parents to make that payment." Unfortunately, this thinking pattern is fairly typical of the way today's families are trying to manage their finances.

Principle 3: *Nothing (no thing) is worth risking the relationship for.*

> For we brought nothing into this world, and it is certain we can carry nothing out. And having food and raiment let us be therewith content. But they that will be rich fall into temptation and a snare, and into many foolish and hurtful lusts, which drown men in destruction and perdition. For the love of money is the root of all evil: which while some coveted after, they have erred from the faith, and pierced themselves through with many sorrows. But thou, O man of God, flee these things; and follow after righteousness, godliness, faith, love, patience, meekness. (1 Timothy 6:7–11.)

One definition of a prenuptial agreement is "a contract between two people who love things more than they love each other." This is not to say that no thought should be given to financial considerations before marriage; but we can hope these considerations are motivated more by a concern with practical financial management than by a lack of trust.

The word *trust,* which originates in the Scandinavian language, means the ability to be comfortable while being vulnerable; it is an essential element in any successful financial or interpersonal relationship. When couples feel a lack of trust, they may feel safer becoming emotionally involved with things than with people. But one of the quickest ways to destroy a marriage, or any other relationship, is to allow a *love of things* to become a higher priority than a *love of each other.* In the beginning of a relationship, being in each other's presence seems to be enough—hearing each other's voice, talking for hours at a time. Unfortunately, as time passes, being together no longer seems to be enough, and complaints and accusations begin to creep into the communication patterns: "I can't live like this any more. How can you expect us to get anywhere on what you bring home?" or "I'm tired of skimping. I deserve to get something that I want once in a while. We always seem to have enough money for the things *you* want, but never for the things *I* want." If this becomes the case, you may very well get the *things* you want, but far too often the acquisition comes at the cost of the relationship.

CASE ILLUSTRATION

A young couple complained to a marriage counselor of not being able to feel close to each other. They felt more like roommates than spouses. As the counselor began to explore their marital relationship, the couple revealed that even after three years of marriage, the wife still had *her* car in *her* name, and the husband still had *his* secret savings account in *his* name. When asked why they had handled their resources this way, the wife answered, "I wasn't sure the marriage would work out, and if it didn't, I didn't want to risk losing my car." The husband was afraid of losing his savings. Unfortunately, although they were safeguarding their possessions, they were losing their love for each other.

Principle 4: Money spent on things you value usually leads to a feeling of satisfaction and accomplishment. Money spent on things you don't value usually leads to a feeling of frustration and futility.

No man can serve two masters: for either he will hate the one, and love the other; or else he will hold to the one, and despise the other. Ye cannot serve God and mammon. . . . Therefore take no thought, saying, What shall we eat? or, What shall we drink? or, Wherewithal shall we be clothed? (For after all these things do the Gentiles seek:) for your heavenly Father knoweth that ye have need of all these things. But seek ye first the kingdom of God, and his righteousness; and all these things shall be added unto you. (Matthew 6:24, 31–33.)

If you know what your values are, you will tend to focus your resources on goals that reflect those values. If you are still not sure what is important to you, you will tend to scatter your resources on a variety of targets, hoping that at least some will pay off.

CASE ILLUSTRATION

The Tanakas sat on the lawn watching their two young children play on the new jungle-gym swing set. They had just finished putting it together, and the children were laughing and shouting gleefully as they tried out each part of their new equipment. Compared to the size of the Tanakas' income, the gym set had cost a lot of money, but watching the children have so much fun made it well worth the price.

The Pavlovics both loved music. Both had grown up in musically inclined families. It was the one thing they had in common. However, they had not gone to a live symphony in over a year. They just could not afford such "luxuries." Their car payments alone were burying them. They blamed social pressure for encouraging them to buy the car in the first place. Before moving into an expensive neighborhood, neither of them had been very interested in cars—taking the bus had been just fine. At least they had been able to ride it to the symphony.

Principle 5: We know the price of everything and the value of nothing.

> Lay not up for yourselves treasures upon earth, where moth and rust doth corrupt, and where thieves break through and steal: But lay up for yourselves treasures in heaven, where neither moth nor rust doth corrupt, and where thieves do not break through nor steal: For where your treasure is, there will your heart be also. (Matthew 6:19–21.)

Unfortunately, the maxim expressed in Principle 5 seems to be all too true about today's world. If it is true of you, you may find it difficult to set your priorities, focus your energy, and define your purpose. Because of social pressures and advertising, you may end up buying what you think you *should* want rather than what you *really* want.

Besides, you couldn't afford what you really want anyway. Could you? Perhaps you remember discussing paying for something important, and had to conclude that you couldn't afford it.

And why not? Because the money had already been spent on something else. For example, as a couple, you'd like to serve a mission together. It would cost about $9,000, and after evaluating you realize you don't have that kind of money. With the payments on the new car, the room addition, recarpeting, and the satellite dish that goes with the new home entertainment center, you just can't afford a mission. Of course, if the money had not been allocated to all of those other things, you probably could have afforded it. You had enough money—it just happened to be committed to other things.

One of the more common side effects of not being able to afford one thing is that you then substitute something else that may not mean as much to you. For example, if a trip to the Caribbean is not affordable at $4,500, you may substitute a trip to Disneyland at $1,500. You may find the next year that again you can't afford the Caribbean trip, so you go to Disneyland once more. In fact, you end up going to Disneyland three years in a row at $1,500 a trip, because you thought you couldn't afford your first choice. Instead, three times you went on a trip that was your second choice—which happened to cost you $4,500 in the end. Are you spending your money on what you *really* want, or are you substituting?

If you believe that substitution is playing too big a part in your life, then the following principle is worth posting on your refrigerator, writing on the cover of your checkbook, or taping to your credit cards.

Principle 6: You can never get enough of what you don't need, because what you don't need can never satisfy you.

> Wherefore, do not spend money for that which is of no worth, nor your labor for that which cannot satisfy. Hearken diligently unto me, and remember the words which I have spoken; and come unto the Holy One of Israel, and feast upon that which perisheth not, neither can be corrupted, and let your soul delight in fatness. (2 Nephi 9:51.)

This principle, of course, applies to many areas of our lives. For example, if you need *respect,* but try to satisfy this need with power, then no matter how much power you get, it will not satisfy you. If you need a feeling of *self-confidence* and you try to attain that feeling through the use of drugs or alcohol, you will never be able to get enough of the artificial substance. If you need *love* but you try to satisfy this need with sex, then no amount of sex will ever satisfy you.

Nor will you ever be able to get enough money to be able to satisfy your need for love. If what you need is to be able to spend more *time* with someone, then no matter how many gifts that person gives you, the gifts will never satisfy your need to share memorable moments. What you don't need will never satisfy you.

CASE ILLUSTRATION

Carol and Phil are both successful in their careers. Unfortunately, their jobs demand long hours and frequent travel. They have two children: Kimberly, age seven, and Michael, age five. Kimberly is watching her mom hurriedly pack a suitcase. "Are you going to be gone very long this time?" she asks softly.

Preoccupied, Carol replies, "Unless something unexpected comes up, this should be a quick one. Two, maybe three days."

Kimberly's lower lip seems to stick out a little farther as she continues to watch the packing. Finally she asks rather nonchalantly, "Then you won't be here to watch me dance, will you?"

Carol looks up quickly from her packing and, with a pained expression on her face, responds to Kimberly's statement. "That's Friday night, isn't it? And Mommy's not going to be able to be there. I'm really sorry, Kimberly, but there's just nothing Mommy can do to get out of this trip. But I promise you—cross my heart—I'll be there the next time you dance. Okay?"

Kimberly looks down at the floor and mumbles, "That's okay. I understand."

Not completely convinced that Kimberly accepts the situation, Carol adds, "How about if I buy you something really special while I'm gone? And I mean something *really* special. Something that will surprise even you. How would that be?"

Kimberly shrugs her shoulders and sighs, "I suppose it'd be all right."

After reading this case, you may want to ask yourself if your needs and the needs of those you love are really being met. If what you need is a feeling of *intimacy* and you and your spouse share confidential information and time with just each other, then you may very well feel satisfied. If you are giving your time and attention to your family members, they may feel happier than if you were to give them all the gifts in the world.

Principle 7: *Financial freedom is more often the result of decreased spending than of increased income.*

> There is treasure to be desired and oil in the dwelling of the wise; but a foolish man spendeth it up. (Proverbs 21:20.)

Having financial freedom is not the same as being financially independent. Financial independence implies having accumulated enough wealth to sustain a high standard of living without further effort on your part; financial freedom implies having enough discretionary income to enable you to select a number of alternatives on which to spend your money rather than having to face financial ultimatums. With financial freedom, you can choose to go to the movies *and* go out to dinner, or to pay off both the Visa *and* the MasterCard, rather than choosing whether to heat *or* eat this month.

Just as it is more difficult to *earn* your way out of debt, it is more difficult to try to *earn* your way to financial freedom. Cutting back on expenses, choosing the less expensive alternative when possible, and using your own talents and ingenuity instead of your checkbook will prove the validity of Poor Richard's proverb: "A penny saved is a penny earned."

Principle 8: *Be grateful for what you have.*

> Giving thanks always for all things unto God and the Father in the name of our Lord Jesus Christ. (Ephesians 5:20.)

The need for "more income to purchase goods and services" can become an endless, futile quest unless you come to grips with who you are and what you really want out of life. Americans are peculiar: we are among the few people on earth who have so much "stuff" that we have to rent storage units in order to have enough space to put it all—and yet we still want more.

Begin appreciating what you already have rather than worrying about what you don't have. Even a crummy job can feel (and certainly *pay*) better than no job at all; renting a small apartment sure beats being homeless; and eating leftovers again is preferable to going hungry.

CASE ILLUSTRATION

Karen and Russ were married college students living in off-campus housing. They both worked part-time, but tuition, books, rent, and utilities took most of what they earned. Food became a luxury. Russ chuckled as he held up a couple of boxes for Karen to evaluate. "Would Madam prefer macaroni and cheese or a selection from our delicious assortment of Top Ramen?"

Karen, assuming an aristocratic pose and a highborn tone of voice, replied, "I do believe I'll partake of the macaroni and cheese, with, I might add, a hot dog, medium well. Thank you." Trying not to smile too broadly, Russ continued, "And would Madam care for dessert? We have an excellent vanilla ice cream available."

Karen looked up in surprise, and dropped the aristocratic pose. Grabbing Russ's arm, she asked, "We've got ice cream? You're not kidding me, are you? We really have ice cream? Where'd we get the money to buy ice cream?"

"Tom had to study for an exam, so he gave me a couple of bucks to run a computer program for him. I decided we deserved a treat at least once in a while, so I got us some ice cream."

Principle 9: The best things in life are free.

> Now we have received, not the spirit of the world, but the spirit which is of God; that we might know the things that are freely given to us of God. (1 Corinthians 2:12.)

As the old song says, "The best things in life are free"—and they are made even better when they are shared with the ones you love. If you have gone through hard financial times with someone special, then you know the importance of thoughtful gestures and humor in trying to creatively make do.

For entertainment one couple liked to go to a local mall and see if they could each "spend" $10,000 on things they really wanted in less than an hour. Of course, they were pretending—they didn't really have $20,000 to spend. But it was fun picking out expensive watches, strange-looking sweaters, and oversized pictures. It didn't cost them a cent, and it was fun—most of the time.

CASE ILLUSTRATION

Seiko, looking out the kitchen window, commented that the storm seemed to be getting worse. Dinner was almost on the table and everyone was about to sit down when the electricity went out. A few of the younger children cried out but were immediately calmed by one of the older children. Their mother began groping in one of the cupboards and in a calm voice said,

"Everyone just stay put for a minute. I know there's a candle around here someplace . . . Aha! Found one. Anyone for a candlelight dinner?" By now the children were feeling the adventure of the occasion, and one offered to be the waiter.

After dinner, they all helped build a fire in the fireplace and took turns reading their favorite nursery rhymes. Some were curling up in their blankets and starting to drift off when the electricity came back on and the magic of the moment disappeared in the glare of the ceiling light. In unison they all bemoaned being called back to the twentieth century.

Principle 10: The value of an individual should never be equated with his or her net worth.

> For what is a man profited, if he shall gain the whole world, and lose his own soul? or what shall a man give in exchange for his soul? (Matthew 16:26.)

> Remember the worth of souls is great in the sight of God. (Doctrine and Covenants 18:10.)

Each individual in a family is unique, one of a kind, and therefore irreplaceable. Some individuals may contribute humor, others may contribute music. One person may provide the family with emotional stability while another may provide financial stability. But the worth of an individual can never be assessed in dollars.

Imagine attending a funeral service in which the eulogy stated, "Frank wasn't worth very much. After all of the expenses of this funeral are deducted, I doubt if his net worth will exceed $10,000. Unfortunately, Frank was struck down in the prime of his consuming. He hadn't had enough time to really accumulate much. All of us who were close to Frank knew there were a lot more things he wanted to buy. With a little more purchasing time, he could have really amounted to something."

We are remembered not for what we consume but for what we contribute—for the difference we make in the lives of others. Our net worth reflects our financial status; our personal worth is reflected in our contributions to the welfare of others.

Personal Values

Is your time and money going to what you really value, or are they merely being spent by default? Far too often, we live our lives *by default:* We lack self-knowledge and merely react to whatever comes our way. A life led *by design*, however, is one in which the consequences reflect thoughtful planning, dedication, and a sure knowledge of our values.

Values are relatively permanent beliefs about what you regard as desirable, worthy, or right. Values tend to reflect early upbringing and often change very little over a lifetime. Your values help determine the relative importance you place on such situations as saving face, saving your marriage, getting a good education, or getting out of debt. They give your life meaning and purpose. As you attempt to develop a sound financial plan, it is essential that you decide which of your values are most important to you.

Replaceables and Irreplaceables

Someone once said, "Values are reflected in how well a person is able to distinguish between what is replaceable and what is irreplaceable." For many, it has become more and more difficult to make this distinction, and they tend to devote more of their resources to attaining things that are replaceable than to preserving what is irreplaceable. They may also fail to receive any personal satisfaction from their possessions or to see any intrinsic value in them. They are then unable to meaningfully connect with the world around them.

A replaceable thing is usually seen as having a utilitarian value only. It is prized only as long as it serves some purpose; once that purpose has been achieved, it is discarded. Something that is not one of a kind is usually considered *replaceable;* something with an intrinsic, personal value, or something that is one of a kind is usually considered *irreplaceable*. Ford fenders, screen doors, most jobs, and money are replaceable; great pieces of art are irreplaceable. Most toys are replaceable; favorite blankets, dolls, or teddy bears are irreplaceable. Most jewelry is replaceable, but Great-grandmother's wedding ring is irreplaceable. Most things built by others are likely to be replaceable, while what is built or created by one's own hands or the hands of a loved one can often become irreplaceable. Individuals are unique, irreplaceable. Relationships that have taken a great deal of time and effort to build, such as an eternal marriage, are irreplaceable. President Joseph F. Smith made a strong declaration about the eternal significance of the marriage relationship:

> I want the young men of Zion to realize that this institution of marriage is not a man-made institution. It is of God. It is honorable, and no man who is of marriageable age is living his religion who remains single. It is not simply devised for the convenience alone of

man, to suit his own notions, and his own ideas; to marry and then divorce, to adopt and then to discard, just as he pleases. There are great consequences connected with it, consequences which reach beyond this present time, into all eternity, for thereby souls are begotten into the world, and men and women obtain their being in the world. Marriage is the preserver of the human race. Without it, the purposes of God would be frustrated; virtue would be destroyed to give place to vice and corruption, and the earth would be void and empty.[16]

Irreplaceables—whether things or relationships—represent something you value, something that justifies hard work or sacrifice, something that provides feelings of gratification, a sense of purpose, or meaning to life.

The Values Inventory

Unfortunately, it is not uncommon to put forth a great deal of hard work to get something you value, such as an adequate income, and then waste it because you have not created a budget that reflects your priorities or considers what you really value. Since you naturally want your resources to go toward what is important to you, a difference in values among members of the family can easily lead to conflicts over how family resources should be spent. While family members will seldom reach total agreement on all issues, a sense of fairness is more likely to prevail if everyone involved feels that his or her values receive equal consideration. It is when significant differences are not discussed that serious problems may arise.

The Values Inventory, Worksheet 1.1, invites you to examine your values and then compare them with those of your spouse. Two copies of the worksheet are provided—one for each individual—to be filled out separately. After you have completed your worksheets, first share your personal responses to the values, and then compare how you each thought the other would respond to a particular value.

Value Conflicts

The necessity for communication in this area cannot be overemphasized. Even if you have a fairly good grasp of your values you may find yourself unable to communicate them effectively to loved ones. As a result, you silently watch as the money is spent on everything but what you want it to be spent on. Things finally come to a head, and only then do you let the other person know—perhaps in anger—how you really feel. Surprised, he or she responds, "If you had told me how important it was to you, I would have let you buy it." Still hurt, you counter with "If you really loved me, you'd have known how important it was to me." With either silence or anger, you are having a difficult time communicating your values to others in a way they can understand or that is helpful to the relationship.

Meaningful Units

One way for you to communicate the relative value you place on different things is to convert them into *meaningful units.*

A meaningful unit represents something that (1) you value, (2) you know how much effort is needed to obtain, and (3) you know how much discomfort and inconvenience are caused by not having it. A meaningful unit, for example, might be a dinner out (something you value), a bike (something you had to work hard to obtain), or a telephone (something that is inconvenient to be without). Almost anything that you value in some way can be used as a meaningful unit.

Once you have determined what represents a "meaningful unit" to you, you can compare it to other "meaningful units" valued by someone else. This is called finding the "relative value" of an item—the amount of value an item has in relation to others.

Meaningful units can help you compare the value of less expensive items to the value of those that are more expensive. For example, to Norma a $35 pair of children's shoes is a meaningful unit. She uses that to compare the relative value of other financial demands, such as her husband Roy's desire to spend $348 on a new shotgun. Norma calculates that she could buy about 10 pairs of shoes for the children with the amount of money Roy would spend on the shotgun. So, to Norma, the relative value of a new shotgun represents, in meaningful units, 10 pairs of shoes.

You can arrive at the relative value of each of your financial demands by calculating how many of your own meaningful units could be bought for the cost of a particular demand.

Meaningful units can also be used the other way around, comparing the value of more expensive items to that of those that are less expensive. For example, you may discover that you could have bought a plane ticket and visited Grandma in person (meaningful unit) for the amount of money you spent on last month's long distance phone calls. You might also find that you could have bought those much-needed tires with what you spent on fast food last month.

It is helpful to compare your meaningful units with your partner's. For example, what was spent on renting videos (your meaningful unit) in the past two months could have paid for a dinner at a nice restaurant (your partner's meaningful unit). By making such comparisons, you will be able to better understand each other's value system—and better work together in establishing spending priorities.

Attitudes

In any relationship, questions about how to allocate resources arise. "Should the money go to mortgage payments or car repairs? To mission funds or home improvement projects?" Arguments can result from a difference in values and a belief that the other person is trying to impose his or her values on you. In most cases, however, couples find they have similar *values* but different *attitudes*.

An attitude is a state of mind based on your opinions and judgments about the world around you. Attitudes can be optimistic or pessimistic, favorable or unfavorable, charitable or hostile. They reflect a position you have taken because of your values, and therefore they are much more flexible than values. For example, you and your spouse may both value education, but you have the attitude that private schools are the way to go, while your spouse thinks public schools are quite sufficient. In such a situation, the arguments you have may be because of attitudes, not values.

As this example illustrates, a person's attitudes can have a major impact on family finances. A decision to send the children to private rather than public schools would greatly increase the cost of education for the family. Saving a specific amount of money for educational purposes would then become a financial goal (see chapter 8).

Approach and Avoidance Qualities

Whenever you are in a situation that demands a decision between two alternatives or goals, you will experience the stress associated with conflict. According to Kurt Lewin, founder of the field theory in psychology,[17] if a goal is attractive, it has *approach*-motivating qualities. If a goal is undesirable, it has *avoidance*-motivating qualities. Most of life's decisions combine the two. In *approach-approach* conflicts, each of the alternatives has desirable characteristics; in *approach-avoidance* conflicts, a choice has both desirable and undesirable characteristics; and in *avoidance-avoidance* conflicts, neither choice is desirable.

Approach-Approach Conflicts

An approach-approach conflict and its accompanying stress occur when a choice must be made between two desirable alternatives. This dilemma is aptly described in the familiar cliché, "You can't have your cake and eat it, too." An example of this kind of conflict is trying to decide which of two great-looking cars you should buy. Both have good qualities, and your goal of driving a new car remains blocked until you make a decision. Your feelings of frustration, stress, and anxiety will continue until you do. You may even make the final decision more from a desire for emotional relief than from a well-considered process of elimination.

When dealing with any conflict, and especially approach-approach choices, keep in mind that goals can often be reached sequentially rather than all at the same time. In other words, what you don't choose at first, you might still be able to choose at a later date.

Approach-Avoidance Conflicts

In this not-so-perfect world, the approach-avoidance conflict is perhaps a bit more common than the approach-approach type. This type of conflict arises when you weigh the desirable against the undesirable. Let's use the new car example again. You have no doubt that you want the new car (approach), but you don't want the years of installment payments that come with such a purchase (avoidance). Another example might be the desire to make a lot of money quickly—but also to avoid high financial risks.

In this kind of conflict, possible gains are weighed against possible losses, the potential for pleasure is weighed against the potential for pain. The "good" is weighed against the "bad"— and you find far too often that you must "take the bitter with the sweet."

Avoidance-Avoidance Conflicts

You can probably remember some unpleasant time in your life when you remarked, "Huh, some choice!" Such a remark usually refers to an avoidance-avoidance conflict—one in which *both* alternatives are undesirable. For example, the judge might say, "Thirty days or $300." You may have to choose between living with a toothache or going to the dentist, or between having the truck repossessed or losing the station wagon. As you might guess, the avoidance-avoidance type of conflict usually creates the greatest amount of frustration and stress.

The ability to resolve an avoidance-avoidance conflict is closely related to your level of maturity. If you are relatively immature, you will go to great lengths to avoid having to make such decisions. You will tend to procrastinate or even try to get someone else to make the decision for you. On the other hand, if you are a relatively mature individual, you will accept the responsibility for the decision and confront the unavoidable with courage. If, for example, you have been laid off work, you can wait until your creditors start pounding on your door. Or you can call them immediately to let them know your situation, so that you can explore their willingness to make adjustments in your payment schedules.

Putting It All Together

From early childhood, you were probably told that it's a cold, cruel world out there, and that physical, spiritual, and economic survival is not easy. What you weren't told was just how hard it was going to be to put it all together.

Physical survival. Your ability to survive physically is determined by your ability to provide the necessities of life, such as food, clothing, and shelter, to provide medical and health care, and to prepare for retirement. To survive physically, then, you must provide the *means* to go on living.

Spiritual survival. To survive spiritually, you must provide a *reason* to go on living. You must be able to find meaning in life, and satisfactory answers to the questions, "Why am I here and where am I going?" and the courage and confidence to have faith in the gospel of Jesus Christ.

Economic survival. Economic survival depends on your ability to convert your mental and physical efforts into goals, services, and money, so that you can take care of your physical and spiritual needs within the framework of your values.

Summary

Understanding basic principles concerning the influence that finances, relationships, and spirituality have on each other is crucial to an effective financial program. Also fundamental is realizing the importance of personal values and the ability to deal effectively with value conflicts. With this foundation you can now evaluate: What part have financial problems played in your marital disagreements? How are your financial dilemmas influenced by your behavior and your spiritual sensitivity? What are your values and how well do you resolve related conflicts?

Knowing what is *really* important to you can conserve time, resources, and emotions. Understanding what is *really* important to the people closest to you—and being able to help them achieve their goals—can bring great happiness to your life and theirs.

Important Terms

Approach-approach conflict: A conflict between two desirable goals.

Approach-avoidance conflict: A conflict over a goal that has both desirable and undesirable qualities.

Attitude: A state of mind based on your opinions and judgments about the world around you.

Avoidance-avoidance conflict: A conflict between two undesirable choices.

Economic survival: Converting your mental and physical efforts into goals, services, and money in order to take care of physical and spiritual needs.

Irreplaceable: Having an intrinsic, personal value, or being one of a kind.

Meaningful unit: Something that (1) you value, (2) you know how much effort is needed to obtain, and (3) you know how much discomfort and inconvenience are caused by not having it.

Physical survival: Provision of a *means* to go on living.

Relative value: The amount of value an item has in relation to other items.

Replaceable: Having a utilitarian value only.

Spiritual survival: Provision of a *reason* to go on living, achieved through faith in the gospel of Jesus Christ.

Value conflict: A situation that demands a decision between two alternatives or goals.

Values: Relatively permanent beliefs about what you regard as desirable, worthy, or right.

Notes

1. Albrecht, 1979; Bader, 1981; Edmondson and Pasley, 1986; Ilfeld, 1982; Wilhelm, Iams and Ridley, 1987.

2. Smith, 1977, p. 208.

3. Blood and Wolfe, 1973.

4. Troelstrup, 1974.

5. Bader, 1981.

6. Albrecht, Bahr and Goodman, 1983.

7. Ashton, 1975.

8. Orthner, 1990.

9. U.S. Department of Commerce, 1994.

10. Hornung and McCullough, 1981.

11. Smith, 1977, p. 274.

12. White, 1990; Coleman and Ganong, 1985; Mueller and Hira, 1984; Pasley and Ihinger-Tallman, 1982.

13. Young, 1954, p. 308.

14. Ibid., pp. 194–95.

15. McKay, 1965.

16. Smith, 1977, p. 272.

17. Lewin, 1935.

VALUES INVENTORY

Read the following list of 30 items. Decide which 10 of the items would be the most valuable to you. Rank these from 1 to 10 (1 being the most valuable) in the appropriate spaces in the *You* column. Next, decide which 10 of the items you think your spouse would choose. Rank these from 1 to 10 in the appropriate spaces in the *Your Spouse* column.

YOU	YOUR SPOUSE	
____	____	A secure and comfortable retirement
____	____	A sense of equality in relationships
____	____	Emotional and sexual intimacy
____	____	A sense of accomplishment in life
____	____	A sense of independence and self-reliance
____	____	A meaningful love relationship
____	____	Financial security for the family
____	____	Happiness or contentedness
____	____	A meaningful relationship with God
____	____	Feelings of self-confidence
____	____	Social recognition and community status
____	____	A fulfilling marriage
____	____	Meaningful purpose in life
____	____	Helping the poor, sick and disadvantaged
____	____	A sense of family togetherness and happy children
____	____	Learning, gaining knowledge continually
____	____	Honesty and personal integrity
____	____	Good health and physical fitness
____	____	Close relationships with extended family
____	____	Traveling and quality vacations
____	____	Companionship, spending time together as a couple
____	____	Success in a job or career
____	____	Freedom to live life as you choose
____	____	New experiences and adventures
____	____	Being outdoors, away from city life
____	____	Satisfying friendships, liking people and being liked
____	____	Living in the city, access to restaurants and entertainment
____	____	Time alone, being by yourself
____	____	Having nice things, such as cars, boats, furniture
____	____	Emotional security, freedom from excessive stress

VALUES INVENTORY

Read the following list of 30 items. Decide which 10 of the items would be the most valuable to you. Rank these from 1 to 10 (1 being the most valuable) in the appropriate spaces in the *You* column. Next, decide which 10 of the items you think your spouse would choose. Rank these from 1 to 10 in the appropriate spaces in the *Your Spouse* column.

YOU	YOUR SPOUSE	
____	____	A secure and comfortable retirement
____	____	A sense of equality in relationships
____	____	Emotional and sexual intimacy
____	____	A sense of accomplishment in life
____	____	A sense of independence and self-reliance
____	____	A meaningful love relationship
____	____	Financial security for the family
____	____	Happiness or contentedness
____	____	A meaningful relationship with God
____	____	Feelings of self-confidence
____	____	Social recognition and community status
____	____	A fulfilling marriage
____	____	Meaningful purpose in life
____	____	Helping the poor, sick and disadvantaged
____	____	A sense of family togetherness and happy children
____	____	Learning, gaining knowledge continually
____	____	Honesty and personal integrity
____	____	Good health and physical fitness
____	____	Close relationships with extended family
____	____	Traveling and quality vacations
____	____	Companionship, spending time together as a couple
____	____	Success in a job or career
____	____	Freedom to live life as you choose
____	____	New experiences and adventures
____	____	Being outdoors, away from city life
____	____	Satisfying friendships, liking people and being liked
____	____	Living in the city, access to restaurants and entertainment
____	____	Time alone, being by yourself
____	____	Having nice things, such as cars, boats, furniture
____	____	Emotional security, freedom from excessive stress

CHAPTER 2

What We Bring with Us

Among the things we bring with us into a marriage are our expectations and our values, our ability to accept and adapt to change, as well as our feelings about ourselves and our experiences. William James, in *The Principles of Psychology,* examined the basis for acquiring a sense of personal identity and well-being:

> In its widest possible sense . . . a man's Self is the sum total of all that he can call his, not only his body and his psychic powers, but his clothes and his house, and his wife and children, his ancestors and friends, his reputation and works, his lands and horses, and yacht and bank account. All these things give him the same emotions. If they wax and prosper, he feels triumphant; if they dwindle and die away, he feels cast down.[1]

James wrote of the dynamics of our lives, of how our feelings shift with good and bad times. But we as Latter-day Saints know that this mortal existence is a momentary stage in our eternal progression, and that we must maintain an eternal perspective about what happens to us here in mortality. Elder Neal A. Maxwell tells us:

> Because our lives are foreseen by God, He is never surprised by developments within our lives. The sudden loss of health, wealth, self-esteem, status, or a loved one—developments that may stun us—are foreseen by God, though not necessarily caused by Him. It is clear, however, that this second estate is to be a learning and a testing experience. Once again, it is relevant to remind ourselves that when the Gods discussed us and our earth

experience, their declaration was, "And we will prove them herewith." (D&C 98:12; Abraham 3:25.)[2]

Unfortunately, many newlyweds tend to bring to their marriages a fairy-tale belief in living happily ever after, a belief that seems to be based on this supposition: "We have been good. God is good. Therefore, only good things will happen to us." This belief seems to completely block out of their minds the fact that their relationship will undergo radical and usually unexpected changes. One partner may even naively ask the other to "stay just the way you are." (If this were to happen, the partner making the request would someday be married to a sixty-year-old spouse with the maturity of a twenty-year-old! Not a pretty picture.)

What usually prompts such a request is the desire to perpetuate the happiness being experienced at that moment. Many erroneously assume that the state of being happy is *static*, rather than *dynamic*, or changing. But life is change, and happiness itself is not appreciated without experiencing contrasting sorrow and hardship. Two people who go through life's ups and downs together grow in ways neither may foresee. Because of each partner's changes, they in actuality do not yearly celebrate just an anniversary, but rather what could be called a "remarriage."

A couple celebrating their fiftieth wedding anniversary, for example, is not necessarily composed of the same two people who married at age eighteen. A pioneer woman who had built sod huts, plowed fields, borne and buried children, fought off Indians, helped dig wells during droughts, and twice nursed her husband back to health would not be the same debutante he first met in a quaint St. Louis sitting room. Having been through such adversity together, however, they would most likely end up loving each other in a deeper, more personal way than when they first met. She would have changed. He would have changed. Their love would have changed, and with each change they would recommit—redeclare—their desire to be married to each other.

Family Rules

As you begin your transition from single life to married life with children, be assured there will be difficulties to overcome. Many of these difficulties may originate in something else you brought with you to your marriage: your separate sets of "family rules."

In the families each of you come from (your "families of origin"), certain rules guide you in your social roles and govern your interpersonal relationships; they set limits on your behavior and enable you to reasonably predict the behavior of others. Among these family rules are expectations about how to manage your finances—and as you might have guessed, the rules each of you has "inherited" will most likely be different.

It is often during the process of making wedding plans that a couple first encounters differences in their family rules. Some of these differences will create conflict *within* the individual and some will create conflict *between* the individuals. Family rules are maintained and transmitted across generations on three levels: explicit, implicit, and intuitive.

Explicit Family Rules

Explicit family rules are expressed verbally or posted on the refrigerator door: "Don't talk with your mouth full. Don't whistle at the table. Sit up straight. Don't spend all your money on candy."

Explicit family rules concerning finances might include "Begin saving for your mission early" and "Always pay your tithing first." As these rules demonstrate, many LDS family rules are founded in the scriptures and the teachings of the prophets. For example, President Lorenzo Snow spoke clearly about the reasons for paying tithing.

> After the law of consecration was given, . . . the Lord gave another law (tithing) six years later which was vastly different from the law of consecration. We are now under that law; and the same promises have been made to us if we will keep that law as were made to the people in Jackson County; the land will be sanctified, and we shall be counted worthy to receive the blessings of the Lord and to be sustained and supported in our financial affairs and in everything we do, temporal as well as spiritual.[3]

In addition to those listed above, many families will include such financial rules as these: "Save some of what you earn. Never buy on credit. Count your change before you leave the counter. Never lend money to a friend. Pay your debts on time. Don't buy things foolishly. And above all, don't talk to others about your personal financial affairs." (In this regard, Sigmund Freud said, "Money [matters] will be treated by cultured people in the same manner as sexual matters, with the same inconsistency, prudishness, and hypocrisy."[4]

Implicit Family Rules

It is the implicit family rules that often have the greatest impact on our lives. Implicit rules are those taught through nonverbal communication. Repeated throughout childhood, implicit rules tend to be just below conscious awareness, so we seldom realize we are following them until someone points it out to us.

One example of an implicit rule is "When Dad leaves the room during an argument, that's the end of the discussion." Other family rules might tell us that when Mom gets a tear in her eye, we do not pursue the issue any farther. We also know which is Dad's chair. We know we should not compare Mom to her sister, bring up the name of a certain relative, or use certain tones of voice when talking to either parent. We know that it is not permissible to sit on a boyfriend's lap, kiss someone in public unless you are at an airport, or leave home permanently unless you're getting married, going to college, or joining the military.

Learning to manage finances begins at an early age. Some lessons are deliberately taught, but most financial management practices are implicitly passed—through example—from one generation to another. Some are "taught" in this way to turn their earnings over to the wife and let her run the house. Others are taught that the father manages the finances, and the rest of the family lives off a specific allowance. Still others learn that each partner takes care of his or her own income and expenses.

Implicit family rules about finances can be detected in such recollections as these: "Dad paid cash for everything. We never talked about money. We never knew how much money Dad made." "Mom never paid more than $20 for a pair of shoes. Mom paid the bills and kept the books. Dad turned his paycheck over to her." "We never went on expensive vacations. The family ate out only on special occasions." "All the relatives owned their own homes. We kept a car for at least five years." "Mom never bought anything for herself. The needs of the kids always came first."

Intuitive Family Rules

Like implicit rules, intuitive rules are also unspoken. But while implicit rules concern more everyday kinds of issues, intuitive rules concern those that are more far-reaching. Based on family heritage—the *emotional legacy* inherited by each person—this kind of rule includes any "ledger" of instinctive obligations that needs to be balanced, any need to "pay back" something "owed" to another, or to "pass on" something of value or importance (such as traditions or beliefs). For example, some children feel an obligation to repay their parents for all of the suffering and sacrifice on the children's behalf, or a need to succeed in order to make sure that all that the parents went through has not been in vain.

Our legacy may also include expectations associated with our ethnic, religious, or vocational background. How much should we contribute toward helping other members of the family come to America? Are we going to serve a mission? Are we going to get married in the temple? Who is to stay on the farm? Who is to become the next doctor? Our legacy can prompt additional questions: Who is to take care of our parents or help pay off their debts? Who is going to see that the siblings get an education?

The intuitive rules category also includes family taboos: "Never marry someone of a different race (or religion, nationality, socioeconomic status)." "Never change your citizenship (or religion, politics, and so on)." "Never sell the land (or the house, a particular heirloom, or such)." "Never gamble and risk losing everything the way Grandpa did." "Even if you declare bankruptcy, your honor will demand that you repay those you owe."

Family Rules Inventory

To better understand how family rules influence your finances, you need to know what rules—explicit, implicit, and intuitive—you and your partner have brought to your marriage.

Following is a list of exploratory questions that will help you identify family rules that govern specific topics and communication patterns. After considering these questions—and any additional ones you may think of—each of you should fill out a copy of Family Rules Inventory, Worksheet 2.1.

To make your answers as thorough as possible, talk to your brothers, sisters, and parents about how they viewed your family's rules. (You may also find this worksheet helpful to list and discuss family rules in areas such as communication, sexuality, morality, health, or education.)

After you have each completed the worksheet, compare and discuss your answers with your partner. Ask yourselves how you feel about these rules. Which ones do you want to keep for your new family and which ones do you want to reject? Determine what compromises and accommodations you need to make.

Exploratory Questions

1. Do you think your family was materialistic? In what ways?
2. Could you ask for financial support? How did family members respond when another family member made a request for help or support?
3. How was affection expressed between you and your parents?
4. How was affection expressed between your parents?

5. Were you allowed to express your feelings? Which feelings were you allowed to express and to whom?

6. How did your parents express approval or disapproval?

7. How did family members respond to change?

8. What kinds of roles were assigned to men and women?

9. How did your family evaluate success? In terms of money, degrees, land, social status, or possessions? In other ways?

10. How did your parents feel about debt?

11. How did your parents manage the family finances?

12. How openly could you talk about finances?

13. In which socioeconomic (middle class, upper class, etc.) group do you think your family belonged? During which period of your life?

14. What was your parents' attitude toward both husband and wife working?

15. What was your family's attitude toward saving and investing?

Rules as a Source of Conflict

Most families have hundreds of spoken and unspoken rules, and in many ways these rules help describe who we are. For instance, a woman raised in a small Japanese village would acquire rules that would provide the social characteristics attributed to being Japanese. Similarly, a man raised in a small Swedish village would acquire rules that would make him Swedish. If both were to emigrate to the United States, they would take a great deal of their heritage with them and would need a period of adaptation before they learned to feel comfortable in their new communities.

A similar process often governs adaptation to a new marriage. In a way, each person's family of origin is like his or her "village" and is the source of the rules brought to the marriage—rules that tend to bias perceptions and govern behavior.

CASE ILLUSTRATION

Sometimes, when money got a little tight, Kent would suggest that Kiesha sell "that old hutch"; the money could then be put to "good use." But Kiesha cherished that old hutch as an irreplaceable heirloom; she would never part with something her great-grandmother had hauled across the prairie in a covered wagon. She would counterattack with "If you really loved me, you would know how much that hutch means to me, and you would never even suggest selling it." Often these opening statements would escalate into a power struggle that would end with such ultimatums as "I honestly think you love that hutch more than you love me. Well, it's either that thing or me. Make up your mind, because you can't have both."

In an attempt to cool things down, Kiesha would suggest borrowing some money from their parents or friends. However, Kent had learned in childhood that you "never borrow money from friends or relatives," since this would inevitably destroy those relationships. Kent's belief in this rule placed powerful restraints on Kiesha's suggestion. Kiesha's lack of understanding of how important it was to Kent to honor this rule and Kent's insensitivity to Kiesha's emotional bond with the hutch were a source of unending conflict. Both of them were merely obeying their family rules.

When Family Rules Are Broken

It is very important that couples understand the rules that bias their perceptions, because these rules influence not only how they expect others to behave, but also the consequences they mete out to those who break these rules. One of the most frequent consequences of breaking family rules is distancing by the other members of the family. If, for example, someone were to wear Scandinavian logging boots into a Japanese house, the hosts may be offended and act somewhat cool and distant.

CASE ILLUSTRATION

Maria invites her new boyfriend, Raphael, to dinner at her home for the first time. Raphael unknowingly sits in Maria's dad's chair, impudently calls him "Pops," and begins to eat before the others have been served or the food blessed. He has broken four family rules within thirty minutes. Some of the family members are not exactly sure why they have not taken to Raphael, but they all sense that he just doesn't fit in.

Jorge is introduced to the family a few weeks later. He remains standing until the mother has been seated, and he calls the father "Sir." Jorge not only waits until after the food has been blessed before beginning to eat, but also compliments the cook and offers to help with the dishes after dinner. Everybody likes Jorge—he seems to be just part of the family.

The difference in the degree of acceptance afforded Raphael and Jorge reflects the degree of irreverence toward or compliance with family rules displayed by each. This is frequently true with regard to in-law relations, and it helps to explain why some sons- or daughters-in-law are accepted into a family and others are not. The degree of harmony between the husband's family rules and the wife's family rules also greatly determines the degree of difficulty in adjusting to marriage.

CASE ILLUSTRATIONS

Example 1. The husband and wife in this case are operating under the rules they brought with them from their families of origin. They do not make the effort to understand or acknowledge each other's rules.

Paul greets Helen coolly. "You're home late."

Helen stretches and tries to ignore his coolness. "I know. I had a lot to do today."

"You're supposed to call when you're going to be late."

Unwilling to ignore the implied accusation, Helen counters, "What are you getting so upset about? I thought you said you were going to support me in this new job. Coming home to harassment is not what I call support!"

Paul's family rule: Spouses call when they will be home late.

Helen's family rule: Spouses support each other's efforts without placing limits.

Example 2. In this case, the husband and wife are also operating under separate family rules, but they make the effort to check out their assumptions about how the other should behave.

Wiping her hands on her apron, Fatima greets Ali at the kitchen doorway. "You're home late."

Ali says tiredly, "I know. I had a lot to do today."

"I know you're busy," Fatima says carefully, "but I'm still upset that you didn't call. Did you know that I'd like you to call when you'll be late?"

"No, I didn't realize that. My dad always just came home as soon as he could, and my mom was always flexible with dinner."

Fatima hesitates for a moment, then presents her position. "I'm willing to be flexible with dinner, but I would also like to know when I can expect you to be coming home. Would you be willing to call me the next time you'll be home later than 6:30?"

"Sure. I'd be willing to do that. I'm sorry I didn't think to call tonight."

Fatima smiles her appreciation. "Thanks. It would make it a lot easier for me to make plans for the evening."

Fatima's family rule: Spouses call when they are going to be late.

Ali's family rule: Spouses do the best they can and need to be flexible with their expectations.

Rule for the new family of Fatima and Ali: Consideration of each other's needs and feelings is more important than loyalty to the way your mom and dad did things.

Coping with Family Financial Rules

It is imperative that you come to know your spouse's family financial rules. In most cases, when a spouse breaks the other's rules, it is out of ignorance and quite unintentional. Nevertheless, it can lead to a state of perpetual discord. Having a knowledge of another's rules can enable you to express love and consideration in ways that can be more fully understood and appreciated by both of you.

The following list of suggestions can help you and your partner make conscious choices about the financial rules and management patterns that will characterize your marriage.

Financial Management Suggestions

1. Be aware that each person has an assortment of divergent values, standards, and goals that tend to influence the way he or she would like to have resources allocated.
2. Accept that each person comes to the marriage with a unique set of financial rules.
3. Appreciate the severe stress placed on individuals and families when family financial rules are broken.
4. Understand that it is possible for families and family members to modify their financial management procedures.
5. Assess your family of origin's financial management patterns and determine which of these you wish to perpetuate and which you wish to discard.

6. Formulate a plan for you and your family that is designed to alter existing, dysfunctional financial patterns and establish functional financial management techniques.
7. Have each member of the family learn how to effectively plan, control, and evaluate the management of financial resources.

Birth Order and Financial Issues

Family rules aren't the only things we bring to our marriages from our families of origin. We also bring the characteristics we acquire through our birth-order position in the family. Personality characteristics associated with your birth order can have a profound influence on how you manage your finances. These characteristics, developed in childhood, are often a permanent part of a person's adult life.

Birth-Order Clusters

The important role that birth order plays in our lives was investigated by Alfred Adler in 1927[5] and became the foundation for his theory of personality development, which he called "individual psychology." Adler believed that birth order is an important factor in the determination of certain personality characteristics, and that these characteristics can be divided into four main clusters: those of the *first born, the second born, the middle born*, and *the youngest*.

The First Born. First-born children are often asked to take care of younger siblings, so being in control and taking charge comes easily to them. Managing the checkbook, giving out allowances, paying the bills, making out a budget (and making sure everyone adheres to its guidelines) are all financial management tasks that come naturally to an eldest child. First-borns are also ambitious and high achievers.[6] Research indicates that first-born individuals attain the highest rate of salary increase, when compared to individuals of other birth orders.[7]

The Second Born. Second-born children, on the other hand, hate being controlled or having someone else try to tell them what to do. Greatly independent, it's important for them to have their own "mad money" to spend as they like and not have to account to anyone for. They have been known to sabotage many a first-born's plans to keep things—including budgets—organized. Second-borns can spend a lot of money trying to look as good as someone else.

The Middle Born. Middle-born children tend to go along with whatever budget has been established. They may resent the fact that their needs have been lost in the "needs of the family," but that is a familiar situation for the middle-born child. However, because they are so sensitive to injustice and unfairness, they are more likely to stand up for the financial rights of other family members.

The Youngest. The youngest, or last-born, child is often used to being pampered and treated like a prince or princess. Credit cards provide instant gratification of almost anyone's whim or impulse, but it is not unusual for youngest children to take their cards to their credit limits—and then some. One study found that last-born children have higher average total liabilities and a higher debt-to-income ratio than individuals of any of the other birth orders.[8]

TABLE 2.1—BIRTH ORDER AND FINANCIAL ISSUES

BIRTH ORDER	CONTROL ISSUES	BUDGETING	NEEDS/WANTS
First Born	Is in control, takes charge, manages the checkbook, pays the bills	Makes out a budget, makes sure everyone adheres to it	Conservative; takes care of needs first, saves to buy wants
Second Born	Hates being controlled, likes to have personal "mad" money	Sometimes sabotages the first-born's budget	Impatient, experiences severe stress if unable to get what is wanted
Middle Born	Assumes responsibility for management tasks	Tends to go along with whatever budget is established	Sensitive to fairness; needs of everyone are considered equally
Youngest	Doesn't like controls, prefers to operate on impulse	Sees budgets as restrictive; avoids responsibility	Does not distinguish between needs and wants

Interaction Patterns

It's not too hard to imagine what kind of interaction patterns might develop as a result of an individual with one set of birth-order characteristics marrying someone of a different set. Preliminary research shows that birth order can have an effect on family finances. For instance, it has been found that a couple's birth-order combination is a significant predictor of family income.

Last-born husbands married to middle-born wives have been found to have the highest family incomes, while middle-born husbands with first-born wives had the lowest.[9]

CASE ILLUSTRATION

Adam and Tashi were on the verge of divorce because of what Tashi saw as Adam's irresponsible use of the checking account. "No one in my family *ever* bounced a check," Tashi would growl. "I've never in my life been so embarrassed as when the bishop returned our tithing check due to *insufficient funds*." Tashi was an eldest child used to acting responsibly, and she expected others to behave in an equally responsible manner.

Adam, on the other hand, was the youngest child in his family of origin. He had a difficult time understanding why Tashi could get so angry with him over a "little" thing like bouncing a check. He countered her accusations with his own indignation. "Lots of people bounce checks. No big deal. It's a perfectly natural, human mistake."

The Birth-Order Exercise

Since birth-order characteristics are likely to influence how you and your spouse interact in your marriage, as well as how you manage your finances, it would be worthwhile to use the Birth-Order Exercises, Worksheets 2.2 through 2.5. It will help you identify the characteristics you developed in your family of origin and apply this knowledge to your marital and financial relationships.

There are four versions of the Birth-Order Exercise—one for each birth-order cluster. Fill out the version that pertains to your own birth order. Then fill out one for your spouse, indicating which of the characteristics for his or her birth order match his or her personality.

The Task Satisfaction Scale

Frequently, people assume responsibility for certain tasks without thinking or discussion, based on observation of their parents or the influence of their birth order. However, they may not necessarily like the tasks they have assumed.

The Managerial Task Satisfaction Scale, Worksheet 2.6, will help you pinpoint how you feel about the allocation of financial management tasks in your family and how you believe your spouse feels about the tasks she or he is asked to perform. You should each complete a copy of the worksheet. Then compare and discuss your responses. If one of you is particularly averse to a certain task, such as balancing the checkbook or paying bills alone, being asked to perform this task may create feelings of resentment and distance. With more open communication, such problems can be avoided. You might either share the task or allocate it to the other partner.

Summary

You and your spouse can bring, consciously and unconsciously, a great number of family rules into your relationship. It is very difficult for two people to successfully develop and maintain a financial management program without taking each other's rules into consideration. Individual characteristics associated with a person's birth order can also have a major impact on our financial and interpersonal behavior.

With the information learned from the questions and worksheets in this chapter, you will be in a better position to evaluate your financial behavior and practices.

Important Terms

Birth order: Position in family of origin, whether first-born, second-born, middle-born, or youngest, the characteristics of which can affect how we manage our finances.

Distancing: Being kept at an emotional distance by other family members; one of the most common consequences for breaking family rules.

Family rules: Accepted standards designed to guide us in our social roles and govern our interpersonal relationships.

Explicit rules: Rules expressed verbally and of which there is conscious awareness.

Implicit rules: Rules taught through nonverbal communication—primarily through repetition throughout childhood; tend to be just below conscious awareness.

Intuitive rules: Rules based on our heritage, the legacy inherited by each person; includes any emotional "ledgers" that need to be balanced—that is, a need to "pay back" what is "owed" to another.

Notes

1. James, 1890, p. 147.

2. Maxwell, 1979, pp. 28–29.

3. Snow, 1984, p. 158.

4. Freud, 1913, p. 283.

5. Adler, 1927.

6. Altus, 1966; Hudson, 1990.

7. Berger and Ivancevich, 1973.

8. Poduska and Allred, 1987.

9. Steggell, Allred, Harper and Poduska, 1990.

FAMILY RULES INVENTORY

List as many financial rules from your family of origin as you can recall in each of the three categories. If you need more space, use the back of the worksheet or other sheets of paper.

EXPLICIT FAMILY RULES
1. _____
2. _____
3. _____
4. _____
5. _____
6. _____
7. _____
8. _____
9. _____
10. _____

IMPLICIT FAMILY RULES
1. _____
2. _____
3. _____
4. _____
5. _____
6. _____
7. _____
8. _____
9. _____
10. _____

INTUITIVE FAMILY RULES
1. _____
2. _____
3. _____
4. _____
5. _____
6. _____
7. _____
8. _____
9. _____
10. _____

FAMILY RULES INVENTORY

List as many financial rules from your family of origin as you can recall in each of the three categories. If you need more space, use the back of the worksheet or other sheets of paper.

EXPLICIT FAMILY RULES

1. _____
2. _____
3. _____
4. _____
5. _____
6. _____
7. _____
8. _____
9. _____
10. _____

IMPLICIT FAMILY RULES

1. _____
2. _____
3. _____
4. _____
5. _____
6. _____
7. _____
8. _____
9. _____
10. _____

INTUITIVE FAMILY RULES

1. _____
2. _____
3. _____
4. _____
5. _____
6. _____
7. _____
8. _____
9. _____
10. _____

BIRTH ORDER EXERCISE—FIRST BORN

Listed here are characteristics common in first-born children. If you are completing this exercise for yourself, read each description and decide how characteristic it is of you. If it is not at all characteristic, circle 1 on the scale. If it describes you exactly, circle 5. If you are somewhere in between, circle one of the numbers 2 through 4. If you are completing this exercise for your partner, indicate instead how characteristic the description is of him or her.

HOW CHARACTERISTIC IS THIS OF ME/MY PARTNER?

	NOT AT ALL				EXACTLY
A first-born person					
1) Needs to be "in charge" or "the boss."	1	2	3	4	5
2) Feels threatened by criticism from others.	1	2	3	4	5
3) Is cautious, does not like to take risks.	1	2	3	4	5
4) Tries to get as much information as possible in order to make plans and lists.	1	2	3	4	5
5) Tends to be intellectual; likes to work with facts and data.	1	2	3	4	5
6) Feels responsible for making sure everything turns out well; fearful of being wrong or making mistakes.	1	2	3	4	5
7) Is obedient, oriented to rules and authority.	1	2	3	4	5
8) Is conservative; does not like things to change or to happen unexpectedly.	1	2	3	4	5
9) Is ambitious and a high achiever.	1	2	3	4	5
10) Has a tendency to think he or she is superior to others.	1	2	3	4	5

BIRTH ORDER EXERCISE—SECOND BORN

Listed here are characteristics common in second-born children. If you are completing this exercise for yourself, read each description and decide how characteristic it is of you. If it is not at all characteristic, circle 1 on the scale. If it describes you exactly, circle 5. If you are somewhere in between, circle one of the numbers 2 through 4. If you are completing this exercise for your partner, indicate instead how characteristic the description is of him or her.

HOW CHARACTERISTIC IS THIS OF ME/MY PARTNER?

	NOT AT ALL				EXACTLY
A second-born person					
1) Is the opposite of his or her older sibling.	1	2	3	4	5
2) Is rebellious, liberal thinking, and willing to try something new.	1	2	3	4	5
3) Is stubborn.	1	2	3	4	5
4) Is very competitive.	1	2	3	4	5
5) Is assertive and outspoken.	1	2	3	4	5
6) Gets bored easily.	1	2	3	4	5
7) Has his or her individual interpretation of the rules.	1	2	3	4	5
8) Is impulsive and often does not think through to the consequences.	1	2	3	4	5
9) Needs to be given choices rather than be told what to do.	1	2	3	4	5
10) Sees situations in terms of black and white; there is no middle ground.	1	2	3	4	5

BIRTH ORDER EXERCISE—MIDDLE BORN

Listed here are characteristics common in middle-born children. If you are completing this exercise for yourself, read each description and decide how characteristic it is of you. If it is not at all characteristic, circle 1 on the scale. If it describes you exactly, circle 5. If you are somewhere in between, circle one of the numbers 2 through 4. If you are completing this exercise for your partner, indicate instead how characteristic the description is of him or her.

HOW CHARACTERISTIC IS THIS OF ME/MY PARTNER?

	NOT AT ALL				EXACTLY
A middle-born person					
1) Is easy-going and does not get upset over the "little things."	1	2	3	4	5
2) Is willing to negotiate and compromise.	1	2	3	4	5
3) Needs to feel appreciated.	1	2	3	4	5
4) Likes to be different.	1	2	3	4	5
5) Is independent.	1	2	3	4	5
6) Tends to be accepting of self and others.	1	2	3	4	5
7) Has an identity problem; often feels "invisible."	1	2	3	4	5
8) Will urge a compromise, and rarely takes a stand in the family.	1	2	3	4	5
9) Sees life as a struggle.	1	2	3	4	5
10) Tends to take a holistic view of things.	1	2	3	4	5

BIRTH ORDER EXERCISE—YOUNGEST

Listed here are characteristics common in youngest children. If you are completing this exercise for yourself, read each description and decide how characteristic it is of you. If it is not at all characteristic, circle 1 on the scale. If it describes you exactly, circle 5. If you are somewhere in between, circle one of the numbers 2 through 4. If you are completing this exercise for your partner, indicate instead how characteristic the description is of him or her.

HOW CHARACTERISTIC IS THIS OF ME/MY PARTNER?

	NOT AT ALL				EXACTLY
A youngest, or last-born, person					
1) Is charming and likeable.	1	2	3	4	5
2) Is impatient; wants something now.	1	2	3	4	5
3) Is very imaginative, creative, and inventive.	1	2	3	4	5
4) Is self-indulgent; believes that he or she is special.	1	2	3	4	5
5) Is irresponsible and undependable; does not believe that he or she should have to pay the consequences for behavior.	1	2	3	4	5
6) Is courageous, not afraid of failure.	1	2	3	4	5
7) Has often been spoiled and pampered.	1	2	3	4	5
8) Does not believe that he or she is taken seriously.	1	2	3	4	5
9) Feels a need to outdo others.	1	2	3	4	5
10) Is manipulative; tries to get his or her own way.	1	2	3	4	5

MANAGERIAL TASK SATISFACTION SCALE

Who performs each of the following management tasks in your home? Are you satisfied with the way responsibilities are shared or divided? On a scale of 1 to 5, with 1 being "completely unhappy" and 5 being "completely happy," rate your satisfaction with each situation by *circling* the appropriate number. Then rate how you believe your spouse would respond by placing an *X* on the appropriate number.

	COMPLETELY UNHAPPY				COMPLETELY HAPPY
1. Shopping for, buying groceries	1	2	3	4	5
2. Obtaining maintenance, service, and repairs for the car(s)	1	2	3	4	5
3. Shopping for, selecting, and purchasing new or used cars	1	2	3	4	5
4. Studying, deciding on, and investing in property, stocks, and bonds	1	2	3	4	5
5. Studying, deciding on, and purchasing life, hospital, and medical insurance	1	2	3	4	5
6. Studying, deciding on, and purchasing car, fire, liability, and other property insurance	1	2	3	4	5
7. Figuring annual federal & state income taxes	1	2	3	4	5
8. Maintaining records of income and expenses	1	2	3	4	5
9. Preparing monthly or annual budget	1	2	3	4	5
10. Paying bills	1	2	3	4	5
11. Signing checks and making deposits	1	2	3	4	5
12. Earning money through employment	1	2	3	4	5
13. Assuming responsibility for the family estate, will, and related matters	1	2	3	4	5
14. Obtaining medical & dental care	1	2	3	4	5
15. Managing family time commitments	1	2	3	4	5
16. Deciding on and performing *inside* chores	1	2	3	4	5
17. Deciding on and performing *outside* chores	1	2	3	4	5

MANAGERIAL TASK SATISFACTION SCALE

Who performs each of the following management tasks in your home? Are you satisfied with the way responsibilities are shared or divided? On a scale of 1 to 5, with 1 being "completely unhappy" and 5 being "completely happy," rate your satisfaction with each situation by *circling* the appropriate number. Then rate how you believe your spouse would respond by placing an *X* on the appropriate number.

	COMPLETELY UNHAPPY				COMPLETELY HAPPY
1. Shopping for, buying groceries	1	2	3	4	5
2. Obtaining maintenance, service, and repairs for the car(s)	1	2	3	4	5
3. Shopping for, selecting, and purchasing new or used cars	1	2	3	4	5
4. Studying, deciding on, and investing in property, stocks, and bonds	1	2	3	4	5
5. Studying, deciding on, and purchasing life, hospital, and medical insurance	1	2	3	4	5
6. Studying, deciding on, and purchasing car, fire, liability, and other property insurance	1	2	3	4	5
7. Figuring annual federal & state income taxes	1	2	3	4	5
8. Maintaining records of income and expenses	1	2	3	4	5
9. Preparing monthly or annual budget	1	2	3	4	5
10. Paying bills	1	2	3	4	5
11. Signing checks and making deposits	1	2	3	4	5
12. Earning money through employment	1	2	3	4	5
13. Assuming responsibility for the family estate, will, and related matters	1	2	3	4	5
14. Obtaining medical & dental care	1	2	3	4	5
15. Managing family time commitments	1	2	3	4	5
16. Deciding on and performing *inside* chores	1	2	3	4	5
17. Deciding on and performing *outside* chores	1	2	3	4	5

CHAPTER 3

Lifestyles and Finances

To manage your finances effectively, you must not only face the task of resolving your immediate financial problems; you must also learn how to cope with personality characteristics that influence the development of these problems. Psychologists have attempted to explain the influence of personality on financial behavior.[1] Their conclusions are incomplete, of course, since they do not represent a spiritual, eternal perspective. God's view of each of us supersedes any of the philosophies of man.

> Before I formed thee in the belly I knew thee; and before thou camest forth out of the womb I sanctified thee, and I ordained thee a prophet unto the nations. (Jeremiah 1:5.)

Not having God's full perspective, however, we often must use those psychological tools made available here in mortal existence to help us progress. Based on several years of observing and working with clients at a family financial counseling clinic,[2] I determined that the way clients manage their finances frequently parallels the lifestyles described by Alfred Adler.[3]

Adler's Concept of Lifestyles

Adler was one of the first personality theorists to recognize that an individual's personality characteristics arise from what he referred to as a *lifestyle*. Your lifestyle is a belief system that gives you a strong sense of where you belong in relation to others, as well as a strategy for achieving a feeling of worth.

Adler believed that while there are many different lifestyles, four themes dominate. These themes are represented by the personality "priorities" (or goals) of *superiority, control, pleasing,* and *comfort seeking.* It is helpful to recognize each of these personality priorities and understand ways of dealing with their possible negative financial effects.

Lifestyle 1: Superiority

Individuals whose lifestyle is based on *superiority* like the limelight and feel significant only when trying to be better than others. This lifestyle can be expensive. Superiority-seeking individuals often find that they are compelled to purchase top-of-the-line items even when they can't afford them. They do not acquire quality merely for quality's sake but rather to gain the recognition and esteem associated with prestigious items. Brand names, labels, and the location and reputation of stores are very important to them.

The Game of One-upmanship

People with a superiority orientation do not want to merely keep up with the Joneses but to surpass them. Such individuals often find themselves participating in an undeclared, progressively more expensive game of one-upmanship. At the beginning of the game the question may be "How do I measure up? Am I as good as other members of this league?" which then frequently leads to competitive purchasing. After playing the game for a while, they often want to move up to an even more competitive comparison group.

Superiority seekers are often trying to compensate for feelings of inferiority; yet in doing so they set themselves up to fail. These owners of Cadillacs will compare themselves to people who drive Ferraris or Rolls Royces—automobiles they can never afford—rather than with owners of Volkswagens or Chevrolets. Although they probably cannot afford a purchase, they make it anyway and set up a pattern of spending beyond their means. They may send their children to the best schools or become members of exclusive country clubs, even though initiation fees or dues exceed what they can manage with their current income. Time-share condominiums or resort programs and vacations to exotic locations frequently attract superiority seekers.

It is difficult not to assume that such personalities are strongly motivated by *pride.* Apparently this was a major concern to John when he taught:

For all that is in the world, the lust of the flesh, and the lust of the eyes, and the pride
of life, is not of the Father, but is of the world. (1 John 2:16.)

As one might expect, this money management tendency can lead to feelings of apprehension and chronic indebtedness. Budgets stretched beyond their limits and frequent harassment from creditors increase the level of stress in any marriage.

The Martyr and the Victim

To justify their conspicuous consumption, superiority-seeking individuals often rationalize to their partners or dependents, "I did it all for you." But of course this defense is meaningless when the "you" referred to does not appreciate the financial gestures. Individuals inclined to superiority often end up feeling that life is meaningless, because after they have bought others everything money can buy, they are still not loved in return.

Because of the stress of such situations, the superiority-seeking person sometimes assumes the role of martyr or victim of the family. The best is usually purchased for someone else—the children or the spouse. For example, a mother may choose to wear the same old, run-down shoes through another winter so that her child can have the latest in ski boots. This martyr-mother then feels more righteous than (i.e., superior to) other parents because of her sacrifices for her children.

When the recipient of the "sacrifices" is the spouse, the superiority seeker's role can switch to that of victim. While the martyr imposes misery upon his or her own self, the victim gets someone else to impose it. For example, the victim may buy gifts for his spouse even though he knows his spouse will not reciprocate in kind. The victim can then feel justified in feeling sorry for himself and in viewing himself as more generous and loving than his spouse. The real intent of the gift is to draw attention to the partner's lack of reciprocation.

In some marriages, both partners base their lifestyles on superiority—but they play different roles. One spouse seeks superiority through consumption and typically satisfies all his or her own wants, while the other spouse seeks superiority through the victim role and tends to satisfy few, if any, of his or her own wants. For example, a husband seeking to be superior may buy an expensive, top-of-the-line shotgun, a four-wheel-drive vehicle, and elaborate camping equipment; meanwhile, his wife, the victim, wears altered dresses bought at a secondhand store because of the heavy debt accumulated by her husband. He is "superior" at consuming; she is "superior" at sacrificing.

Overcoming a Superiority-Seeking Lifestyle

If this lifestyle describes you and you wish to overcome its undesirable characteristics, you must first become aware of how this priority affects your spending behavior. It may be helpful to review the social motivations behind particular purchases or buying habits, and then compare these motives with practical reasons for making a purchase. For example, what is your motive for buying a car? Is it to impress neighbors and relatives and to drive up to the country club in something that looks like it belongs there? Or is your motive to have a dependable means of transportation? From a practical standpoint, a five-year-old Chevrolet will get you across town about as well as a brand-new BMW. The social reasons for wanting to drive the BMW may originate in the need to feel superior.

It may also be helpful to look into childhood circumstances that may have fostered such personality traits. Competition with siblings may have been significant and may still be an active force. The feeling of not being good enough for a certain social group at school or in the community may have played a great role in your selection of a superiority-seeking lifestyle.

It may be enlightening to check out just how impressed others actually are with your efforts to be superior. You may learn that most people are so preoccupied with their own challenges and struggles that your efforts to impress them go unnoticed or receive only a passing acknowledgment. You might ask a neighbor, "Hey, what do you think of my new car?" and your neighbor might answer, "Did you get a new car? Well, how about that? How long have you had it?" You tell him you've had it a couple of weeks and your neighbor replies, "Is that a fact? This car seems a little bigger than that little whatchamacallit you used to have." You then feel obliged to point out that the little whatchamacallit was a BMW 325i.

If you tend to be a victim or a martyr, you may think about asking others, after you have related a tale of financial woe, to judge your pitiable performance—in much the same way Olympic performances are judged. If they are not impressed with your "misfortune," perhaps you should give it up.

Once you've gained greater insight into your motivations, you may realize that you have a choice: You can continue behaving as you have in the past, which would mean more futile comparisons, heavy debt, and stress from feeling over-responsible and overburdened. Or you can begin trying to identify how much status would—or should—honestly be "enough" for you (see chapter 6). Keep in mind Principle 6: *You can never get enough of what you don't need, because what you don't need can never satisfy you.*

Lifestyle 2: Control

Those whose lifestyle is based on *control* have three primary areas of focus: (1) control of self, (2) control of others, and (3) control of situations.

Control of Self

Financially, a focus on control of self often translates into *not* giving in to the urge to purchase wants or luxuries. Self-control means sticking with the basics—purchasing only needs. To a controller, impulse buying is an absolute no-no, and those who so indulge are perceived as weak and are severely criticized. Those who exercise this type of control to the extreme live a miserly existence characterized by exaggerated savings programs and austere surroundings. In some cases, a point of negative returns occurs: the cost of maintenance begins to exceed the cost of replacement. Maintaining an older car, for example, can end up costing more than buying a new one; or heating a home without adequate insulation might cost more than installing additional insulation.

Control of Others

Control of self sometimes assumes a rather passive-resistant orientation: a "you can't make me do anything I don't want to do" attitude. In contrast, control of others is much more active and far more common.

The controller's dilemma stems from being overwhelmed with the responsibility of managing the finances, yet afraid of losing control if some responsibilities are allocated to others. Some control-oriented people believe that the one who controls the purse strings controls all. Their intent is to make others subservient, often through control of the checkbook, credit cards, allowances, or the distribution of inheritance.

Such manipulations can be explicit or implicit. Explicit control occurs when one spouse determines how much the other will be allowed to spend and for what purpose. The controlling spouse maintains control by persistently making the subservient spouse feel guilty and incompetent about his or her management of finances. Explicit control can also occur when the controller manipulates others into borrowing money from him or her. The indebtedness of others assures the controller a position in which others "owe him (or her) one."

With a controlling personality, the possibility of exercising unrighteous dominion is ever present. Most Latter-day Saints are well aware that the power of the priesthood is to be discharged with patience and love, and not in an attempt to take away another's free agency.

> Behold, there are many called, but few are chosen. And why are they not chosen? Because their hearts are set so much upon the things of this world, and aspire to the honors of men, that they do not learn this one lesson—That the rights of the priesthood are inseparably connected with the powers of heaven, and that the powers of heaven cannot be controlled nor handled only upon the principles of righteousness. That they may be conferred upon us, it is true; but when we undertake to cover our sins, or to gratify our pride, our vain ambition, or to exercise control or dominion or compulsion upon the souls of the children of men, in any degree of unrighteousness, behold, the heavens withdraw themselves; the Spirit of the Lord is grieved; and when it is withdrawn, Amen to the priesthood or the authority of that man. . . .

> We have learned by sad experience that it is the nature and disposition of almost all men, as soon as they get a little authority, as they suppose, they will immediately begin to exercise unrighteous dominion. Hence many are called, but few are chosen. No power or influence can or ought to be maintained by virtue of the priesthood, only by persuasion, by long suffering, by gentleness and meekness, and by love unfeigned. (D&C 121:34–37, 39–41.)

When the control is implicit, the manipulator becomes the "power behind the throne." The controlling spouse subtly prompts the other to buy things without the manipulated one being aware of what is happening. For example, a wife may want to drive a new car but may not want the responsibility of assuming such a debt. So she prompts her husband, "I suppose now that you've got that raise you're already thinking of ways to spend it. You've got to promise me you won't go near Bob's Car Lot, because I know how you operate. The moment you sit behind the wheel of that red convertible with the tan leather interior, you'll just have to have it. Oh, I know how you've always wanted a car like that, and I know how you love the wind and the sun. But even with the raise it wouldn't be practical, so even if you drive by just to look at it, you have to promise you won't stop." In like manner, a husband may wish to go on an expensive vacation but wants his wife to believe that the idea was hers. "Honey, you've been working really hard lately," he says. "I don't know how you do it. I'd be absolutely exhausted if I tried to accomplish just half of what you do. Don't you ever think about taking a break from the daily grind and getting away from it all? I mean *really* getting away from it all?"

Control of the Situation

Control of the situation is often closely associated with control of others. Controlling income and expenses is one way of controlling the situation. While income is sometimes kept confidential, expenses are often made public in a gloomy, pessimistic light. For example, a husband may keep an ample net worth and income a secret from the rest of the family, yet insinuate that they do not have much money for nonessentials. The rest of the family may then feel reluctant to ask for things they want.

Controlling the situation also means making plans, preparing schedules, and laying out the future in an inflexible, often unrealistic manner. In some instances, controllers of the situation become overinsured in an attempt to be prepared for any and all catastrophes.

Unfortunately, some people who are subjected to control-oriented individuals go on spending sprees, while others juggle the books so that even a bank auditor would be unable to decipher what took place. Many who live under the influence of a controller feel tense and frustrated at being stifled by rigid financial programs, and as a result they become defiant and disobedient.

Overcoming a Controlling Lifestyle

If you think you have controller tendencies and encounter feelings of defiance in others, you may wish to (1) bring financial matters into open discussion, (2) develop a financial management plan where financial responsibilities are shared with all family members, and (3) encourage programs where each member of the family has at least some money (an allowance, mad money, or such) free of all accountability.

If you have this personality, one of the most difficult but beneficial things you must do is reorient your thinking. You must realize that your worth as an individual does not come from your ability to control. If you truly want others to respond to you, you must change from a controller/dictator role to a leader/teacher role. You will want to become an educator who imparts skills to others rather than a tyrant who criticizes their ignorance.

For instance, a controller tries to get results by complaining about the high utility bills and nagging about lights left on and thermostats turned up. A leader would instead educate the family on what it costs per day for electricity and gas, then help them set goals for reducing the utility bills for one month. As an incentive, half of the amount saved could be shared with the children. In this way, individual family members would be able not only to make a contribution but also to develop a greater sense of personal responsibility.

Gradually develop a more cooperative, democratic perspective toward finances and relationships. The technique of "trading places," or rotating leadership roles, can be useful in achieving a more egalitarian atmosphere while managing finances. Controllers have a strong desire to avoid ridicule or humiliation, so it is very important that they learn to accept their human weaknesses. A control-oriented family must develop the courage to be imperfect, to make mistakes and still feel lovable. Everyone needs to agree that the world will not end if one of you makes a costly decision. No one is immune to buyer's remorse.

Even more important than accepting your humanness is the ability to accept the will of God. "Having it your way" may be all right when it comes to hamburgers. But when to comes to fulfilling your earthly mission and progressing eternally, you would be wise to remember that your Father in heaven has a wider perspective than you do, and that he desires you to gain an understanding of the power of faith. You need to learn to respond to the Lord as Moroni did:

> And I, Moroni, having heard these words, was comforted, and said: O Lord, thy righteous will be done, for I know that thou workest unto the children of men according to their faith. (Ether 12:29.)

It has been said that *impatience* is when we want things to go by our schedule, and *patience* is when we accept that things will go by God's schedule. Jesus Christ—our great example—trusted in the will of his Father, saying in the garden of Gethsemane, "O my Father, if it be possible, let this cup pass from me; nevertheless not as I will, but as thou wilt" (Matthew 26:39). The control-oriented individual needs to develop this greater trust in God.

If your goal is to eliminate, or at least reduce, your use of control-oriented behaviors, the technique of catching yourself to bring behavior into conscious awareness can be helpful. At first, you may catch yourself only *after* you have behaved a certain way. A verbal acknowledgment of "I did it again, didn't I? But I'm catching myself" will generate words of encouragement from other members of the family. Continue through a progression of catching yourself *during* to catching yourself *before* acting in the old, undesirable ways.

For example, as a control-oriented person, you may tend to tell others how they should spend their money, or to judge their choices if the money has already been spent. Since habits usually don't disappear overnight, if you make a vow (something the self-control impulse is prone to encourage) that you will *never* criticize the spending behavior of others again, you may be setting yourself up for failure; but acknowledging that you criticized again, that you are criticizing again, and finally, that you were about to criticize but thought better of it, allows you to remain human while making progress.

Lifestyle 3: Pleasing

Those who have chosen *pleasing* as their first priority do all they can to avoid rejection. Believing that one can buy the love and acceptance of others, they often use gifts to gain recognition or affection, or as a substitute for giving time to those they love. Such individuals unfortunately see love as a commodity that can be bought, sold, and exchanged for goods and services, and their attempts to *buy* love can lead to financial disaster. Pleasers unable to afford their own generosity find themselves on a treadmill, managing to pay off last Christmas at about the time the next Christmas rolls around.

The world of pleasers is often frustrating. If they give a gift and it is not well received, they feel rejected. On the other hand, when pleasers receive a gift, they may pretend to like it so as not to offend, regardless of their true feelings.

Difficulty Saying No

Pleasers find it difficult to say no to the requests of family members. This situation seems increasingly prevalent in today's world of dual-income families, reconstituted families, and divorced or separated parents. Love is measured by the cost of gifts, or money is allocated as his, hers, or ours.

Pleasing-oriented parents often accrue heavy debt to satisfy their children's wishes, believing that if they say no, the children will interpret it as a lack of love. They may buy gifts for their spouses even if it requires extra work to pay for them. Unfortunately, the gifts are never enough, because the desires of the indulged are usually insatiable.

The "generosity" of pleasers sometimes extends well beyond their immediate family. Even if their own families are in great financial need, pleasing-oriented people often lend money to friends. The situation worsens if the pleaser becomes reluctant to ask for repayment for fear of offending the debtor. Problems can arise when a pleaser co-signs loans, puts up collateral for other people's loans, or takes out loans to provide money for others.

The pleaser's attempts to avoid rejection may also create problems with clerks and sales-people. In some cases, pleasers buy things they don't want or need simply because they want the salesperson to like them. This also makes them susceptible to high-pressure sales promotions and get-rich-quick schemes.

Overcoming a Pleaser Lifestyle

As long as you are pleasing-oriented, you will find it difficult to distinguish between being valued for your personality and being valued for your presents or possessions. Do your "friends" come over to be with you or to be in your pool? Do they enjoy your company or just your ski boat? Are your children as glad to see you when you are empty-handed as they are when you come "bearing gifts"?

As a way to confront your pleasing tendencies, you may wish to find out if a failure to "come through" with a gift or loan would end a particular relationship. If so, you may ask yourself, "What is the merit in maintaining such a relationship?" Rather than being afraid of rejection, you may find it helpful to actually seek it: See how many "friends" you can lose in a week by request-ing payment from those who owe you money or by saying no to requests for financial aid.

You must realize that a need to be liked by everyone (including those you dislike) indicates low self-esteem. Only by presenting yourself without gifts will you ever know the true basis of your relationships. Whether another person is happy, sad, loving, or rejecting is a choice that per-son makes; it is not within your power to generate lasting feelings. When you recognize that you cannot *buy* love and friendship, and that you cannot *make* someone else happy, you become more able to question the motivation behind your gift exchanges and loans. With enough encourage-ment and change in outlook, your primary concern can become the welfare of others rather than whether they accept or reject you.

"False charity" means giving in order to get approval and acceptance rather than to show true love and concern. It is self-serving manipulation under the guise of charity. Our first stewardship is the welfare of spouse and family. For them to suffer due to a pleaser's generosity toward others, without their consent, is cruel. For the pleaser's creditors to go unpaid is tantamount to theft.

This, of course, does not mean that you should not be charitable and give what you can. But you must be realistic and prayerful in your giving so that you don't end up placing additional individuals on the receiving end of a charitable exchange—and so that you don't end up giving what is not really needed. True charity—the pure love of Christ—involves more than just giving material goods. As Paul so beautifully explained, true charity understands *all* the needs of those to whom the charity is extended:

> And though I bestow all my goods to feed the poor, and though I give my body to be burned, and have not charity, it profiteth me nothing. Charity suffereth long, and is kind; charity envieth not; charity vaunteth not itself, is not puffed up. Doth not behave itself unseemly, seeketh not her own, is not easily provoked, thinketh no evil; Rejoiceth not in iniquity, but rejoiceth in the truth. (1 Corinthians 13:3–6.)

Lifestyle 4: Comfort Seeking

Often, those who choose comfort as the basis for their lifestyle were pampered as children. As a result, they tend to be self-indulgent and to make little discrimination between needs and wants. Comfort-oriented people sometimes have a history of impulse buying: the very desire for something is, for them, sufficient reason to purchase it. People buy impulsively partly to acquire the desired item as soon as possible, and partly to reduce the stress from frustration at not having what they want.

Comfort seekers live for today and often believe that there really is such a thing as a free lunch and that the piper doesn't necessarily have to be paid. In spite of these mistaken beliefs, however, eventually there comes a day of reckoning.

Reducing Stress

Stress reduction is one of the primary goals of comfort seekers—but they go about it all wrong. They often procrastinate, hoping that whatever is causing the stress will go away if they ignore it. As a consequence, they accumulate unfinished business, unresolved problems, and unmade decisions. Thinking to ease their stress as quickly as possible and at any cost, they refinance loans, take out additional loans, or consolidate existing loans. They ask for cash advances on salaries, delay payments on less stressful bills, and pawn valued possessions. They do not open mail or answer the phone, and they can get good at lying.

Comfort-oriented people seek to take the so-called "easy" way out. They may walk out on current debts, move to another state, and start all over again. They often view bankruptcy as a way to escape the stress of heavy indebtedness rather than as a way to solve current financial problems and get a fresh start. Usually they see their negative financial situation as only temporary; they believe their ship will come in "any day now."

Overcoming a Comfort-Seeking Lifestyle

As a comfort seeker, you dislike being pinned down or cornered, especially on details. You have become skilled at avoiding having to provide specific financial information. You are also pretty good at getting others to back off by convincing them that you cannot handle stress very well. You might even carry this "I can't handle stress" theme to an extreme, expecting others to solve the financial problems that have taken you years to create. As with the controller, it is important for you to learn to trust in your Heavenly Father and his plan. You need to remember Paul's words:

> There hath no temptation taken you but such as is common to man: but God is faithful, who will not suffer you to be tempted above that ye are able; but will with the temptation also make a way to escape, that ye may be able to bear it. (1 Corinthians 10:13.)

Along with a renewed faith in God, you need to recognize that one of the most efficient ways to reduce stress is to act responsibly. Ask yourself, "How would things be different if I were to have all of my debts paid off and I were no longer being harassed by creditors?" or "How would my life be different if I were able to increase my income by 10 to 20 percent? How would it be if I were self-reliant?" President Ezra Taft Benson addressed this issue when he said:

> I would respectfully urge you to live by the fundamental principles of work, thrift, and self-reliance, and to teach your children by your example. It was never intended in God's divine plan that man should live off the labor of someone else. Live within your own earn-

ings. Put a portion of those earnings regularly into savings. Avoid unnecessary debt. Be wise by not trying to expand too rapidly. Learn to manage well what you have before you think of expanding further.[4]

As a comfort-oriented person you may resist structured or limiting corrective programs, so any remedial programs you adopt should not be too austere. You may find that increasing your income is more effective than trying to reduce expenditures.

You may also wish to recall one of the reasons you came to earth—to continue your eternal progression through *overcoming* challenges, rather than avoiding them. The challenges others confront may be even greater than yours, and learning to help them with their struggles may help you to have a better perspective on the ones you have been given.

Financially Effective Personality Characteristics

My neighbor, a certified public accountant, was once heard to say that from a financial standpoint, there are really only two kinds of people: *spenders* and *savers*. He maintained that spenders tend to be in debt, live from paycheck to paycheck, and have little or nothing available for investment. Savers, however, tend to pay cash for what they buy, maintain a savings account, and remain financially secure thanks to long-term investments.

This concise perspective may allow financial planners to quickly appraise their clients, and is therefore useful from a certain point of view. However, from a celestial perspective, we cannot make such quick judgments. The diversity found among individuals seems to be infinite, each personality having been formed over eons of time. (One set of parents, noting the emergence of specific personalities in their children almost from birth, acknowledged that "the cake is baked by the time we get them. As their parents, we can decide what kind of frosting to put on them, but we cannot change an angel food cake into a devil's food cake, or a carrot cake into a German chocolate.")

We are all here to face our particular challenges and to complete our particular missions. Each is given specific talents and gifts to help us meet our goals.

> For all have not every gift given unto them; for there are many gifts, and to every man is given a gift by the Spirit of God. To some is given one, and to some is given another, that all may be profited thereby. (D&C 46:11–12.)

Perhaps some personalities have matured more than others, but it is quite apparent that none of us has yet reached perfection. Imagine three personalities emerging into mortal existence. Imagine that the first personality enters mortality 80 percent perfect and leaves mortality 85 percent perfect. The second personality enters mortality 70 percent perfect and leaves 80 percent perfect. Now imagine that you are the third personality; you enter mortality 50 percent perfect and leave 75 percent perfect.

From your perspective, you may view your life as less perfect than the other two. However, from another perspective, the amount of growth experienced in mortality has been greater. The first individual experienced only a 5 percent growth and the second individual a 10 percent growth. In comparison, you experienced a 25 percent growth during your mortal probation! What an accomplishment! Can you imagine having that kind of growth take place without challenges to overcome—specific challenges, designed around each person's individual needs?

President Spencer W. Kimball taught:

> We should be able to understand this, because we can realize how unwise it would be for us to shield our children from all effort, from disappointments, temptations, sorrows, and suffering. . . . If we looked at mortality as the whole of existence, then pain, sorrow, failure, and short life would be calamity. But if we look upon life as an eternal thing stretching far into the premortal past and on into the eternal post-death future, then all happenings may be put in proper perspective.[5]

Since we do not know what another person's challenges are, or the nature of his or her mission, it is not for us to judge another's personality and then demand that they live up to our expectations. They are not here in mortality in order to live up to our expectations, but to fulfill their probationary progression in the judgment of God.

But while we may not judge others, we *are* responsible for our own self-improvement and progress. We must periodically evaluate our own strengths and weaknesses, and remember that there will be consequences for maintaining certain personality characteristics. In contrast to the foregoing inept personalities, the following personality characteristics contribute to effective financial management programs.

Self-reliance. If you are self-reliant, you try to be your own banker whenever possible, establishing a savings program and setting aside "payments" toward the purchase of an item long before you actually buy it. In this way, you can earn interest rather than pay it.

To be an efficient banker, you must be able to maximize the use of your assets. You may find it advantageous, for example, to borrow money to buy now rather than later; there is often a cost advantage to buying at current prices during an inflationary period. Or you might find that it costs you less to make payments on a washer and dryer than it would to use a laundromat.

Accurate perception of reality. It's important to appreciate the need to live on your *net income* (what's left of your paycheck after state and federal taxes, Social Security, pension payments, and dues are taken out). You also need to accurately appraise the *true* cost of a purchase (including taxes, interest, operation costs, insurance premiums, and accessories; see chapter 6), and to recognize any change in your financial situation and adapt accordingly.

Flexibility. If you live below your means, you are able to draw on uncommitted funds as the occasion arises. You are then able to enjoy the freedom and flexibility that come from a lack of indebtedness. As you grow and change, your plans and goals are able to grow and change with you.

Problem-centeredness. Problem-centered people are able to distinguish between those things they can do something about and those they can do nothing about. For example, not much can be done about factory shutdowns or layoffs, but a great deal can be done to establish a family emergency fund for use in such a situation.

Active appreciation. Active appreciation means that you consistently value what you own. You remember that "new and improved" models are not necessarily preferable to what you already have. You appreciate the utilitarian value as well as the aesthetics of possessions. You recognize the importance of taking care of your possessions and maintaining them properly to prolong their life expectancy and keep replacement costs at a minimum.

Strong sense of ethics. You know how important it is to be honest in all of your financial dealings. You believe that no financial gain is worth sacrificing valued relationships, self-respect, or your standing with your Heavenly Father. Elder Bruce R. McConkie stated:

> Perfect *honesty* is one of the invarying characteristics exhibited by all who are worthy to be numbered with the saints of God. Honest persons are fair and truthful in speech, straightforward in their dealings, free from deceit, and above cheating, stealing, misrepresentation, or any other fraudulent action. Honesty is the companion of truth, dishonesty

of falsehood; honesty is of God, dishonesty of the devil, for he was a liar from the beginning. (D&C 93:52; 2 Ne. 2:18.)[6]

Strong sense of self. By maintaining your individuality and a strong sense of self, you can suppress the urge to waste money on fads, status symbols, or competing with others.

Imagination. By being imaginative and creative in increasing your income or decreasing your spending, you can better cope with changes in the economic climate. You are willing to try a variety of things, from being artistic to taking classes in home and car maintenance, from holding garage sales to making needed items at home.

Appreciation of emotional costs. It is essential to develop the ability to evaluate not only the monetary costs of an item, but the emotional costs as well. Consider the emotional strain placed on a family because of increased indebtedness or additional work hours. Consider what others may have to give up because of someone else's spending habits.

Charity. You have a sense of belonging to humanity. Giving to charitable causes is part of your resolution to serve the needs of others as well as your own. You recognize that your own well-being is intimately involved with that of others—especially members of your family. You find little comfort in being physically satiated while watching others starve, and if you are surrounded by ignorance, you cannot expect to realize your own intellectual hopes.

With regard to charity, King Benjamin taught that we must teach our children to:

> . . . walk in the ways of truth and soberness; ye will teach them to love one another, and to serve one another. And also, ye yourselves will succor those that stand in need of your succor; ye will administer of your substance unto him that standeth in need; and ye will not suffer that the beggar putteth up his petition to you in vain, and turn him out to perish. Perhaps thou shalt say: The man has brought upon himself his misery; therefore I will stay my hand, and will not give unto him of my food, nor impart unto him of my substance that he may not suffer, for his punishments are just—But I say unto you, O man, whosoever doeth this the same hath great cause to repent; and except he repenteth of that which he hath done he perisheth forever, and hath no interest in the kingdom of God. For behold, are we not all beggars? Do we not all depend upon the same Being, even God, for all the substance which we have, for both food and raiment, and for gold, and for silver, and for all the riches which we have of every kind? (Mosiah 4:15–19.)

Summary

Different personalities, or lifestyles, can greatly affect how each person manages his or her finances. A couple's combination of these characteristics can influence how finances are handled in their relationship. Learning which category—superior, controlling, pleasing, or comfort-seeking—best describes you is the first step toward getting rid of personality characteristics that adversely affect your finances. Acquiring and developing desirable personality characteristics will greatly increase your ability to effectively manage your resources.

Important Terms

Comfort seeking: Lifestyle based on trying to reduce stress, often by buying impulsively, procrastinating, and taking the "easy" way out.

Controlling: Lifestyle based on trying to control oneself, others, and situations.

Lifestyle: Term used by psychiatrist Alfred Adler to describe a belief system that gives one a strong sense of where one belongs in relation to others, as well as a strategy for achieving a feeling of worth.

Pleasing: Lifestyle based on trying to gain others' approval and affection, often by buying their love with gifts and money.

Superiority: Lifestyle based on trying to be better than others; involves one-upmanship and perhaps playing the victim or the martyr.

Notes

1. Jourard, 1971; Bornemann, 1976.

2. Poduska, 1985.

3. Adler, 1927; Eckstein, Baruth and Bahrer, 1978.

4. Benson, 1988, p. 262.

5. Kimball, 1972, pp. 96–97.

6. McConkie, 1966, p. 363.

CHAPTER 4

Relationships and Finances

C hapter 1 pointed out that many surveys find finances to be one of the major causes of marital discord and dissatisfaction—and even the leading cause of divorce. Why is this so? The answer often centers on the financial issues of *allocation* and *control*—which have roots in our personal relationships.

Allocation and Control

The process of allocating funds is linked to the principle of scarcity: the more resources you commit to A, the fewer you have to commit to B (for example, the more you spend on new clothes, the less you have to spend on food). When faced with decisions related to this principle, you weigh the cost of giving up one option against the cost of giving up another; this is commonly referred to as *opportunity costs*.

Along with distinguishing between wants and needs (see chapter 9), opportunity costs need to be considered when establishing allocation, or spending, priorities, such as what gets purchased first, who gets paid first (or at all), and whose values get satisfied first. But in the very act of trying to establish such priorities, you will find concerns about control arising almost automatically.

Allocation

For the most part, allocation issues are a middle-class phenomenon. Most of the time the poor have only enough to provide for their basic needs (food, clothing, and shelter); setting priorities for wants is usually not an issue, simply because there is nothing left to spend. The rich usually have enough not only to take care of their needs but to satisfy their wants as well, so there is not much need for them to set priorities either. For the middle class, however, allocation is a problem, because although they may have enough for their basic needs, they seldom have enough left over to satisfy everyone's wants. They must then decide how to allocate the remaining resources.

Control

Control deals with the problem of deciding not only who will establish the priorities, but also who will actually oversee the allocation of funds. The possibility always exists that whoever has control may try to satisfy his or her own values before considering the values of others. To effectively cope with this inherent problem, we must look at the issue of dominance and submission.

Dominance and Submission

Essential to solving the problems of allocation and control are the elements of cooperation, understanding, and consideration. Partners cooperate most effectively when they consider themselves equals, and when both are capable of assuming dominant or submissive roles depending on the circumstances. Dominant and submissive roles should not be seen as positions of superiority and inferiority but as *reciprocal roles of responsibility,* as described in these guidelines:

1. Dominance does *not* mean being superior or a dictator.
2. Dominance means *consenting* to assume responsible leadership regarding the welfare of others.
3. Submission does *not* mean being inferior or a slave.
4. Submission means *consenting* to follow as long as your feelings and needs are considered.

Only in relationships based on equality can trust and intimacy exist. A dominant position in this kind of relationship, therefore, is not a tyrannical one, and submissiveness is not slavery. Self-appointed dictators are primarily concerned with their own welfare; those who *consent* to accept a dominant position—by a mutual decision of those involved in the relationship—are consenting to assume responsibility for the welfare of the others. Similarly, individuals who consent to submission in a relationship are *not* abdicating their right to self-determination. On the contrary, they have consented to be submissive because they believe their feelings and needs will be considered. When individuals suspect that this is not the case, they usually withdraw their consent.

The person who has consented to be submissive may find it helpful to ask the following questions of the person who has consented to be dominant:

1. Have you made a decision?
2. Were my feelings considered?
3. Was the decision made with love (and not power)?

If the answer to all three questions is yes, the one in the submissive role can often sustain the decision even before finding out what was decided. The submissive party believes the dominant person has made the best decision he or she can—and then does not indulge in recriminations if the decision results in problems. (We may not always know what is the best decision or the worst. We may never know, for instance, what might have happened had we chosen differently. We only know what has happened as a result of the alternative we chose. So it is only in retrospect, after we see the consequences of a decision, that we can accurately evaluate our choices.)

Consenting to be submissive or dominant obviously requires a great deal of trust, the courage to be vulnerable, a willingness to exchange the roles of leader and follower, and a commitment to establishing a relationship based on love rather than one based on control. President Ezra Taft Benson, speaking to priesthood holders, reminded them that:

> Love means being sensitive to [your wife's] feelings and needs. She wants to be noticed and treasured. She wants to be told that you view her as lovely and attractive and important to you. Love means putting her welfare and self-esteem as a high priority in your life.[1]

Love versus Power

If you trust the love in your relationship, you trust that the other person will not only try to satisfy your needs but will also *want* you to have what would make you happy. Even when you have no way of obtaining what you seek, the person who loves you will still *want* you to have it.

If, however, you do not trust the love in your relationship, you feel you must rely on yourself to satisfy your own needs. You rely more on power than on love. If the other person won't give you what you want, then you feel that you have to either get it yourself or manipulate the other person into getting it for you. In this case, you may succeed in getting what you want, but you can never succeed in making that other person *want* you to have it. Only when we love someone does his or her happiness become *as important as* our own.

Imagine trying to sustain a marriage based solely on power. The attitude of one partner might be, for instance, "I'll be the only one to write checks," "I'll decide how the money will be spent," or "I'll decide whether or not to tell you how much I earn." Imagine the following saying—handed down from generation to generation—done in needlepoint and hung on your wall: *I want you to have power over others as I have had power over you.*

Now imagine a relationship based on love. Topics of discussion include "How would you feel about my buying a new set of reference books?" or "Now that we have come into a little extra money, how would you like to see some of it spent?" Imagine the needlepoint saying *I want you to love others, as I have loved you.* When the feelings of all family members are considered in decision making, the family can experience solidarity and cohesiveness.

Moral Reasoning and Relationships

The need to be loved is the need for understanding from someone who cares. To be loved is to know that someone else is interested in your problems and frustrations as well as in your dreams and ambitions. It is to have another person show concern for your welfare and appreciation for your efforts.

If reciprocation or consideration is lacking, however, concern can become indifference, appreciation can become contempt, and caring can turn into feelings of bitter sacrifice. These unfortunate transitions are usually the result of selfishness and a lack of moral maturity.

German philosopher Immanuel Kant, in his 1781 *Critique of Pure Reason,* said, "Morality is not the doctrine of how we may make ourselves happy, but how we make ourselves *worthy* of happiness."[2] We can make ourselves worthy of happiness partly by increasing the level of morality that governs our interpersonal relationships. The relative success or failure of a couple's relationship depends greatly on the degree of moral maturity each partner possesses.

Child development specialist Lawrence Kohlberg saw moral maturity as the ability to accurately perceive the appropriateness of one's action or inaction,[3] an ability developed from social maturation and the growth of *moral reasoning*. Kohlberg believed that an individual's moral reasoning progresses through six stages. We can use these stages of moral reasoning to evaluate interpersonal relationships.

Stage 1: Avoiding Punishment

At the lowest stage, Stage 1, moral reasoning is based on personal fear and the desire to avoid punishment. If your relationship operates at this level, you act morally only if you think you would be caught if you were to act otherwise. For instance, you may be faithful to your spouse while in your hometown, but when you are out of town, you may think that anything goes. Or you may reveal to your spouse all income from your regular job, but if you were to make a little money on the side (which is less easily detected), you may keep it secret.

This lowest level of moral reasoning involves some very fundamental choices. Each of us must decide the direction our lives will take, as Joshua declared to those who followed him:

> And if it seem evil unto you to serve the Lord, choose you this day whom ye will serve; whether the gods which your fathers served that were on the other side of the flood, or the gods of the Amorites, in whose land ye dwell: but as for me and my house, we will serve the Lord. (Joshua 24:15.)

Stage 2: Self-gratification

Stage 2's moral reasoning also has an *egocentric*, or self-centered, motive: "What's in it for me?" Operating at this level, you are nice to someone only if it will benefit you. You give to someone only if you think you will be getting something of equal or greater value in return. For instance, you are nice to your boss, to rich friends, and to those with influence because of their potential to reward you. But you see no purpose in being nice to those who work under you, to "friends" who are temporarily down on their luck, or to those with little or no influence.

A person at this level of moral reasoning clings to a childhood perspective that survival depends primarily on *getting* rather than *giving*. Children often believe that in order to survive, they must be able to get others to serve them, love them, and give to them. Such a perspective, however, places them in very dependent, insecure positions in their relationships.

Those who are able to achieve higher levels of moral reasoning have accepted childhood's end and more easily make the transition from a getting to a giving orientation. Paul, in extolling the importance of giving and charity, declared:

> When I was a child, I spake as a child, I understood as a child, I thought as a child: but when I became a man, I put away childish things. For now we see through a glass, darkly; but then face to face: now I know in part; but then shall I know even as also I am known. And now abideth faith, hope, charity, these three; but the greatest of these is charity. (1 Corinthians 13:11–13.)

Stage 3: Peer Pressure

In Stage 3, moral values are based primarily on living up to the expectations of others; their values become yours. At this stage, you think and behave as you believe your peers would think or behave in a given situation. For instance, if someone you know lied to his spouse about how much he paid for something, then you might conclude it would be all right for you to do the same.

The temptation to surrender to social pressure is constant. There will always be those who will attempt to turn us away from a righteous path. Lehi's dream of the tree of life, the precious fruit, and the pointing fingers in the "great and spacious building" describes this situation very clearly.

> And after they had tasted of the fruit they were ashamed, because of those that were scoffing at them; and they fell away into forbidden paths and were lost. (1 Nephi 8:28.)

Likewise, many may find themselves attending church meetings, doing their home or visiting teaching, and even going on a mission, not because of a personal testimony, but because everyone else is doing it.

Stage 4: The Letter of the Law

In Stage 4, you begin to think and behave according to established authority; moral reasoning is very rigid and inflexible. Characterizing this stage are statements such as these: "I believe it because it says so right here in the Bible." "I don't make the rules, I just obey them." "You have to do it because I said so."

Spouses may confront each other with what they perceive as the other's "duty" as a husband or wife. They may become defiant: "In this state, the law says everything is split fifty-fifty, and that means *everything*—including income!" "It's your responsibility to make enough money to feed and clothe this family, not mine." "Look, I give you $400 a month to buy groceries. It's your job to make it stretch far enough to feed the five of us for the entire month. My mother was able to feed six on less than that."

Living by "the letter of the law" shows some progress in the development of moral reasoning. But, as the above examples show, doing so still keeps one in the realm of self and does not necessarily foster concern for the feelings and welfare of others. Jesus taught that a rigid observance of the letter alone, in the absence of the spiritual intent of the law, was not sufficient (see Matthew 5:17–48, John 6:63; also Romans 2:29, 2 Corinthians 3:6). To live by "the spirit of the law," as well as the letter, involves higher intentions, and a greater desire to do what is right for the right reasons.

Elder Neal A. Maxwell clarified the relationship between the letter of the law and the spirit of the law when he wrote:

> One of the ironies which is fostered, at times innocently, in the Church, is the feeling we have that the spirit of the law is superior to the letter of the law because for some reason it seems more permissive or less apt to offend others. The reverse is true. The spirit of the law is superior because it demands more of us than the letter of the law. The spirit of the law insists that we do more than merely comply superficially. It means, too, that we must give attention to the things that matter most and still not leave the others undone.[4]

Stage 5: The Contract

In Stage 5 you are basing your moral reasoning on a more cooperative, unselfish interpretation of rules, regulations, and standards. At this level you are willing to enter into a "contract" with another person and you pledge to keep that commitment. While there are legal and financial factors to consider, your willingness to honor your agreement is a matter of self-respect and personal integrity. In taking out a loan, for example, you are giving your word that you will pay back the money you have borrowed. Even if you had to declare bankruptcy someday, you would still make every effort to pay back each creditor in full. It might take many years, and it might be very difficult financially, but you would intend to honor your commitment and preserve your good name.

Of course, the most important contracts we can enter into are those with God. A contract with God is commonly referred to as a covenant, and throughout the Bible, Book of Mormon, and the Doctrine and Covenants the Lord makes and keeps covenants with his people.

> Thanks be to thy name, O Lord God of Israel, who keepest covenant and showest mercy unto thy servants who walk uprightly before thee, with all their hearts. (Doctrine and Covenants 109:1.)

Unfortunately, his people have, from time to time, tried to unilaterally release themselves from such covenants. We sometimes become discouraged, impatient, and misinterpret the Lord's will. We may declare that we have kept our part of the bargain: We have gone to church, said our prayers, read our scriptures, gone on a mission, and married in the temple—so why aren't "good things" happening to us? Why are we not getting what we want, when we want it? Because of such thinking, we may decide, "If being good doesn't pay off, I'm no longer going to be good."

Such a decision, of course, would be an example of moral reasoning at the self-satisfaction level. At the contract level of reasoning, we would honor our covenants with God—no matter what—as well as the ones we have entered into with those we love on earth.

> Search diligently, pray always, and be believing, and all things shall work together for your good, if ye walk uprightly and remember the covenant wherewith ye have covenanted one with another. (Doctrine and Covenants 90:24.)

Stage 6: The Golden Rule

If your moral reasoning has developed to Stage 6, your moral values are based on universal principles of compassion and mutual trust and respect for humanity. You recognize the dignity and worth of others, and your moral reasoning is founded on one of the oldest, simplest moral principles of all, the Golden Rule:

> Therefore all things whatsoever ye would that men should do to you, do ye even so to them: for this is the law and the prophets. (Matthew 7:12.)

At this stage, you treat others well simply because they are *human,* not because of their sex, race, age, wealth, social status, or relationship to you. You treat them as you would want to be treated.

Relationships and Financial Priorities

Unfortunately, many people operate at Stages 3 and 4 throughout their lives; even worse, many others operate at Stages 1 and 2. But many people are operating, or aspiring to operate, at Stages 5 and 6. In each case, an individual's moral reasoning shows in the types of relationships he or she forms, and influences the financial priorities he or she establishes.

To form relationships with others is one of the most basic of human needs. We need others in order to gain greater security, to perpetuate ourselves through our posterity, and to expand our ideas and perspectives. Psychoanalyst Erich Fromm believed that one of our greatest needs is to escape from loneliness by relating to others.[5] But conflict between our need for emotional security (to love and be loved) and our need for financial security can have a profound effect on our relationships. For example, some people marry primarily for love, others for money.

These two needs do not always conflict. You can express feelings of love through the use of money, but you need to be aware of the *metamessage*—the message about the message—that is being sent along with the money. For example, if you share with others only on a very limited basis and refuse to be inconvenienced, then others may get the feeling that they are not a very high priority in your life. Similarly, if you are willing to share only with the understanding that somehow the gesture must be repaid, the recipient may end up feeling obligated rather than befriended.

On the other hand, charitable love can also be expressed monetarily. At this more caring level, the donor makes it known that the recipient is completely free of any obligation and that the satisfaction of having helped someone in need is sufficient payment.

Relationships can be classified according to the financial priorities of those involved—by the relative importance of satisfying one's own financial needs versus satisfying the financial needs of others. Thus, relationships can be based on selfishness, convenience, commitment, altruism, or devotion.

Selfishness

Selfish people seldom consider the needs and wants of others. Your relationship is based on selfishness if resources are allocated to satisfy just one individual—you or someone else whom you favor above others. This egocentric relationship is characterized by passive involvement with others, with more *getting* than *giving* taking place.

President Spencer W. Kimball, in his book *Marriage,* discussed the importance of motive when two people marry:

> The marriage that is based upon selfishness is almost certain to fail. The one who marries for wealth or the one who marries for prestige or social plane is certain to be disappointed. The one who marries to satisfy vanity and pride or who marries to spite or to show up another person is fooling only himself. But the one who marries to give happiness as well as receive it, to give service as well as to receive it, and looks after the interests of the two and then the family as it comes will have a good chance that the marriage will be a happy one.[6]

CASE ILLUSTRATION

Linda and Bill are living in student housing and are one month behind on their rent. Linda is working to put her husband through college, so money is scarce and "making do" has become routine. When she comes home from work, Bill meets her at the front door. Stopping her before she can get through the doorway, he excitedly tells her, "Don't come in yet! I've got a surprise for you." Bill then asks her to shut her eyes and, taking her by the hand, leads her into the living room. "Stand still and keep your eyes shut," he says. A moment later Linda is blasted with 100 watts of compact disc high fidelity generated by state-of-the-art matching tweeters and two 18-inch woofers. The stereo was something Bill had really wanted, and besides, it was on sale.

Convenience

Your relationship is based on convenience if you allow only *limited access* to your resources—if you consider the needs of others only if it is convenient for you. You may have consented, either implicitly or explicitly, to be useful, but the needs of others are not your top priority. You want to be addressed only when you feel like being available.

CASE ILLUSTRATION

Larry asks his wife, Marilyn, if he can borrow her car. Marilyn asks, somewhat critically, "Why don't you use your own car?"

Larry tells her, "It's almost out of gas."

"Well," Marilyn counters, "I don't want you using up all of my gas cruising around. I'm going to the mall in about an hour, and I can drop you off then."

"Can't we leave any sooner?"

"Hey, I'm offering you a lift. Take it or leave it."

Commitment

Your relationship is based on commitment if you have agreed to allow your partner *unlimited access* to your resources, even if to do so becomes inconvenient. In a relationship based on commitment, you have consented, implicitly or explicitly, to be *used* (not exploited, which is to be used *without* your consent). In this type of relationship, you say, "When you are hungry, *use* my food. When you have no place to go, *use* my place. When you are lonely, *use* me as a companion. After all, you are my friend."

Jesus Christ put forth one of the greatest descriptions of friendship when he declared:

> Greater love hath no man than this, that a man lay down his life for his friends. Ye are my friends, if ye do whatsoever I command you. Henceforth I call you not servants; for the servant knoweth not what his lord doeth: but I have called you friends; for all things that I have heard of my Father I have made known unto you.

> Ye have not chosen me, but I have chosen you, and ordained you, that ye should go and bring forth fruit, and that your fruit should remain: that whatsoever ye shall ask of the Father in my name, he may give it you. These things I command you, that ye love one another. (John 15:13–17.)

Of course, to avoid one-sided depletion of resources, this agreement must be *mutual* and *reciprocal* between the partners involved. In addition, the person being granted unlimited access to your resources must remain sensitive to the price you must pay in order to honor your commitment.

CASE ILLUSTRATION

Hilda approaches her husband, Hector, with an excited report about the beautiful blouse in the store window—the one he had said would look so terrific on her. Hilda exclaims, "It's on sale!"

Hector puts his arm around her and cautions, "On sale or not, we really can't afford it."

Hilda is thoughtful for a moment. Then, remembering the jar that Hector puts his loose change in each night, she asks, "Couldn't we use some of the money in your change jar?"

At first he protests, reminding her that that money is being saved for a computer program he has wanted for some time. But after a moment of reflecting and seeing the anticipation and excitement in her face, Hector smiles and agrees to use the money to buy the blouse. As Hilda leaves for the store, Hector calls out jokingly, "You owe me one."

Months later, Hilda surprises Hector with a small package containing the computer program he had been saving for.

Altruism

Your relationship is based on altruism if your first priority is a willingness to be *charitable*, to give without expecting reciprocation. When you are charitable, the needs of others are considered to be at least as important as your own.

The philosopher Alamshah defines the desire to be charitable as "the urge to exercise feelings of gentleness, compassion, the higher levels of sympathy, and tenderness, . . . a kind of tension which motivates the self to identify with other beings." He believes that since all people possess the same inherent needs, "empathy enables us to know or to sense the feelings or intentions of the other."[7] With empathy, you are better able to act or react appropriately, to relate in a sensitive and caring manner and to understand the impact of your behavior on others.

If you keep these principles in mind when giving or receiving gifts, then you will be less likely to offend or be offended and more likely to keep your expectations of reciprocation within appropriate bounds. It is empathy that enables us to experience *philos*, or brotherly/sisterly love, and to develop a strong sense of responsibility within a relationship. Paul, teaching others the principles which had been taught to him by Christ, counsels us:

> Put on therefore, as the elect of God, holy and beloved, bowels of mercies, kindness, humbleness of mind, meekness, long suffering; Forbearing one another, and forgiving one another, if any man have a quarrel against any: even as Christ forgave you, so also do ye. And above all these things put on charity, which is the bond of perfectness. (Colossians 3:12–14.)

CASE ILLUSTRATION

Jan has been accepted to a university and is to receive a partial scholarship. She and Satoshi are already working as much as they can and their resources are really limited. Things are not looking too promising and Jan is feeling discouraged, when Satoshi comes into the room holding a check. "What do you have there?" she asks.

"Enough to make up for what your scholarship doesn't cover."

In a state of disbelief, Jan hesitantly asks, "But where—where did you get this kind of money?"

Satoshi has sold his car—the one he had dreamed of owning for several years. With tears quickly forming in her eyes, Jan throws her arms around his neck and softly tells him, "Oh, how I love you. Thank you. Thank you so much." Then she leans back and asks, "How can I ever repay you?" Satoshi looks at her and says, "You owe me nothing."

The desire to be charitable stems from our ability to feel what others feel, recalling times when we were the ones who received help. Charity follows the same principle that governs sharing food at the dinner table: Take some and pass it on.

Devotion

Your relationship is based on devotion if you seek opportunities to serve, anticipating the needs of your partner even before they arise. President Kimball, counseling a young married couple, declared:

> Your love, like a flower, must be nourished. There will come a great love and interdependence between you, for your love is a divine one. It is deep, all-inclusive, most comprehensive. It is not like that association of the world which is misnamed love, but which is mostly physical attraction. . . . The love of which the Lord speaks is not only physical attraction, but also faith, confidence, understanding, and partnership. It is devotion and companionship, parenthood, common ideals and standards. It is cleanliness of life and sacrifice and unselfishness. This kind of love never tires nor wanes. It lives on through sickness and sorrow, through prosperity and privation, through accomplishment and disappointment, through time and eternity.[8]

CASE ILLUSTRATION

Indira and Pandit worked, scrimped, and saved for four years to get enough money for a down payment on their first home. Indira tended other people's children during the day and typed resumés for pay at night. Pandit worked as a bricklayer's assistant during the summer, worked construction during the fall and spring, and did brake jobs for neighbors in his garage at night. He would call Indira during the day, realizing that she might need to hear an adult's voice after being surrounded by children all day.

Indira would drape big bath towels on the bathroom counter and set out lotion to rub on Pandit's back after a hot soaking in the tub. She knew the work he did was strenuous; a massage would help avoid a stiff back the next day.

Pandit and Indira were devoted not only to each other but also to their common goal. They each cut back on their spending and were willing to set aside many of their wants. Willing to sacrifice many things during those austere times, they were not willing to sacrifice their love for each other.

Values and the Exchange of Resources

Far too many people in today's world seem to believe that how much they are loved is represented by how much money is spent on them. Many a hardworking parent, bending from the pressure of such a belief, will combine money and affection in ways that further aggravate the family's already difficult financial situation.

Social scientist Uriel Foa proposes an economic model (see Figure 4.1) explaining some of the difficulties in trying to exchange certain resources within a family unit.[9] Some resources are concrete, some symbolic; we care very much about who gives us some things (they are associated with a particular person), very little about who gives us other things (they have a universal value). Foa shows in his model why an exchange of related resources (such as love and service) is more likely to be effective than an exchange of unrelated resources (such as love and money).

Money can be easily exchanged for goods, for example, but attempts to exchange money for love are likely to fail. Gifts (goods), being a little closer to love, might be a more effective exchange— but thoughtfulness and consideration (service) in exchange for love is most likely to succeed.

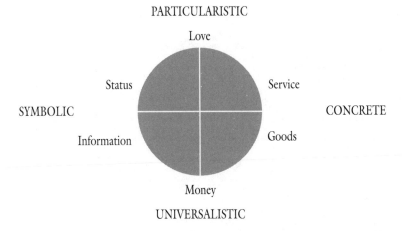

Figure 4.1. *Resource exchange model. Adapted from Foa, 1971. Copyright © 1971 by the AAAS. Reprinted by permission.*

Acting Responsibly and Being Considerate

To manage finances successfully within a relationship, a couple must achieve a balance between *acting responsibly* and *being considerate*. To act responsibly is to satisfy your needs and obligations without interfering with the ability of others to satisfy theirs. To be considerate is to have a genuine concern for the feelings and welfare of others.

Figure 4.2 illustrates the four possible combinations of these two characteristics and their opposites, as well as the emotional results of these combinations. Examples of these combinations are given in the following pages.

Considerate but Irresponsible

You are considerate but irresponsible when you think about the needs of others but are careless of the consequences of your actions. For instance, a husband buys his wife the new 21-gear mountain bike she would like (considerate) at a time when they cannot even make the rent payments (irresponsible). As a consequence, the wife will most likely feel frustrated rather than pleased, because the husband has acted immaturely.

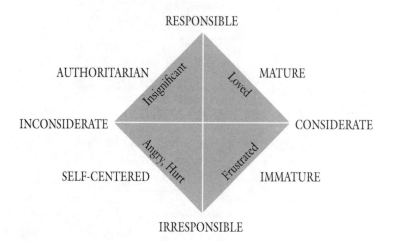

Figure 4.2 *Possible combinations of the characteristics* **responsible** *and* **considerate** *(and their opposites) and the effects of these patterns on a relationship.*

CASE ILLUSTRATION

Tom sometimes pleads with Carol, "I've bought you everything that money can buy, and you still don't act like you really love me. What do you want from me?" These are the desperate words of someone trying to buy love.

Carol tries again to explain to him that although she appreciates his gifts, they are gifts they cannot afford. She tells him that to be considerate, he doesn't have to buy her *things*. Unfortunately, Tom still insists on buying gifts for her.

This example demonstrates that people can give money a symbolic meaning. Tom's gifts are intended to symbolize his love for Carol. But from Carol's perspective, his gifts are symbolic of how irresponsible he is. Until they can talk openly about the feelings behind their actions—and reactions—harmony between them will be impossible.

Irresponsible and Inconsiderate

When you care neither about the possible consequences nor about someone else's feelings, you are irresponsible and inconsiderate. For example, one spouse may be angry with the other and decide to get even by "maxing out" the credit cards on a spending spree. The couple has no way of paying off the debt, and could possibly face bankruptcy (irresponsible). It does not matter to the angry spouse how the other may feel about the spending spree (inconsiderate). After all, in this person's view, the other deserved it. In such cases, the "punished" spouse will usually feel angry and hurt because the other is self-centered.

CASE ILLUSTRATION

Marquita believed for years that economic fluctuations in Juan's business dealings affected his commissions. Not until she received a call from a salesman who worked with Juan did she learn of his gambling habits. The salesman had loaned Juan a considerable amount of money to cover some of his debts and wanted her to influence Juan to pay him back.

Marquita felt betrayed. When she confronted Juan about his gambling debts, he became angry and defensive. "Listen, what I do with *my* money is *my* business. I doubt I'll hear you complaining if I come home with some big winnings. So stay off my case while I'm in a slump."

Marquita felt as though she didn't really know the man she was married to. She wondered how else she had been deceived and whether or not her whole marriage was just a sham. She also wondered whether or not she would ever be able to trust him again.

Habitual gamblers have a tendency to lose it all. Being irresponsible and inconsiderate usually leads to both financial disaster and the destruction of relationships.

Responsible and Inconsiderate

As the head of the household, you may act responsibly simply because someone has to pay the bills and put food on the table. But because of the stress associated with these tasks, you may find yourself being inconsiderate of your family's feelings. Because of excessive debt, for example, you may decide to take a second job to repay the debts (responsible), without recognizing how your spouse and children might feel about not being able to spend time together as a family (inconsiderate). (You also may end up irritable and unpleasant because of stress and exhaustion.)

The others may voice their complaints about not seeing you as much, but you tell them that you would not have to work so much if they would just turn off the lights when they leave a room and turn the thermostat down. Even though you are "doing it all for them," they may feel insignificant, and you will be seen as authoritarian.

CASE ILLUSTRATION

Samuel, upset about their chronic indebtedness, criticizes his wife, Sarah, for not showing more restraint in spending. Waving an unpaid bill at her, Samuel accuses, "You act as if money grew on trees. You're spending it faster than I can make it."

Sarah responds defensively, "I've cut back on everything I can think of short of making underwear out of old pillowcases. I'm not sure what more I can do to help."

Without thinking, Samuel retorts, "If you really want to help out around here, get a job and start bringing in some money so we can pay off these debts."

Responsible and Considerate

When you are not only acting responsibly but also being considerate of your partner's feelings, the chances are very good that you will achieve success in both your financial and personal life. Assume, for instance, that you want to withdraw funds from your savings account in order to gain what you think would be a higher return on an investment. However, being sensitive to your partner's need for a feeling of security, you first ask how he or she would feel about such a decision. In this situation, the spouse being asked would most likely feel loved, and you would be seen as mature and caring.

CASE ILLUSTRATION

Martha thinks it would be wiser to spend the $1,000 Christmas bonus on debts than to put it into savings. "I am afraid it would take us until March or April to pay off our Visa card," she tells Kirk, "but if we use the bonus money, we could pay most of it off right away. What would you like to do with the bonus?"

Kirk is concerned about how well the company he works for will perform during the upcoming year. "I know how you feel about being in debt and paying all that interest," he explains. "But I'm a little worried about possible layoffs. I'd like to put at least some of it into savings. How about if we were to put $500 on the credit card and the other $500 into savings?"

Summary

The issues of allocation and control are integral to family finances—and the quality of a relationship is integral to resolving issues of allocation and control. Appropriate questions to ask yourselves might be: What roles am I willing to play when it comes to financial management? Is our relationship based on power or on love? How do our financial priorities affect our relationship? Do I truly care about the needs of others? How do I show it?

These issues can be satisfactorily settled by: reinterpreting dominance and submission, understanding levels of moral reasoning, and working together responsibly with love and consideration rather than power and selfishness. The words of our Savior and of his prophets can guide us in reaching these goals.

Important Terms

Acting responsibly: The ability to satisfy your own needs and obligations without interfering with the ability of others to satisfy theirs.

Allocation: Commitment of resources, linked to the principle of scarcity—the more resources you commit to *A*, the fewer you have to commit to *B*.

Being considerate: Having a genuine concern for the feelings and welfare of others.

Control: Power wielded by the one who establishes the priorities and oversees the allocation of funds.

Dominance: Consenting to assume responsibility for the welfare of others; does *not* mean being superior or a dictator.

Financial priorities: The relative importance of satisfying one's own financial needs versus satisfying the financial needs of others. Financial priorities in a relationship can be based on selfishness, convenience, commitment, altruism, or devotion.

Love: Basis of a relationship in which the other's happiness is as important as one's own.

Moral reasoning: The process one goes through in deciding how to act (or not act) in a given situation. Kohlberg identified six stages of moral reasoning: Stage 1, avoiding punishment; Stage 2, self-gratification; Stage 3, peer pressure; Stage 4, the letter of the law; Stage 5, the contract; and Stage 6, the Golden Rule.

Power: Basis of a relationship in which each person must rely on himself or herself to satisfy his or her own needs.

Submission: Consenting to follow as long as one's feelings and needs are considered; does *not* mean being inferior or a slave.

Notes

1. Benson, 1988, p. 508.

2. Kant, 1982, p. 347.

3. Kohlberg, 1963, 1969.

4. Maxwell, 1970, p. 46.

5. Fromm, 1970.

6. Kimball, 1980, pp. 41–44.

7. Alamshah, 1963.

8. Kimball, 1982, p. 248.

9. Foa, 1971.

CHAPTER 5

Communication and Intimacy

Good communication is crucial to effective money management. Communication cannot be accomplished alone; at least two people must interact to create communication. When we have trouble communicating, it is not the fault of just one person; it happens because of the interaction process. For communication to improve, all involved parties need to take responsibility for their own contributions.

Circular Communication Systems

While we often think of events and their causes as linear (A causes B), this is often not true in the context of relationships. With people influencing each other as they interact, causality is often circular: Person A's actions influence person B's, B's influence C's, C's influence D's, which in turn may influence A's (see Figure 5.1).

The following interaction sequence, an example of the circular model of causality, might occur in a family:

    A. The mother is having an argument with the father over their daughter's behavior and, during the course of the argument, the mother begins to withdraw.

    B. The father, frustrated by the withdrawal, begins to yell.

    C. The daughter begins to cry.

    D. The father becomes more frustrated and yells louder.

E. The daughter cries harder.

F. The mother defends the daughter.

G. The daughter, holding on to her mother, cries more.

H. The father withdraws by stomping out of the room.

I. The mother begins to yell at the father—and where it stops, nobody knows.

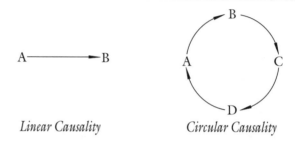

Linear Causality   *Circular Causality*

Figure 5.1. *Two models of causality.*

In this illustration, father, daughter, and mother have developed a system of interaction in which each influences the behavior of the other. However, since each person is part of the cycle that perpetuates the pattern, there is no single "cause" for the mother's or the father's withdrawal or for their yelling. Systems such as this usually resist change. The pattern seeks to maintain a familiar state of equilibrium, and each person plays his or her part in the process.

If you have ever found yourself thinking, "Here we go again," or "We've been over all of this before," then you have encountered circular communication systems. To achieve a different pattern, at least one participant needs to change his or her part in the cycle.

Changing the System

The characteristics of a particular circular communication system are guided by family rules about communication. In our example family, one rule is that the mother will defend the daughter. The mother may or may not be aware that such a rule operates in her family, but her behavior is nevertheless governed by it. For this communication system to change, at least one participant will need to behave differently. One individual's change will influence changes in the other members.

For example, if the father were to stop yelling, the pattern would change, and the daughter might be influenced to try something besides crying. If the daughter didn't cry, but negotiated instead, the mother would no longer have a reason to play her familiar "protector" role in the pattern. Instead, the mother might choose to talk to the father about what's bothering him. The father would not "cause" these changes by altering his behavior. Instead, when he changed *his part* in the system (or changed a rule that governed his behavior), the system would adjust to his change in ways he could not predict.

Be aware that such changes in family communication rules are often difficult to make. Frequently, when one person breaks out and tries something different, other family members try, either overtly or covertly, to bring the "wayward" member back so that the old, familiar balance can be maintained.

Perpetuating the System

Continuing this example, let's say that the daughter leaves her family to marry. Her marital communication system will likely be different from her family of origin system, but she may try to perpetuate some of her old, familiar patterns in her new system. If her new husband should yell at her for some reason, she may initially break down and cry, hoping that someone else (possibly her mother or her best friend) will take her side. If the daughter's husband comes from a family in which people tend to yell back and then later apologize, he may be confused or even hurt by his wife's behavior.

In this example, family communication rules are in conflict (see chapter 2). The daughter is following the rule "When someone yells at me, I will cry and go find help." The husband is following the rule "After I yell at someone, they can yell back, but then we both need to apologize." The difference between these two rules is likely to leave both spouses wondering what to do next.

Since these are not the kind of household rules that are written and hung on the refrigerator, neither spouse may understand that they are operating from different, unstated patterns. This conflict is not "caused" by either spouse independently of the other. They interact and influence each other's behavior in a circular way.

The "Dance"

CASE ILLUSTRATION

Francine shakes an accusing finger at Ralph and critically points out, "Whenever I try to talk to you about finances, you just get mad and stomp off." Ralph counters with "Well, you usually throw the checkbook at me, and tell me that if I'm so smart I can balance it myself." Both Ralph and Francine would probably agree on at least one thing: they have a problem talking about finances.

The communication pattern between Ralph and Francine could be compared to a dance. Any two people who have been together for an extended period of time tend to develop interaction patterns. These patterns are like dance steps, and, like dance partners, spouses get used to responding to each other in certain ways. The "dance" involves both parties, and both are responsible for the patterns they have created. If a certain "dance step" isn't working, both partners have the power to choose new steps. When one spouse takes a different step, the partner has an opportunity to respond differently. Even small changes on the part of one or both provide opportunities to create new patterns and to improve the relationship.

Of course, the best "new step" that battling couples can take is to act with patience and forgiveness toward each other. As Paul wrote to the people of Ephesus:

> Let no corrupt communication proceed out of your mouth, but that which is good to the use of edifying, that it may minister grace unto the hearers. And grieve not the holy Spirit of God, whereby ye are sealed unto the day of redemption. Let all bitterness, and wrath, and anger, and clamour, and evil speaking, be put away from you, with all malice: And be ye kind one to another, tenderhearted, forgiving one another, even as God for Christ's sake hath forgiven you. (Ephesians 4:29–32.)

CASE ILLUSTRATION

Example 1. Katya, looking frustrated, complains loudly, "This checkbook is a mess."
Boris complains back, "Ha! You've got no room to be criticizing me for the way *I* keep a checkbook."

"Look who's talking," Katya counters. "Your biggest problem is that you can't take constructive criticism."

"That's because you never know what you're talking about," Boris snaps.

Katya comes in from the kitchen and says, "You never listen to me long enough to know. I think it's a trait that runs in your family. You're just like your mother."

"*My* mother? If we're on the subject of mothers, let's talk about *your* mother . . . "

Each spouse continues to respond without attempting to understand the problem. The "dance steps" center on blame and irrelevant issues that hurt.

Example 2. Katya says, "This checkbook is a mess."

Boris, looking over her shoulder, responds, "What's the problem?"

With frustration in her voice, Katya continues, "I sat down to balance our checking account and noticed that nothing was recorded for check number 728. Do you remember when it was written?"

"You bet I do," Boris answers. "It was last Thursday when I took the kids to the doctor. I was so involved with how high their fevers were and how pale they looked that I just wrote out a check to the receptionist and bundled them back into the car."

Katya smiles knowingly. "It sounds like you had your hands full."

Boris smiles back and nods. "It was like trying to keep puppies in a box."

Each spouse has attempted to understand and support the other—and the content of their discussion remains relevant to the initial problem.

Today's world is filled with the pressures of too many things to do and not enough time to do them. Mistakes are bound to happen. Our ability to look past the mistakes to see the effort put forth by another in our behalf allows us to be empathetic rather than critical.

Communication That Works

The Communication Goals Exercise

Take some time during the next week to look at your own communication patterns and the responses you personally make to the "dance" that you and your spouse perform. Write your observations on the Communication Goals Exercise, Worksheet 5.1.

The Zap Rule

To help yourselves become more aware of any problems being caused by ineffective communication patterns, you may also want to employ the "zap rule." A tool to help you communicate more effectively, the zap rule will let each of you know when he or she has said something hurtful or demeaning and allow him or her the chance to express the same idea in a more loving, supportive way.

A *zap* is anything that makes you feel as if you're not being treated as an equal or with dignity and respect, or as if you are being blamed, punished, or ridiculed. The zap rule requires that the conversation stop immediately when a participant perceives a zap, and that an attempt be made to rephrase the comment. This is how it works:

1. When you feel you have been *zapped*, raise your hand or stop the discussion.
2. Tell the other person, *in a non-accusatory way*, that you felt zapped. You need not justify your feelings. The zapped person is assumed to be right; therefore, the zapping person should not attempt to convince the other that the comment wasn't really a zap.
3. Ask the zapping person to rephrase the statement, or modify the tone of voice used to express the statement, so as to remove the zap characteristics.
4. The zapping person should attempt to rephrase the comment so that the zap is removed.
5. Thank the person for rephrasing.
6. Only three zaps are allowed per discussion. If more than three zaps occur, then take time out from that particular topic (at least 30 minutes), but agree to come back to it later.

Levels of Communication

One of the most common sources of dissatisfaction in communication is partners expressing themselves on different levels of intimacy. For example, after an evening of dinner and dancing, one spouse says, "I had a good time tonight. Getting out like that really means a lot to me." The other spouse responds at a different level of intimacy: "The music was okay but I thought the price of dinner was outrageous. We could feed the whole family for a week on what it cost us tonight." The first spouse is communicating at a *feeling* level while the second is communicating at a *cognitive* level. The most effective communication occurs when both partners communicate on the same level.

Harold Bernard and Wesley Huckins, in *Dynamics of Personal Adjustment*, discuss five levels of communication.[1] Each level has its own combination of content, meaning, and emotional involvement, and each level can play an important part when discussing finances.

Level 5: Clichés and Greetings

Level 5 is the least intimate level of communication. Most commonly used in casual conversations, it includes greetings and clichés such as "Easy come, easy go," and "Money just seems to burn a hole in my pocket."

Level 4: Information and Directions

Level 4 is used primarily to give directions and exchange information. Financially compatible couples inform each other of pertinent details: "I stopped by the bank today. The reason our checkbook doesn't balance is that we're not recording our automatic teller withdrawals."

Level 3: Feelings about External Events

Level 3 is the first level at which you express individual feelings, but only about the *external* world. You may share likes and dislikes, and feelings associated with values, attitudes, and beliefs. You may say, for example, "I hate going into debt as much as you do, but how else can we afford to get the car repaired unless we put it on a credit card?"

Level 2: Feelings about Internal Events

Level 2's attempts to express emotions go to a deeper level—that of your *internal* world: what is going on inside you rather than what is going on outside. At this level, you may express high-risk feelings such as love, loneliness, and hurt. You might tell your spouse, "I have never felt so unloved, so unimportant as when I saw you drive up in that new car, after I had pleaded with you not to buy it, not to bury us further in debt. For a moment I actually hated you."

Level 1: Intuition

Level 1 is the most intimate level of communication; it communicates a sense of oneness and togetherness. In contrast to the other levels, this level is usually nonverbal. Because of the intensity of emotions, communication often takes place through eye contact, embrace, and touch. Children are very good at interpreting this level of communication. When giving someone a gift, a child will immediately look up at the person's face to evaluate how the person *really* feels about the gift. They seem to know intuitively that most of what we communicate is nonverbal.

In general, 95 percent of what we communicate is nonverbal (tone of voice, gestures, posture, facial expressions, personal possessions, and so forth), while only 5 percent is verbal (words). When verbal and nonverbal messages contradict each other, we tend to believe that the nonverbal is the more valid message.

The Importance of Communicating on a Feeling Level

Unfortunately, many married couples seem to spend most of their time trying to communicate on levels 5 (clichés) and 4 (information), which keeps their relationship on a fairly superficial level. For greater intimacy, couples must communicate as much as possible on the feeling levels (levels 3, 2, and 1).

Each of us is responsible for our own willingness to commit to a relationship, to risk being vulnerable, and to express our feelings openly and honestly. You are responsible for what communication you send to your partner, and for interpreting what you receive. But you are *not* responsible for how your partner receives what you send. In handling these responsibilities, it is helpful to tell the sender what the communication *represented* to you and then ask if that was his or her *intent*.

CASE ILLUSTRATION

After putting the kids to bed, Jeff returns to the kitchen to confront his wife, Pat. "When you told me that you had already paid this month's bills, I felt like a complete failure. It came across as if you thought I had been doing a lousy job of it and therefore you were going to take over. Is that what you really think?"

Pat, with a look of surprise at such an accusation, replies, "For heaven's sake, no. I think you're doing a fine job paying the bills. But I knew how time-consuming and upsetting paying the bills can be, and I thought that since your final exams were at the beginning of the month, I'd save you the time and frustration by paying them for you."

Finding out what a person *means* by what he or she says is crucial. The same words can mean different things to different people. Verbal misunderstandings sometimes stem from confusion between the *denotative* and *connotative* meanings of a word. The denotative meaning is the dictionary definition of the word; the connotative meaning includes the emotional overtones, or personal meaning, that the word carries. For example, the word *collateral* is defined in the dictionary as the security provided by a borrower in the form of pledged assets or endorsement by a co-signer. From a connotative standpoint, *collateral* means something that can be repossessed, such as the tractor or the furniture, and thus may generate feelings of anxiety, anger, and helplessness.

Communicating on the feeling levels is especially important when dealing with what is *expected* from the relationship in comparison to what is being *provided*. Most relationships that fail were built on promises that could not be kept and expectations that could not be met. When someone promises to *make* someone else happy, the person to whom the promise was made expects to be made happy. When that person remains miserable, he or she doesn't have to look far to find someone to blame.

One love-struck individual may say, "I've been miserable all my life," and the other replies, "So have I." In unison they exclaim, "Let's get married and make each other happy!" If one of them is not happy, he or she assumes that the other is withholding the "happy power." This assumption, of course, releases the unhappy one from any personal responsibility for the current state of affairs.

In many cases, happiness is associated with being something, doing something, or having something. Happiness can be a result of being important to someone, feeling special or irreplaceable. It can come from having your feelings appreciated or having consideration given to your need to do something or have something. In the latter case, however, "happy power" can often translate into financial power. If you have the ability to meet the needs of your spouse and yet selfishly withhold resources—depriving your spouse of activities or things that make him or her happy—you are misusing your power and are very likely leaving your partner disillusioned with the marriage.

Negotiations

One of the most effective ways of meeting each other's needs within a relationship is through the process of *negotiation*. A cooperative decision-making process in which two or more parties talk in an effort to resolve their differences, the primary purpose of negotiating is to achieve agreement; the secondary purpose is to establish and maintain long-term relationships. As with building a house, building a marriage requires a willingness to negotiate and compromise to reach mutually satisfying solutions.

Negotiating is an essential part of everyday life; the better you become at it, the more often you can peaceably settle misunderstandings, including financial problems. Many of the problems associated with meeting needs within relationships, as well as some of those encountered when dealing with creditors, can be avoided by using some basic negotiation guidelines.[2]

First of all, know that negotiations are *not* intended to be win-lose battles, but a means of arriving at solutions that are *mutually beneficial*. To avoid developing a "win-lose" mentality, you must separate the *people* from the *problem*. Remember that you are together for the purpose of attacking your financial problem and not each other. So one of the first things you need to negotiate is how you are going to treat each other. From the first encounter, you should make every effort to ease tensions, safeguard the other person's self-esteem, and show appropriate consideration for the other person's position.

When negotiating, if one person insists on "winning it all," that person will ultimately lose, in terms of the relationship. The parties involved are *opponents who need each other*, and must be able to treat each other with dignity—something that is especially important in the many negotiations called for within a family. The dignity with which a member of the family was treated during past negotiations has a major effect on how willing that person will be to negotiate future impasses. No one should ever be left with feelings of resentment or the belief that she or he was totally defeated.

Pre-negotiation Planning

A number of factors contribute to successful negotiations. One of the most essential is pre-negotiation planning, which should include at least the following:

1. Know what you want and what the other person wants.
2. Know what is negotiable and what is not.
3. Establish priorities; know the relative importance of various items to be negotiated.
4. Know what you are willing to give up.
5. Acquire the necessary facts and information about each issue or item.
6. Develop a reasonable defense for your position.
7. Develop alternatives.

The Opening Proposal

The opening proposal should be realistic and should show some consideration for the opposing position. It should also be credible—the other person must believe you are sincere. The degree of sincerity you project depends a great deal on your reputation: In the past, have you been ethical, fulfilled commitments, and acted expeditiously?

After you make the opening proposal, be prepared to settle for less than you expected. Then if negotiations result in more, you will be pleasantly surprised. But you will never get more than you ask for *originally*, so open a little high. The positions you take later may then appear more reasonable or generous, and you will be able to give up more during the process. In this way, the "give and take" principle can more easily work, and the other person is more likely to make a greater number of counter proposals.

Making Concessions

Making a concession means changing your offer in favor of the other party. The change (1) reduces the benefits you are seeking, and (2) encourages the other party to either come to an agreement or make a concession in exchange. Keep in mind that the very fact that your opponent has agreed to negotiate is a sign of readiness to make concessions. So look for areas of common interest and solutions that might be beneficial to both parties.

Keep your concessions small and infrequent. Your first concession should be your largest, and each subsequent concession should be smaller than the previous one. For example, if you were negotiating a selling price, you might propose a price of $200 and then make a $30 concession, bringing the price down to $170. For your next concession, though, you should come down only $20, and only $10 for your third concession. Meanwhile, the buyer will increase his or her offers by a similar progression. As a consequence, both the seller and the buyer will soon be able to project the optimal, mutually satisfying price.

Similarly, when negotiating the distribution of financial responsibilities within a relationship, you might open with "I'll pay two of the fixed bills," followed by a proposal to pay four of the fixed bills but none of the variable bills. Later, you might concede to pay all the fixed bills and two of the variables.

Counter Proposals

Before making a counter proposal, review what has already been proposed and evaluate how your counter offer can serve a *common good*. Above all, do not phrase your counter proposal as a threat. If someone has made a concession in good faith, for example, do not reciprocate with an ultimatum: "You'd better come up with something better than that or I'm walking out of here," or "Carrying just one check with you and leaving the rest at home may work, but if you bounce one more check, your name is coming off the account, and that's final!"

Reaching an Agreement

Remember that your ultimate objective is to arrive at a mutually acceptable agreement, not to get the other person to let you have your way. If you are willing to lower initial demands, make frequent concessions, and consider the interests of the other person, you can greatly improve your chances of reaching an agreement.

Sometimes negotiations become *deadlocked*—neither side willing to move from a particular position. Perhaps attitudes have become hostile because feelings have been needlessly hurt or past experiences have contributed to an atmosphere of distrust. When this happens, apologies are generally the most effective way to get beyond the deadlock.

Closing

Closing a negotiation becomes possible when both parties have achieved most of their objectives. For instance, a creditor hoping to receive immediately 100 percent of what was owed may settle for 80 percent in three equal installments. Or one spouse, who had hoped to avoid paying bills alone, may succeed in convincing the other spouse to assume responsibility for the fixed-payment debts. In both cases, the negotiations will have closed successfully.

Sometimes you can close by proposing an overall final offer that ties smaller items into one cohesive package. Such a proposal is usually made when one party perceives that the other has made all the concessions he or she is willing to make, so a package of special concessions is included as an incentive to close. For example, one spouse may propose, "I'm willing to do it all: pay the bills, write the creditors, and do the shopping for one month while you study for your entrance exams, if in return you will use the extra time for studying and nothing else."

Closing can also take place when a solution is proposed that is unique and simple, yet substantially different from the alternatives that have already been suggested: "Rather than arguing over whether you or I should manage the finances, why don't we hire an accountant to do it?"

Once you reach an agreement, record the details in writing and *do not try to make any changes.* Try to maintain a sense of acceptance toward the outcome and avoid thinking about what you might have done or said differently. Above all, try to view both sides as victorious.

Reframing

The real success of the negotiations lies in how each person chooses to interpret the outcome. In many cases, it is far easier for us to change our perspective on an event than it is to change someone else's behavior. The process of changing perspectives is called *reframing*. Family therapist Paul Watzlawick believes that by *reframing*—changing one's conceptual or emotional point of view on an event—family members can gain greater understanding about some old family processes.[3]

John Milton, in *Paradise Lost*, provided us with perhaps the most poetic definition of reframing:

> The mind is its own place, and in itself
> Can make a heaven of hell, a hell of heaven.

Milton's view suggests that it is we who, through our ability to interpret the world in a variety of ways, determine the way we see the world around us.

CASE ILLUSTRATION

Amanda was feeling very frustrated and angry over the fact that her father was putting 15 percent of his paycheck into savings every month. She felt the family needed at least some of it for clothes and entertainment. Her father, however, was adamant about the amount to be set aside for savings and would not consider withdrawing any of it.

Amanda saw her father as stingy and mean, and she doubted that he really loved her and the other children. But when she talked with her father, he revealed that when he was a child, his family had gone through the Great Depression. Having witnessed the agony and trials that his parents, brothers, and sisters had gone through, he had vowed that when he grew up he would make sure that this kind of hardship would never befall his family. Reframing her father's behavior within the context of his experience with the Depression enabled Amanda to see his saving money as an act of love and concern for the family rather than as an act of selfishness.

Reframing can also be very helpful when trying to communicate differences in how you each perceive the relative importance of a particular purchase. The concept of *meaningful units*, as discussed in chapter 1, is an example of reframing. The cost of a pair of shoes for one of their children was that couple's meaningful unit. They were able to arrive at the relative value of other wants by appraising how many pairs of shoes they could buy with the amount paid for other items. A new garbage disposal, for example, cost six pairs of shoes, subscribing to cable TV for a month cost two pairs, and one month's supply of soft drinks cost four pairs.

In another case, a couple realized they could have opened an individual retirement account (IRA) with what they had spent on credit card interest alone in the past year. An IRA became this couple's meaningful unit.

The relative value information provided by meaningful units is often more useful than knowing an item's cost in money alone. With an increased understanding of each other's values, a couple can achieve an even greater level of sensitivity and intimacy.

Intimacy and Communication

Communication and intimacy go hand in hand. Before you can be emotionally intimate with others, you must first understand and accept their feelings, their aspirations, and their values. But gaining such understanding with regard to another person's finances can be difficult. According to a study by Blumstein and Schwartz, "Money is often a more taboo topic of conversation than sex, and courting couples may discuss their prior sex lives while never raising the question of their economic histories. . . . [Personal finances] are the last frontier of self-disclosure."[4]

Intimacy is created through the process of sharing and a willingness to trust. Trust is the ability to feel comfortable while being vulnerable. When partners communicate ineffectively, each may develop a distorted view of the other and of their relationship. This distortion blocks true understanding, and lack of understanding can result in a low level of intimacy in the relationship.

CASE ILLUSTRATION

Maria throws her purse on the chair as she comes into the room. She sighs tiredly, "I had a really bad day today."

Jose doesn't look up from his paper, but mutters, "Really? Well, you should hear what my day was like. I can't believe I survived it."

Maria doesn't respond immediately, but starts for the medicine cabinet in the bathroom. "I have this horrible headache. I wonder if I'm getting sick or something."

Jose puts his paper down and raises his voice so she can hear him from the bathroom. "A headache's nothing. I almost got hit at a four-way stop. These out-of-state drivers act like they learned to drive on another planet."

Maria comes out of the bathroom and heads for the kitchen. "I'm hungry. Maybe I just need to eat something."

Jose reaches for the phone as he comments half to himself and half to Maria, "I need to call my brother tonight . . ."

Effective communication skills result in a higher level of intimacy.

CASE ILLUSTRATION

Marsha comes in and flops down on the nearest chair. "I had a really bad day today."

Paul puts down his paper and asks, "Really? That's too bad. What happened?"

Marsha sighs, "I got this really horrible headache around lunchtime, and I haven't been able to get rid of it."

Paul grimaces, "That doesn't sound too good. That's the second headache this week. Is there anything I can do?"

Marsha gets up and heads for the kitchen. "I think I just need something to eat. I've had to work right through lunch a couple of times this week. Thanks for the offer. How about starting some toast while I get the eggs? How was *your* day?"

Paul puts a couple of pieces of bread in the toaster and replies, "I can't believe I survived it."

"That bad? What happened?"

Paul continues, "I almost got hit at a four-way stop."

Marsha's eyes widen, then she puts her arm around him. "That almost happened to me a couple of weeks ago," she says. "Scared the heck out of me."

Paul agrees. "Believe me, I was scared. The rest of my day was pretty well shot."

You can probably see the difference in the level of intimacy being experienced by each couple. It is quite possible that there was a time when Paul and Marsha communicated with the same low level of intimacy that Jose and Maria use. Perhaps Paul and Marsha consciously decided they wanted a more celestial marriage—and then dedicated themselves to developing a greater level of intimacy through more responsive communication. A long time ago, another Paul, a disciple of Christ, spoke of such efforts.

> Seek those things which are above, where Christ sitteth on the right hand of God. Set your affection on things above, not on things on the earth. . . . When Christ, who is our life, shall appear, then shall ye also appear with him in glory. . . . But now ye also put off all these; anger, wrath, malice, blasphemy, filthy communication out of your mouth. Lie not one to another, seeing that ye have put off the old man with his deeds; And have put on the new man, which is renewed in knowledge after the image of him that created him. (Colossians 3:1–2, 4, 8–10.)

Characteristics of Intimate Relationships

Clinical psychologist Gerald Corey assembled the following list of characteristics of intimate relationships.[5]

1. Each person in the relationship has a separate identity—each can give and receive without losing separateness.
2. Each is able to talk openly about matters of significance.
3. Each assumes personal responsibility for his or her level of happiness and doesn't blame the other for unhappiness.
4. The couple are able to play together.
5. The couple are able to fight constructively.
6. Each makes some attempt to keep romance in the relationship.
7. Each considers the other an equal.
8. Each actively demonstrates concern for the other.
9. Each is growing, changing, and open to new experiences.
10. Each is able to find meaning outside of the relationship.
11. Each avoids manipulating the other.
12. Each recognizes the need for solitude and space.
13. Each avoids assuming an attitude of ownership toward the other.
14. Each shows flexibility in role behavior.

15. Neither expects the other to do for them what they are able to do for themselves.
16. Each discloses inner feelings and thoughts to the other.
17. Each allows the other a sense of privacy.
18. Each has a desire to give to the other.
19. Each encourages the other to become all he or she is capable of becoming.
20. Each has a commitment to the other.

Relationship Intimacy Exercise

After you and your partner have reviewed the preceding list, discuss the following questions:
1. Which of these characteristics do you believe are part of intimacy?
2. Which of these do you have in your relationship?
3. What links do you see between communication and intimacy?

Choose one of the characteristics of an intimate relationship, write it on an index card, and carry it with you for the next week. Work toward implementing this characteristic to a greater degree in your marriage. After one week, choose another characteristic to work on. Continue this exercise until you have achieved the degree of intimacy you desire to have in your relationship.

Summary

Effective communication skills and intimacy in a relationship go hand in hand. Recognizing and changing circular communication patterns and evaluating your level of communication are important aids to greater intimacy. Learning to reframe and to negotiate will be effective means of achieving favorable compromises with both creditors and members of your family.

Personality, feelings, and relationships are tremendously significant to financial behavior. With this understanding, you are ready to explore your financial past, present, and future.

Important Terms

Circular causality: A model of causality that acknowledges that one event may influence another event, which in turn influences another, which in turn influences the first. Communication patterns show circular causality.

Communication, level of: The degree of intimacy expressed. Bernard and Huckins identified five levels of communication: Level 5, clichés and greetings; Level 4, information and directions; Level 3, feelings about external events; Level 2, feelings about internal events; and Level 1, intuition.

Intimacy: Closeness to and understanding of another person. A low level of intimacy is usually due to ineffective communication skills, while a high level of intimacy is usually a result of effective communication skills.

Negotiation: Talking with another person in order to settle some matter; a cooperative decision-making process consisting of pre-negotiation planning, the opening proposal, making concessions, counter proposals, reaching an agreement, and closing.

Reframing: Changing one's conceptual or emotional point of view on an event or circumstance.

Zap: Any message that makes you feel you're not being treated as an equal or with dignity and respect, that you are being blamed, punished, or ridiculed. Zaps interfere with the communication process and are to be avoided.

Zap rule: If a zap is perceived during communication, the conversation stops immediately and the offender then makes an attempt to rephrase the comment in a considerate and respectful way.

Notes

1. Bernard and Huckins, 1975, pp. 330–37.

2. Poduska, 1987.

3. Watzlawick, Weakland and Fisch, 1974.

4. Blumstein and Schwartz, 1983, p. 51.

5. Corey, 1990, pp. 225–28.

COMMUNICATION GOALS EXERCISE

Decide independently of each other what communication goals you and your spouse would like to achieve. After you complete your separate lists, select and discuss three goals you hold in common. (The common goals may be chosen from the individual goals, or they may be some combination of the individual goals.)

I would like to see us achieve these three communication goals:

1. _____

2. _____

3. _____

My spouse would like to see us achieve these three communication goals:

1. _____

2. _____

3. _____

These are the three communication goals we have in common that we would like to achieve:

1. _____

2. _____

3. _____

PART 2

Your Financial Past, Present, and Future

One reason most budgets simply do not work is that they are developed around a time frame that is too limiting. Budgets often focus on the current month only, as if what happens during *that* month portrays the entire financial picture. This restricted view inhibits the development of a successful financial management program. For a truly effective budgeting process, you must work with three different, but interrelated, time frames.

First, take a look at your financial *past* to better understand how you got where you are today, and to learn to cope effectively with the debt load you have accumulated. Next, look toward the *future* to get some idea of how to avoid those budget-sabotaging "eight balls" that always seem to come along just when you think you are getting your finances under control. Dealing with the future also includes making plans for retirement, missions, insurance, and educational needs. It is important to decide where you eventually want to be financially, what kind of effort you will need to make in order to get there, and how much time it will take. During this process, it is essential that you maintain an *eternal* perspective in order to preserve a balance between your temporal and spiritual objectives.

After you have a better understanding of how the past and the future can affect your current situation, you will be ready to begin managing your budget in the *present*.

CHAPTER 6

Understanding Why You Have Financial Problems

*T*t is important to explore your past as you attempt to understand what behavior has been responsible for your current financial situation. Major considerations in this chapter are two principles from chapter 1—Principle 1: *Financial problems are usually behavior problems rather than money problems,* and Principle 2: *If you continue doing what you are doing, you will continue getting what you are getting.*

If you find yourself saying, "I've been trying to get out of debt for the past 12 years, but I haven't made it yet," then, although you may *talk* about getting out of debt, you are most likely set in a pattern of *behavior* that perpetuates chronic indebtedness. According to Principle 2, you will have to change what you have been doing or you will continue in debt for the rest of your life.

How Did You Get into This Mess?

We get into financial messes for many reasons, most stemming from our emotions—impatience, envy, anger, love, craving, inadequacy, insecurity, and loneliness. For example, the interest you pay on a loan is often the cost of impatience, the "I want it, and I want it now" syndrome. Impatience can be a very expensive emotion, and so can others. It may be wise to consider again, as was mentioned in chapter 3, the adage "*Impatience* is trying to make things occur on *our* schedule while *patience* is accepting that things will occur on *God's* schedule."

The following list of questions indicates some of the reasons people get themselves into financial messes. Try to identify the emotions associated with each type of behavior—and which behaviors most closely match your own.

1. Do you buy items that are usually associated with a higher socioeconomic level than your income warrants? Do you compete with someone else or with a particular comparison group? Do you buy things to compensate for feelings of inadequacy or because of a need to impress others? This behavior is identified as **trying to move too far, too fast.**

2. Do you habitually live beyond your means, and are any increases in income already committed? Do you buy into "get-rich-quick" schemes or high-risk investments? Does your financial system lack emergency funds or savings programs? This is identified as **failure to determine what is sufficient.**

3. Do you **lack basic financial management skills?**

4. Do you have a history of **impulse buying?** Have you been self-indulgent in an attempt to compensate for loneliness or the feeling that no one cares about you?

5. When you buy something, do you neglect to take into account the hidden, indirect, and relationship costs? This is identified as **failure to determine the true cost of a purchase.**

6. Do you buy things that you use infrequently and that you could have rented for much less? This is called **failure to analyze the cost per use.**

7. Do you **lack sufficient medical or liability insurance coverage?**

8. Are you staggering under your debt load? This may be because of **credit abuse.**

9. Do you have **addictive behaviors,** such as gambling, hoarding, or substance abuse (alcohol, illegal drugs, nicotine, prescriptions)?

Trying to Move Too Far, Too Fast

Most of us live in an upwardly mobile society; however, the pace at which we attempt to move from one socioeconomic level to another can have a dramatic impact on our financial situation. For the sake of simplicity, assume that there are only five socioeconomic levels and that these levels can be identified primarily by the amount of income earned and the types of purchases made, as shown in Table 6.1.

TABLE 6.1
SOCIOECONOMIC LEVELS AND TYPES OF PURCHASES

SOCIOECONOMIC LEVEL	ANNUAL INCOME	BOAT PURCHASE	HOUSING
5. High	$100,000+	Yacht	Mansion
4. Medium high	$50–99,000	Cruiser	Large house
3. Medium	$30–49,000	21' inboard	Medium house
2. Medium low	$15–29,000	12' outboard	Small house
1. Low	below $15,000	Canoe	Rental unit

The amount of effort (represented by the amount of change in income) needed to move from Level 1 to Level 2 or from Level 2 to Level 3 is relatively small compared to the effort needed to move from Level 3 to Level 4, or from Level 4 to Level 5. As a consequence, more people live at levels 2 and 3 than at levels 4 and 5. But this doesn't seem to discourage people with lower level incomes from trying to purchase things normally associated with the more luxurious lifestyles of the higher income levels. Unfortunately, those at the lower income levels must go into debt to buy these expensive items.

Purchasing items corresponding to your own level of income is possible, although it usually means saving for a while first. Buying items corresponding to a lower level of income than your own usually means paying cash and being able to buy immediately. For example, if your income were around $45,000 per year and you wished to buy a 21-foot inboard powerboat—a purchase within your income level—you would have to save for a while, but it would be attainable. If you wanted to buy a 12-foot outboard—a purchase within a *lower* income level—you could probably pay cash for it without having to save. But if you were to attempt to purchase a cruiser—which corresponds to a *higher* socioeconomic level—you would have to go into debt to buy it.

Financial problems are inevitable when you try to move too far, too fast, and begin to consume at a rate that exceeds your current level of income. The remedy is simple: To avoid unnecessary debt, *make purchases that are appropriate to your income level.* To help you become converted to this fundamental principle, consider the following issues.

Assets and liabilities

For the most part, debt is a symptom of trying to live beyond your means—trying to obtain status symbols that are beyond your level of income. It's like going to a bank and explaining, "I'm going to be honest with you loan officers. I cannot possibly live the lifestyle I want to live or buy the things I'd like to buy unless you agree to contribute thousands of dollars toward making my dreams come true. It's obvious that I cannot afford to live in the manner to which I would like to become accustomed on my current salary. So how about it? Do I get the loan?"

You need to realize that, in actuality, your *equity* is your own contribution, and your *liabilities* are the contributions others make, toward maintaining your lifestyle. Assume you—and the bank—buy a $10,000 car, for example. You must divide this asset into the portion you own and the portion the bank owns: Your $2,000 down payment represents your equity in the car. The loan you received from the bank ($8,000 paid to the dealer) counts as a liability.

The Cost of Belonging

"Buying up" is often an attempt to gain acceptance from those you admire. Trying to buy a sense of belonging can be very expensive, both directly and indirectly. Direct expenses are the costs of "membership" in the group. They might include joining a country club, spa, or private or professional organization, as well as purchasing privileged seating at sports, entertainment, or political events.

Indirect expenses come through other consumer practices, such as buying a house in a particular neighborhood. The make and model of the car you drive may represent an attempt to be included in a particular group, as may the logos on your clothes and shopping bags. Quite often, the indirect costs of membership in a social group are even higher than the direct costs.

Unfortunately, the truth of Principle 6—*You can never get enough of what you don't need because what you don't need can never satisfy you*—often defeats misguided efforts to buy acceptance and belonging. Spending to achieve a higher status, to control others, or to feel important is expensive and wasteful—and, for most, unaffordable. In the long run, such spending is futile and ungratifying, partly because of the inherent lack of intimacy associated with it, and partly because of the gradual development of a dependence on the things that money can buy.

Conspicuous Consumption

The need to impress others is often found in people who want to be accepted by those at a higher economic level and who, at the same time, loathe being regarded as equals by their peers at a lower socioeconomic level. Pride and envy play a big part in their lives.

Prideful individuals engage in what is commonly referred to as *conspicuous consumption*—acquiring goods and services not because they are needed but because they are expensive, generate attention, and provide the appearance of affluence. Such individuals often see themselves as less successful than a particular group of high achievers and are constantly trying to catch up with them. In the process, they tend to "compare to lose": if they drive a Buick, they notice the Cadillac; if they are in a Cadillac, they want a Mercedes; if they drive a Mercedes, they compare themselves to Rolls Royce owners. Regardless of how high they climb, they inevitably lose in the comparison—those in higher brackets see to that!

Self-Worth

Comparing ourselves to others is counterproductive in another way: some of those who do so may feel like impostors when they finally achieve professional and financial success. They believe that others really deserve their successes, while they have just been lucky.[1] They fear that sooner or later their "secret" will be discovered, and others will find out that all of the things they have surrounded themselves with have no substance behind them.

Far too many people believe that their self-worth rests on the numbers found on their balance sheets rather than on the mutual respect found in their relationships. They believe that people are worth more if they have lots of money and are worth less if they don't. But in most cases, you express your true self-worth by what you can *do;* you try to impress others by what you can *buy*. The need for belonging can be satisfied through what you can *contribute*, not through what you can *consume*.

You may wish to explore your own beliefs by asking yourself these questions: How do you judge your own worth and that of others? What are your intentions when making purchases—to *express* your self-worth, or to *impress* others with your financial worth?

Elusive Happiness and Security

Psychotherapist David Krueger notes that "One will desire more and more money as long as nothing challenges the belief that money can command emotional as well as material goods from others. . . . The desire for it is insatiable."[2]

The pursuit of personal affluence can be an insatiable goal. Yet, an ever-increasing number of us have come to place our faith in the belief that if we could only acquire enough (whatever that is), we would find happiness and security. President Spencer W. Kimball addressed this quest for material security:

> Few men have ever knowingly and deliberately chosen to reject God and his blessings. Rather, we learn from the scriptures that because the exercise of faith has always appeared to be more difficult than relying on things more immediately at hand, carnal man has tended to transfer his trust in God to material things. Therefore, in all ages when men have fallen under the power of Satan and lost the faith, they have put in its place a hope in the "arm of flesh" and in "gods of silver, and gold, of brass, iron, wood, and stone, which see not, nor hear, nor know" (Daniel 5:23)—that is, in idols. This I find to be a dominant theme in the Old Testament. Whatever thing a man sets his heart and his trust in most is his god; and if his god doesn't also happen to be the true and living God of Israel, that man is laboring in idolatry.[3]

Far too often the hoped-for happiness eludes the carnal man; only a fortunate few ever come to understand that true happiness and security is more likely to be achieved through trust in God. Nephi, while acknowledging his own weakness and susceptibility to temptation, declared:

> O Lord, I have trusted in thee, and I will trust in thee forever. I will not put my trust in the arm of flesh; for I know that cursed is he that putteth his trust in the arm of flesh. Yea, cursed is he that putteth his trust in man or maketh flesh his arm. (2 Nephi 4:34.)

Failure to Determine What Is Sufficient

When you buy a car, your main concerns are what you can afford and what would be *enough* car (how many of the amenities you can live without). But determining what would be enough income is more complex—you must decide whether you are referring to an *open-ended* or a *closed-ended* amount.

Open-ended versus Closed-ended Budgets

With an open-ended budget, you have not determined how much money is enough. No matter how much your current income is, you are probably thinking in terms of making more, and your budget is unrealistically based on anticipated increases in income. Take, for example, the words of this overly optimistic planner: "Can you believe that between the two of us we made over $52,000 last year? If we play our cards right, we ought to make at least $60,000 this year, and maybe $70,000 next year. The size of that new house is looking bigger and bigger. If it keeps going like this, it won't be long before we're talking about a pool and a sauna."

In about 340 B.C., Aristotle, observing the people of his day, almost prophetically described the financial world that today's families face.

> Some persons are led to believe that getting wealth is the object of household management, and the whole idea of their lives is that they ought either to increase their money without limit, or at any rate not to lose it. The origin of this disposition in men is that they are intent upon living only, and not upon living well; and, as their desires are unlimited, they also desire that the means of gratifying them should be without limit.[4]

In contrast, when you consider a closed-ended amount of money, you have decided how much income you would consider *sufficient*. With the necessary income predetermined, you are in a position to regulate your expenditures accordingly and to experience the freedom that comes from living within your means. (Specific skills for accomplishing this are included in chapter 8.) For instance, if you determined that $30,000 per year were a sufficient income and adjusted your spending to that figure, then any additional income would be uncommitted and could be saved or spent as you saw fit. Imagine the result: "I can't believe how much we have in savings already. Our decision to put half of every salary increase into savings and to use the other half to compensate for cost-of-living increases has worked out beautifully."

Open-ended budgeting—in other words, living beyond your means and having any increases in income already committed—eventually leads to financial insecurity. It's like walking a tightrope—if you have no financial safety net, a fall will kill you. Nobody wants to live in a world that precarious.

Financial Security

To make your world a little safer, you must prepare for the unexpected. Financial planners recommend that an emergency savings fund of at least three months' expenses be maintained at all times. Unfortunately, too few people have such a savings program. And too many people have no savings program to provide them with sufficient retirement funds. As a result, many never achieve a feeling of financial security.

Just about everyone dreams of someday being financially secure. But since there are no guarantees in life, in most cases what we really achieve is a *feeling* of security rather than actual security. For example, many workers have placed large amounts of savings in pension funds, but, through no fault of their own, because of poor management or fraud by others, the workers have been left destitute. Money in a pension fund does not necessarily mean you are financially secure. It may mean that for the time being, you just *feel* financially secure.

Feelings of security or insecurity are generated as much by what is going on inside you as by what is happening on the outside. Internal threats, for the most part, come from a series of "what-ifs": What if I lose my job? What if I can't keep up the payments? What if I don't get the raise? Fortunately, most of these fears are seldom realized; nevertheless, the stress from the worry is very real.

Feelings of security can come from inside you as well—from the self-confidence that results from knowing you can cope with whatever *does* happen in life, rather than from futile attempts to control what *might* happen.

What Is Enough Home?

Included in the quest for security is the issue of safeguarding whatever we call home. Being able to pay the rent, build a house, or pay the mortgage is often paramount in maintaining a sense of well-being and security. Your security in your home is directly related to how your income compares with your outgo.

While most lending institutions recommend that home buyers limit their mortgage liability to no more than 25 to 30 percent of their gross income, many people carry mortgage liabilities in excess of 50 percent of their income.

Attempting to impress others is often a major cause of excessive mortgage indebtedness. You may want to ask yourself, "How much of the house is for me and how much is for impressing others? If these 'others' were not involved, how much house would I really need?" Whether you are buying a home, renting an apartment, or leasing a condo, the primary questions are the same: "What is sufficient? What is enough house? Enough money? Enough security?"

It is helpful to establish a "goal alignment" between you and your spouse to determine what would be *sufficient* in your lives, regardless of what others have. Each of you separately list what you would consider a sufficient income, house, car, and so on. Then share, negotiate, and compromise to make a mutual list of what it would take for both of you to be financially satisfied with your lives. The primary goal is to set limits on your needs and wants.

LDS scholar Hugh Nibley, declaring "enough is enough," quotes both scriptures and prophets:

> "Having food and raiment," says Paul to Timothy, "let us be therewith content" (1 Timothy 6:8). We must have sufficient for our needs in life's journey, but to go after more is forbidden, though you have your God-given free agency to do so. "Our real wants are very limited," says Brigham; "When you have what you wish to eat and sufficient clothing to make you comfortable you have all that you need; I have all that I need." How many people need to eat two lunches a day? We all eat too much, wear too much, and work too much. Brigham says if we all "work less, wear less, eat less, . . . we shall be a great deal wiser, healthier, and wealthier people than by taking the course we now do."[5]

Lack of Budgeting and Management Skills

Over a lifetime, the average family will manage between $1.5 and $2 million ($35,000 to $50,000 per year for 40 years in current dollars). Imagine running a business that will gross a couple of million dollars and deciding that it is not necessary to write anything down—"We'll just wing it." Far too often this is exactly what families do.

Most families have only a rough idea of where their money goes. They simply live from paycheck to paycheck, regardless of the paycheck's size. As long as the money keeps coming, or until something unexpected happens, all is well.

Most people have never been taught how to manage their money—only how to earn it. Such ignorance can mean losing in two minutes what it took you two weeks to earn. For example, you may be talking to a car dealer who has just shifted from "sales price" to "monthly payments." He tells you, "For just $10 a month more you can have the stripes *and* for only an additional $5 a month you can have the tinted mirrors." If you say, "Hey, what's an extra $15? I'll take both!"

you have just added $900 plus interest to the price of the car over a five-year contract ($15 x 60 monthly payments).

A more effective way of dealing with situations like the one just described is to use the concept of *analyzing marginal (or additional) costs*. Compare the amount of additional value you would receive to the money it would cost you to buy the extra items. For the above example, you would ask yourself if the addition of the stripes and tinted mirrors add an extra $900 to the value of the car. Or, considering your personal preferences and desires, would having these items on your car be worth $900 to you? In other words, would you be getting your money's worth? One of the ways to increase your chances of accurately answering this and other related questions is to take advantage of community educational resources such as libraries, schools, and seminars. The more educated you become and the more skills you acquire, the closer you will come to financial wisdom and security.

Impulse Buying

Most phone solicitations and late-night TV $19.95-plus-shipping-and-handling ads sell items very few people would ever put on their shopping lists. So the manufacturers, in hopes of selling their products, bring them to the buyer. You have probably never made out a shopping list that included, for instance, time shares in an Icelandic condo, an inflatable raft with a battery-operated outboard motor (batteries not included), or a year's supply of avocado pits as a treatment for gout. But you just might buy such items on impulse. Similarly, most supermarkets place items that are least likely to be on your list at eye level or near the checkout stand to encourage you to buy on impulse.

For some people, buying things whenever they want them gives them a sense of power or control over their lives. For others, impulse buying represents a way of coping with an emotional craving that is not otherwise being satisfied. (They need to remember Principal 6: *You can never get enough of what you don't need, because what you don't need can never satisfy you.*) For most people, however, impulse buying is merely a reflection of poor shopping habits and a lack of self-discipline.

Such habits can often be overcome simply by making out a shopping list and sticking to it, by not carrying credit cards or checkbooks with you, and by agreeing to establish built-in time delays proportional to the size of the purchase—for example, waiting 24 to 48 hours before making large purchases. Ask yourself, "Do I really need this, or do I merely want it?" A quick review of consumer products reveals that more than 50 percent of the items you have the impulse to buy today didn't even exist ten years ago. Apparently there was a time when you got along without them.

A very real consideration should be to ask in prayer about the wisdom of a pending purchase, especially if it is an important one. Remember the promise made in the scriptures, "If any of you lack wisdom, let him ask of God, that giveth to all men liberally, and upbraideth not; and it shall be given him" (James 1:5). This scripture can very well be applied to our temporal as well as our spiritual needs.

Failure to Determine the True Cost of a Purchase

It's amazing how much denial and rationalization we use to convince ourselves that we can afford something we know we cannot afford. We might say, "The computer only costs $1,200, and it will pay for itself with what it saves us on balancing the checkbook." That's quite an expensive calculator! And the $1,200 price tag is not even the *true cost* of the computer. In addition to taxes and interest charges, there are the costs of a color monitor, a printer, paper, printer ribbon, software, a computer desk, floppy disks, disk storage boxes, and so on, ad infinitum. It could take a lifetime before the money saved from balancing your checkbook makes up for the cost of the computer.

This example may be an exaggeration—no one buys a computer just for the purpose of balancing the checkbook—but the principle is true. Most people can barely afford many of the things they buy, and the true cost of the items often turns out to be far greater than the initial purchase price. The *true cost* includes the initial cost, hidden costs, indirect costs, and relationship costs. When these costs are taken into account, they can easily move you from the realm of "just barely" to "just buried."

Hidden and Indirect Costs

After the initial purchase, there are often additional things you must buy to make an item work better, so it is imperative that you calculate the cost of add-ons with the original purchase price. For instance, if you buy a stereo, you soon discover that to get full fidelity you need to add a compact disc player. Then you need compact discs to play. By then the speakers are no longer adequate, and so on. A large part of your indebtedness may be a result of the *hidden* costs of buying something.

Similarly, *indirect* costs such as operating, maintaining, and repairing an item must be taken into account as part of the true cost. One definition of a boat is a hole in the water that you pour money into—and swimming pools have also been known to be bottomless from a financial point of view.

Ask yourself the following questions to determine the hidden and indirect costs of a contemplated purchase:

1. When purchasing a car, do you need extras like undercoating, pin-striping, and extended warranties? These items, tacked on in what is called "back-end loading," can cost you.
2. What items are included in the closing costs when you purchase a home? Is the buyer or the seller going to pay for certain items such as repairs, taxes, appraisals, and inspections?
3. What accessories are needed for the item to operate as intended? Does it require battery packs, transmitters, additional games, software, printers, saddles, trailers?
4. What are the legal costs, such as registration, insurance, license fees, and property taxes?
5. What are the operational costs, such as fuel consumption, tire replacement, electricity, updating, depreciation, food requirements (for example, hay or oats)?
6. What are the maintenance and repair costs, such as oil changes, antifreeze, air conditioning, veterinarian fees, storage facilities?
7. What are the costs of holiday extras: long distance calls, cards, stamps, travel, special foods, decorations, and additional electricity?

Relationship Costs

More subtle, but equally important to consider when determining the true cost of a purchase, are *emotional* and *time* costs: How might the new purchase affect relationships? For example, you may have gotten a real bargain, from a dollar-cost standpoint, on a "four wheeler" (all-terrain vehicle). Yet, since a second income is required to pay for it, the time costs may interfere with your ability to take the vehicle out in the country and enjoy it. You may also have less time to spend with loved ones. You may be more tired. And feelings of resentment may develop. These emotional costs are very high.

Resentment is especially likely when you make a purchase in spite of the protests of your spouse, or when he or she feels that the purchase is more important than the relationship. Statements such as these may be warning signs: "Maybe if I wore a hood ornament, you'd spend as much time with me as you do with that car." "Just where am I supposed to sit, since I can't sit on your white satin couch?" Relationships with *things* might appear safer than relationships with *people,* but they cannot be as satisfying. Remember Principle 3: *Nothing (no thing) is worth risking the relationship.*

We must always view things from an eternal perspective. Imagine arriving at the celestial kingdom with a TV under one arm and a VCR under the other. (No, you say, your spouse is not with you, but you have some really terrific video of him or her that was taken just before the divorce.) Those who have been married in the temple must never lose sight of the fact that exaltation involves both husband and wife, and that being sealed in the temple is only the promise— a truly celestial marriage depends on oneness and faithfulness.

Failure to Analyze the Cost Per Use

You want to finish off a section of your basement. To frame the walls you need to attach the two-by-fours to the basement floor. To accomplish this, you buy a nail gun that fires nails through wood into concrete. The gun costs almost $400 and you use it on this *one* project. The cost per use is $400. If you use the gun on two projects, the cost per use drops to $200 ($400 divided by 2). But you could *rent* the gun for $20 per use.

Cost-per-use consideration should be given to just about everything you have the urge to buy, including mountain cabins, boats, four-wheel-drive vehicles, cellular phones, airplanes, scuba gear, high-powered night vision scopes, and so on. For example, you may be considering a $25,000 mountain cabin. The cabin is snowed in much of the year, and the roads are too muddy to use during the spring, so the primary use time is summer and fall.

Interest charges, property taxes, organizational dues, plus maintenance and repair can easily bring the *true cost* to between $50,000 and $75,000, not including furnishings. If your family went to the cabin one weekend each month during those two seasons, the cabin would be used six times per year. The mortgage payments would run about $375 per month ($25,000 at 13 percent for 10 years). Taxes, dues, and maintenance cost about $125 per month, for a total of

$500 per month or $6,000 per year. This means that the six visits to the cabin would have a cost per use of $1,000, not including travel costs. You could rent a fantastic cabin for $100 per night or $200 per weekend—a fraction of the cost of purchasing your own cabin.

Cost-per-use calculations can let you determine if there are more economical ways to fulfill your needs, such as renting, borrowing, sharing, or simply doing without. Sharing can be especially effective between cooperative neighbors and extended family members. Only *one* Rototiller could be used for five yards, for example, or *one* snowblower for three driveways.

Lack of Adequate Insurance Coverage

Lack of adequate insurance can put people in financial straits almost as fast as unemployment. Some of the most neglected forms of coverage are major medical, disability, liability, and life. In many cases, the car and house are adequately covered, but the people in them are not.

Insurance protects us from rare but potentially very costly events. The rarity of these events leads many to believe that they do not need insurance, so they try to get by without it, leaving themselves open to financial disaster. It's important to review medical, life, and property insurance policies on a yearly basis or whenever there is a change in the size or composition of the family. (For more on insurance needs, see chapter 8.)

Credit Abuse

Many people don't realize until it's too late that they're getting into serious financial difficulties. Because of the behaviors already discussed, they live beyond their means, abuse credit, and one day find themselves staggering under a heavy load of debt. Following are danger signs that warn of impending financial disaster, as well as suggestions for effective use of credit.

Credit is not thought of as debt. More than two-thirds of all families use some type of credit card, and nearly 50 percent of them pay off their account balance each billing period.[6] Those who don't pay off the balance on a monthly basis see credit cards not as a short-term substitute for cash but rather as a convenient means of taking out a loan. Many don't realize that when they make statements such as "I'll just put it on the Visa" or "Let's just charge it," they are in reality saying, "Let's go into debt for it."

Stop thinking of your credit card's limit as a line of credit, and begin thinking of lines of credit as lines of debt.

You have to borrow to make payments to creditors. Picture yourself on a boat in the middle of the ocean. The boat has ten holes in the bottom and you have only nine corks. No matter how you move the corks around, endlessly pulling a cork out of one hole in order to use it to plug another, your boat will eventually sink. The same principle applies to using cash advances from one credit card to make payments on another, or taking out a new loan on the car to make mortgage payments.

To avoid getting into this kind of financial bind, determine affordable payment amounts *before* you acquire a debt.

You have more than seven consumer-credit loans. If this is the case, you are living beyond your means and expecting others to support your lifestyle (see **Trying to Move Too Far, Too Fast**, this chapter). As each creditor says, "That is all I care to contribute," you must find someone else who is willing to bankroll your excesses. To avoid such pretentious living, limit credit use to major purchases only, involving no more than two or three creditors all together.

More than 20 percent of your take-home pay is used for credit payments. Excluding your mortgage payment, installment debt should not exceed 20 percent of what you take home after taxes. For a person taking home $1,500, monthly payments for debt should total no more than $300. In many cases, car payments alone meet or exceed this limit, but for some reason car payments are often thought of separately from other consumer debt items, such as furniture, household appliances, and clothes.

Be sure to include everything but the mortgage when you total up your credit payments, and keep these payments to no more than 20 percent of your take-home pay.

All of the secondary earner's income goes to pay debts. The actual amount realized from the secondary earner's income varies with the income group to which the wage earners belong.[7] Dual-income families in the lower-income group lose about 46 percent of their increase to job-related expenses, while those in the middle-income group lose about 56 percent, and those in the upper-income group lose about 68 percent. Job-related expenses include tax, Social Security, and health care deductions, life insurance premiums, contributions to retirement funds, union or professional dues, extra clothing plus uniforms and cleaning, meals out, additional transportation costs, and child care expenses. What's left will usually pay just some of the bills.

(Not surprisingly, even with these additional expenses, the dual-income family has some advantage over the single-income family. Again, the size of this advantage varies with the wage earners' income group. Dual-income families in the lower-income group usually realize a 70 percent increase in income over a single-income family. Those in the middle-income group realize a 38 percent increase, while high-income families realize only a 16 percent increase.)

Since a second income yields less in actual usable funds than you may have thought, the amount you are then able to use for debt repayment may not be large enough. It is important that you realize this before taking on a second income for the purpose of debt repayment.

Credit cards are used impulsively. A good rule of thumb is that the item purchased should last longer than the payments do. Paying for vacations and meals usually lasts longer than the trip or dinner. Imagine reading a restaurant's menu to a loan officer and saying, "The New York steak looks good to me, but then the fresh lobster is always superb. What do you think? Can we qualify for a loan that's big enough to get both?" At first this may seem a little ridiculous, but when you charge your dinner rather than pay cash for it, you are in effect asking the bank if you can borrow money to pay for your meal.

As a mark of your dedication to using sound financial principles, agree to use credit cards only for preplanned purchases of durable goods, or in emergencies.

Accounts are not paid on time. From time to time, even large businesses experience a cash flow problem when the costs of purchases and overhead exceed the amount of money coming in. If this condition is only temporary, the businesses can ask their creditors for some additional time to fulfill their financial obligations. But if this condition continues over a long period of time, the businesses go bankrupt. They spend faster than they earn; eventually it catches up with them. The same rule is true for individuals.

There are few things in life that cause more stress than getting behind on bills. Past due notices and calls from collection agencies can create financial, emotional, and social stresses that can be devastating to feelings of self-esteem.

To avoid this kind of outcome, create a reserve account or subtract credit card purchases just as you would checks (see chapter 8).

No more than the minimum due is paid each month. Many bank card repayment plans are set up so the cardholder must pay only 1/36 of the principal due plus interest. In effect, the bank is saying, "We don't want you to pay off your outstanding balance too quickly, because there is no other way we could loan the money out and make as much profit as we are making." The cardholder might pay up to 21 percent interest, in addition to an annual fee that is equivalent to another one to three percent. This, plus the 3 percent that the retailer pays to the bank, can result in a hefty 27 percent return for the bank. That obviously beats the interest rates that could be earned on a home loan.

To avoid paying high interest rates, accelerate payoff schedules by adding as much extra principal as possible to each payment (see chapter 7).

Debt repayment schedules are longer than one year. Excluding your home mortgage, student loans, and most car loans, the duration of a loan should not exceed *one year.* Ideally, this should apply to car loans as well, but with the average cost of a new car approaching $15,000, it's unrealistic to expect to pay off a car in one year. In the "good old days," the car manufacturers operated on a three-year style-change cycle, and car loans were made for one- or two-year periods. But the price of cars has risen faster than has the buyers' ability to pay for them. To compensate for this discrepancy, car loans are now offered for five-, six-, and even seven-year periods. The car dealer is basically saying, "On your income, you couldn't possibly make the payments necessary to pay the car off in one year" (translated: "You can't afford it—period"). So the amount of the monthly payments has been reduced, allowing you to make more payments over a longer period of time.

Three consequences of these financial manipulations must be considered:

1. The buyer can end up with interest charges amounting to almost as much as the purchase price of the car.
2. It is not until three or four years into the loan that the value of the car begins to exceed the amount still owed on the loan. (Of course, a large down payment can decrease both the size of the loan and the amount of interest you pay.)
3. The longer the term, the harder it is to count on financial stability. How stable can you expect your financial world to be during the next five to seven years? As you look back over the past five years, do you find that life has gone the way you expected, or did you have a few surprises?

If you would like to buy a $5,000 car but you have only about $200 per month available for payments and you still want to be able to pay the car off in one year, try the following: Make a $210 payment to your *savings account* each month for one year. At the end of that year, you'll have approximately $2,600 (including 3 or 4 percent interest). Put the $2,600 down on the car and finance the remaining $2,400 for 12 months at $211 per month ($2,345 at 10 percent = $2,532 divided by 12).

If you were to finance the whole $5,000, you could make monthly payments of $231 for 24 months (at 10 percent interest). But by saving for a year you were earning interest for a year instead of paying it, and you were in debt for only one year instead of two. Thus your car is paid for in the same two-year period and your net interest payments dropped from $544 to about $132.

Whenever possible, calculate and commit to only a one-year payoff schedule—except for most car and education loans.

Consolidation of loans is being considered. Consolidation loans are helpful only if the behavior that led to the problem in the first place has been corrected. Otherwise it will be just a matter of time before the problem resurfaces and drives you even deeper into debt. You may find that you are better off using the fold-down method described in chapter 7 to decrease your debt load and the amount of your monthly payments.

Addictive Behavior and Finances

Faithful Latter-day Saints who keep the Word of Wisdom and live the gospel in other ways as well have definite advantages over people who don't—and one of those advantages is financial.

Sixty-six percent of the people in the United States over 15 years of age drink alcoholic beverages on occasion. Fifty-eight percent drink at least once a month, and 10 percent drink at least one ounce of alcohol per day (the equivalent of two mixed drinks, two glasses of wine, or two cans of beer). One in ten users becomes an alcoholic.[8]

All addictive behaviors are costly, in both financial and human terms. The financial and personal costs of cocaine addiction are well known, as are the costs of becoming addicted to other illegal drugs, prescription drugs, alcohol, and tobacco. The financial devastation of an addiction stems not only from the exorbitant costs of some of these substances, but also from the personal deception created to justify maintaining such habits. If the substance abuse involves an illegal drug, trying to create a family budget is useless because *all* of the family resources will eventually be devoted to obtaining more of the drug.

If legal drugs (alcohol, tobacco, or prescription drugs) are involved, the cost of the substance should actually be included in the budget. In this way those both directly and indirectly involved will realize exactly how much money is being spent on addictive substances. For example, two or three cans of beer per day add up to two or three six-packs a week. At $5 or $6 a six-pack, this can add up to between $40 and $80 per month.

In many instances, users deny how expensive their habit has become or that the rate of consumption has increased. With the costs of the addictions being recorded as part of the family budget, denial becomes impossible. In addition, the accumulated costs of the habitual consumption can be assessed from a relative value standpoint (see chapter 1). For instance, the previously noted beer consumption costs could reach $1,000 per year. Is there some other way you would have preferred to spend that $1,000? Is your money, as Principle 4 admonishes, going to what you value?

Gambling and compulsive buying are other addictive pathological behaviors that can bring financial ruin and personal heartache both to those directly involved and to their loved ones. In most cases, it is necessary to seek professional help to overcome addictive or compulsive behaviors.

Behaviors Associated with Effective Financial Management

Let's review the behaviors this chapter has recommended to replace those that may have gotten you into your current financial mess:

1. Make purchases appropriate to your income.
2. Set limits on your needs and wants; decide what would be "enough" house, car, income, and so on.
3. Take advantage of educational resources—such as libraries, schools, and seminars—to learn budgeting and management skills.
4. Agree to build in time delays proportional to the size of the purchase being considered.
5. Calculate hidden and indirect costs along with the original purchase price.
6. Consider whether renting, borrowing, or sharing might be more economical than buying.
7. Periodically review medical, life, and property insurance policies to make sure they are adequate in light of your present circumstances.
8. Think of lines of credit as lines of debt, and use them only for emergencies and pre-planned purchases of durable goods.
9. Seek professional help regarding addictive or compulsive behaviors.

Latter-day Saint Families

For active LDS families, the financial dynamics described above have a twist that is a distinctive consequence of being a "peculiar people." Because of our understanding of the eternal nature of our lives, and because of commandments and covenants we hold sacred, an active Latter-day Saint family has other priorities than trying to keep up with the nonmember "Joneses."

The Lord himself aids us in knowing where our time and resources should be spent. To begin with, he instructs:

> Thou shalt not covet thy neighbor's house, thou shalt not covet thy neighbor's wife, nor his manservant, nor his maidservant, nor his ox, nor his ass, nor any thing that is thy neighbor's. (Exodus 20:17.)

Because of their desire to receive and extend blessings to others, many Mormons assume the extra cost of travel to and from temples. They also willingly accept a number of financial obligations closely associated with their temple covenants, such as contributing to fast offerings, supporting missionaries, and paying a full tithe.

Paying tithing may be difficult at times; therefore, such commitments need to be made early in the marriage. In *The Miracle of Forgiveness*, President Spencer W. Kimball clearly stated how important it is for young families to realize the impact their spiritual and temporal priorities will have on their future happiness.

> Many people build and furnish a home and buy the automobile first—and then find they "cannot afford" to pay tithing. Whom do they worship? Certainly not the Lord of heaven and earth, for we serve whom we love and give first consideration to the object of our affection and desires.[9]

Most Latter-day Saint parents have consented to prayerfully consider the number of children they are to bring into the world. President Kimball continued:

> Young married couples who postpone parenthood until their degrees are attained might be shocked if their expressed preference were labeled idolatry. Their rationalization gives them degrees at the expense of children. Is it a justifiable exchange? Whom do they love and worship—themselves or God? Other couples, recognizing that life is not intended

primarily for comforts, ease, and luxuries, complete their educations while they move forward with full lives, having their children and giving Church and community service.[10]

Obedience to such spiritual counsel frequently results in having larger families to support than would be found in a comparison of the national average. And the financial obligation assumed by such families is not just the cost of raising each child. For many families, there is the additional expense of supporting missionaries.

With the average mission—including pre- and post-mission expenses—running about $10,000, a family that sends five children on missions adds approximately $50,000 to the traditional family budget. This may mean dedicating $75–85,000 of the family's gross (pre-tax) income to missionary efforts.

This willingness to devote such a large portion of one's income to spiritual endeavors may seem bewildering to some. But to the devoted, such behavior is a tangible manifestation of the strength of their testimony and their love of Jesus Christ and his gospel. It also exemplifies the importance of fully comprehending and practicing Principle 4: *Money spent on things you value usually leads to a feeling of satisfaction and accomplishment.*

Again, the Lord himself teaches us what to value. In his Sermon on the Mount, he admonished:

> Lay not up for yourselves treasures upon earth, where moth and rust doth corrupt, and where thieves break through and steal: But lay up for yourselves treasures in heaven, where neither moth nor rust doth corrupt, and where thieves do not break through nor steal: For where your treasure is, there will your heart be also. . . . No man can serve two masters: for either he will hate the one, and love the other; or else he will hold to the one, and despise the other. Ye cannot serve God and mammon.
>
> Therefore I say unto you, Take no thought for your life, what ye shall eat, or what ye shall drink; nor yet for your body, what ye shall put on. Is not the life more than meat, and the body than raiment? . . . (For after all these things do the Gentiles seek:) for your heavenly Father knoweth that ye have need of all these things. But seek ye first the kingdom of God, and his righteousness; and all these things shall be added unto you. (Matthew 6:19–21; 24–25; 32–33.)

Summary

The basic premise of financial counseling is that financial problems are behavior problems, rather than money problems.[11] Our individual, interactive, and financial behaviors are related. Principles that govern one aspect of our behavior are likely to affect other areas of our lives as well.

Evaluate how you may have acquired your current debt load and what you can do to avoid accumulating additional debt. Does your behavior show signs of credit abuse? Do you understand how to calculate the true cost of a purchase? Do you realize the implications of having an open-ended rather than a closed-ended budget? Are you free of habits and addictions that would adversely affect your finances? How does your testimony of the gospel help you effectively manage your life and your finances?

Important Terms

Closed-ended budget: Budget based on living within your current income.

Conspicuous consumption: Acquiring goods and services not because they are needed but because they are expensive, generate attention, and provide the appearance of affluence.

Cost per use: Purchase price of an item divided by the number of times you use it. The cost-per-use calculation provides a basis for comparing the wisdom of buying versus renting or borrowing.

Equity: Your contribution toward the maintenance of your current lifestyle.

Liabilities: The contributions others make toward the maintenance of your current lifestyle.

Open-ended budget: Budget that is unrealistically based on anticipated increases in income.

True cost: Purchase price plus hidden, indirect, and relationship costs.

Notes

1. Krueger, 1986.

2. Krueger, 1986, pp. 25–26.

3. Kimball, 1982, p. 76.

4. Aristotle, 1952, p. 452.

5. Nibley, 1989, p. 235.

6. Canner and Cyrnak, 1985.

7. Hanson, 1991.

8. U.S. Department of Health and Human Services, 1990.

9. Kimball, 1969, p. 41.

10. Ibid., p. 41.

11. Reeves, 1983.

CHAPTER 7

Debt Management

*S*ome people equate the process of managing debt with juggling in a dark room: you never know what's going to come down on you next. Some seem to accept the stress associated with managing debt as a fundamental component of the life of the twentieth-century consumer. Others avoid debt as they would the bubonic plague; debt to them is a destructive force capable of abolishing the American promise of life, liberty, and the pursuit of happiness. To appreciate one way of looking at debt, a brief look at one aspect of history might prove helpful.

Debt as Indentured Servitude

When America was first being settled, many wished to come to the new land who didn't have enough money to pay for passage. Yet the desire to come to America was so great that many offered to work off the cost of their passage by becoming someone's servant if that person paid their way. These immigrants were called *indentured servants*. Such a servant might be defined as anyone who contracted to pay off a debt by working for the creditor for a specified period of time.

A number of similarities can be found between indentured servants and borrowers in today's financial world. Let's say you want to buy a car. The price of the car is about $13,500, and the bank agrees to finance the loan at a 13 percent interest rate for a period of five years. The total price of the car will come to about $18,400, made up of 60 monthly payments of about $305 each. You will have to earn around $500 per month in order to clear enough (after taxes are deducted) to make the $305 payments.

Assume your gross income (before deductions) is about $2,000 per month. So the $500 you need to make the car payment represents 25 percent of your monthly salary. In essence, this means *you have agreed to work one week (25 percent of your time) out of every month for the next five years for the bank so you can have the new car.* You have just become an indentured servant for the next five years of your life. This is what indebtedness really means.

It is important to remember that freedom of choice is an integral part of our mortal condition, and anything that diminishes our freedom of choice diminishes the quality of our existence. Our Heavenly Father, in order to enhance our lives and encourage us to use our free agency, will consistently increase the number of alternatives from which we can choose. In contrast, Satan, who has always been against the use of agency, will do his utmost to limit our choices in an attempt to enslave us and thereby rob us of our birthright.

If you don't like the idea of being an indentured servant, you will want to get your debts under control. The first step is to stop going farther into debt. Then you must decide whether to increase your income or decrease your expenses to get out of debt. Based on this decision, you must then develop a plan to start getting out of debt. Throughout the process, you can learn to cope with the stress that accompanies a financial crisis.

Stop Going Farther into Debt

Remember Principle 2? *If you continue doing what you have been doing, you will continue getting what you have been getting.* This is especially true for chronic indebtedness.

Imagine two people trying to survive in a boat in the middle of the ocean. One of them asks the other, "What are you doing?" and is told, "I'm plugging the holes in the bottom of the boat. What are you doing?" The first person answers, "I'm poking holes in the bottom of the boat." This analogy clearly describes what happens when one person tries to get out of debt while a partner continues to increase the debt. To become free of debt, *everyone* involved must stop doing whatever it is that has been getting them into debt.

It stands to reason that if you are an alcoholic and wish to recover, you must stop drinking. If you are a compulsive gambler, you must stop betting. And if you are chronically in debt, you must stop borrowing. Otherwise, things will just go on as before. Those who truly want to get out of debt must decide to get out now: *no more charging, no more borrowing, and no more buy-ing until you have enough money to pay for the purchase.*

Delay Buying

One of the prime causes of debt is impatience: "I want it and I want it NOW!" And for that we are willing to pay enormous interest charges. *Impatience can be a very expensive emotion.* In many cases, with the passage of time and a look at the consequences, "I want it" can become "I *thought* I wanted it." For this reason, delays should be built into your decision-making process when you make a major purchase. You may want to use the principle "The larger the purchase, the longer the delay." In other words, if something is going to cost $500, then agree to wait at least 24 hours before making the purchase. If the cost is over $1,000, wait 36 hours; over $5,000, wait 48 hours, and so on. You may be surprised at how many times you'll be glad you decided to wait and didn't make the purchase after all—and didn't apply for yet another loan.

Stop Qualifying for Loans You Don't Really Qualify For

When you take out a loan, you are usually asked to fill out a balance sheet, or statement of financial status, that lists your current assets and liabilities. You are asked to disclose your current income and to list your current debts, such as credit cards and car loans. After you have com-pleted your loan application, the bank runs a credit check and takes a look at your income-to-debt ratio to decide whether or not you qualify for (i.e., can handle the expenses of) the new loan.

However, as the old saying goes, "The only time a bank is willing to give you a loan is when you don't need one." Because of this, when filling out loan applications, some people try to make themselves appear better off than they actually are. A real problem arises when they exaggerate their income, "forget" to list certain expenses—and then just barely qualify for the loan. Suppose a couple's take-home pay is about $2,000 per month. Twenty percent of that amount, or $400 per month, is the maximum amount most banks would allow them to commit to consumer debt. Their credit card, car loan, and furniture payments add up to $350, and they are applying for a new loan for a hot tub. The loan officer recognizes that the hot tub loan would put them slightly above the credit-limit guideline. But if they have been good customers, she may reluctantly approve their loan.

After they sign the papers, the husband nudges the wife and whispers, "It's a good thing we didn't list our $200-a-month boat payments on the application. If we had, we probably wouldn't have qualified for the loan." And he's absolutely right—they wouldn't have gotten the new loan if they had included anything near $200 more per month on their list of liabilities.

You may think that you would never be dishonest enough to neglect to list such an obligation. Yet many people are making "boat" payments that they neglect to list on a loan application. The "boat" can be a financial obligation that is not written down in the form of an official contract but that nevertheless epitomizes high-priority values. For instance, for those with religious affiliations, the "boat" may be called the *USS Tithing* or the *USS Church Offerings*. For some, it could be called the *USS Home Care*, representing their share of nursing home expenses for an elderly parent; for others, it could be called the *USS Friendship*, representing payments to friends or relatives who were generous enough to loan them money when they were in a bind.

The point is, you may assume some financial obligations without contracts or official records. These agreements are as much a part of your financial indebtedness as is a loan from a bank. But if you don't list these informal obligations on loan applications, you may "qualify" for a loan you do not really qualify for. Even worse, as pointed out in chapter 6, the actual loan payments probably represent only a fraction of what your new toy will eventually cost you each month. As a consequence, you will find yourself sinking deeper and deeper into debt, and you may end up needing to earn even more money in order to meet all of your financial obligations.

Decide Whether to Increase Your Income or Decrease Your Expenses

One of the overriding truths of debt management is that to get out of debt, you must either *increase your income* or *decrease your expenses*. Most of those who find themselves buried in debt tend to favor increasing their income over decreasing their expenses. Usually, though, decreasing expenses is far more effective.

To illustrate the difference between these two debt management approaches, look again at the situation in which you had to earn $500 to clear a car payment of approximately $300. Continuing this line of reasoning, you would have to earn $1,000 to make $600 worth of payments. But if you were to decrease your debt load by $600 per month (perhaps by selling a car, the boat, or one of the horses), it would have the same effect as increasing your income by $1,000 per month. That would be almost the same as getting a $12,000-a-year raise!

CASE ILLUSTRATION

The way one California family handled their debt problems illustrates beautifully the principle of decreasing expenses. The father taught school and the mother tended neighborhood children whose parents both worked outside the home. One of the couple's two sons was spiritually moved to go on a mission even though he was already 19 and had not saved for a mission. The parents were thrilled with his decision, but knew that meeting the additional costs of supporting a mission would be difficult. The pre-mission costs accumulated rapidly, and once the monthly mission contributions of $375 began, the financial burden became unmanageable. At first the father tried working evenings at a convenience store to increase his income, but the combined stress of the extra hours and constant worry began to take their toll on his health.

As an alternative to trying to earn enough to cope with the mounting debt, they decided to sell one of their cars. The car payments were $300 per month, insurance for the car was almost $100 per month, and monthly gas bills were over $50. In addition, the costs of registration, licensing, and maintenance easily amounted to $50 per month. All together, selling the car saved the couple about $500 per month—just what they needed to pay for the pre-mission costs and monthly contributions. From that point on—even after the mission was completed—the father carpooled with other teachers at his school.

This example illustrates how one couple learned not only to manage their debt problems but also to cope effectively with an unexpected increase in expenses: Often the best way out of the hole is to decrease expenses, rather than increase income. An additional point worth making here is that your attempts to "earn" your way out of debt could end up putting you in a higher tax bracket, which, because of taxes, would leave you with an even smaller percentage of your extra income available for debt payments.

Meet Your Obligations to the Lord

Finding themselves in an anxious, debt-ridden, short-of-funds situation, many Church members are tempted to make a serious mistake: to decrease expenses by *not* paying their tithes and offerings. "I don't see how we can pay our tithing this month," they may say. "With that 10 percent gone, the rest is just not going to stretch far enough. Once we get back on our feet, we'll make it up." Such reasoning can be very persuasive—but how can the Lord bless us if we do not exercise faith in him? Here is the perfect opportunity to prove to the Lord that we believe his promises, and that we depend on him and not on "the arm of flesh."

We must heed these words of President Joseph F. Smith:

> It is highly proper for the Latter-day Saints to get out of debt. . . . Wherever I have had the opportunity of speaking, I have scarcely ever forgotten to hold out to the people the necessity—that I feel, at least—of our settling our obligations and freeing ourselves from debt. . . . I would say, in connection with this subject, that one of the best ways that I know of to pay my obligations to my brother, my neighbor, or business associate, is for me first to pay my obligations to the Lord. I can pay more of my debts to my neighbors, if I have contracted them, after I have met my honest obligations with the Lord, than I can by neglecting the latter; and you can do the same. If you desire to prosper, and to be free men and women and a free people, first meet your just obligations to God, and then meet your obligations to your fellowmen.[1]

Start Getting Out of Debt

The basic idea behind getting out of debt is to pay off as much as possible, as fast as possible, without acquiring any additional debt. Two helpful techniques can make getting out of debt much more achievable: *accelerated repayment* and *the fold-down plan*.

Accelerated Repayment

The basic idea behind accelerated repayment is to pay off the principal quickly in order to reduce the interest charges. In a new long-term loan, most of the money included in the payment goes toward interest charges, and only a small amount goes toward paying off the principal. But when extra money is added to a regular payment, *all* the extra money goes toward paying off the principal, thus accelerating the repayment of the loan and reducing future interest charges. The accelerated repayment method can be applied to almost any loan.

Table 7.1 illustrates this concept with a mortgage of $100,000. It shows that, by adding an extra $25 to the mortgage payment each month, you reduce the term to maturity from 30 years to 25 years and 10 months and the total interest paid over the life of the loan by about $36,000. By paying an extra $100 per month toward the principal, you reduce the term to maturity to 19 years and 3 months and the total interest by about $90,000. Of, if you take out the mortgage for a 15-year period, payments increase to $1,075 per month (about $197 more than for the standard 30-year mortgage), but you save $122,500 in interest compared to a 30-year mortgage.

In three of the four cases above, payments per month are higher, but the savings in total interest is much greater than the total payment increases. The high cost of interest cannot be overemphasized. Note that with the 15-year loan you end up paying nearly $200,000 for a $100,000 house. With the 30-year loan, you pay over $300,000—enough for three $100,000 houses!

TABLE 7.1—FOUR WAYS TO PAY OFF A MORTGAGE (ASSUMING A $100,000 LOAN AT A 10 PERCENT RATE OF INTEREST)

Payment Period	Payment Amount	Interest Paid	Interest Saved
30-year loan	$878	$216,000	0
Adding $25 per month: 25 years 10 months	$903	$180,000	$36,000
Adding $100 per month: 19 years 3 months	$978	$126,000	$90,000
15-year loan	$1,075	$93,500	$122,500

The Fold-Down Plan

The fold-down plan of debt elimination entails paying off one debt and then applying (folding down) that payment to another debt in a cumulative progression. The first step in this plan is to pay off one of your debts, perhaps by using your tax refund, reallocating money budgeted for entertainment, or riding the bus. Then, when the first debt is paid off, the money that had been allocated to making those payments is now applied to paying off a second debt. When the second debt is paid off, the amount for payments on that debt *and* the first debt are folded down into paying off a third debt, and so on until all of the debts are paid off. During this process, monthly expenses remain constant, but debt payments progressively focus on fewer and fewer debts.

Table 7.2 gives an example of a fold-down repayment plan. On the left side of the table are listed creditors and the dollar amounts owed to each. To the right of the creditors are the monthly payments. In this example, $50 each month goes to Visa, $100 to MasterCard, $25 to Sears, and so on—a total of $1,075 per month is distributed in loan payments.

TABLE 7.2—FOLD-DOWN REPAYMENT PLAN

CREDITORS	MONTHLY PAYMENTS								
	Jan	Feb	Mar	Apr	May	Jun	Jul	Aug	Sep
Visa $50.00	50	paid							
MasterCard $250.00	100	150	paid		(Interest payments saved)				
Sears $225.00	25	25	175	paid					
Furniture $850.00	100	100	100	275	275	paid			
Car loan $2,650	300	300	300	300	300	575	575	paid	
Second mortgage $5,650	500	500	500	500	500	500	500	1,075	1,075
Total owed $9,675	1,075	1,075	1,075	1,075	1,075	1,075	1,075	1,075	1,075

After the January payments are made, the Visa bill is paid in full. However, instead of using that $50 somewhere else in February ("Now that we have our Visa card paid off, we can afford to buy the dining room set"), the amount of the Visa payment is applied to the MasterCard bill. As a result, in February a total of $150 is applied to the MasterCard bill, paying it off. All other payments remain the same for that month. In March, the $150 that had been allocated to the credit cards can now be added to the regular $25 payment to Sears, paying off that debt. Again, regular payments are made to all other creditors during the month of March. In April, the extra $175 now available can be added to the $100 furniture payments. After only two months of $275 payments on the furniture, it is completely paid off. This process continues until the entire $1,075 is being applied to the second mortgage.

In this example, all debts have been repaid after eight months. The amount of time it will take for you to pay off your debts varies with the total amount of indebtedness and how much extra money you can use to begin a fold-down program. (Remember, *all* of the amount you pay over and above your regular monthly payment goes toward paying off the principal.) Extra money might come from income tax returns, garage sales, cutting back on long-distance phone calls, playing less golf, brown-bagging lunch instead of eating out, or reducing the utility bills.

By using the fold-down method, you save a great deal in interest charges (the sooner you pay off a debt, the sooner you stop paying interest on that debt). However, for this method to be successful, *it is absolutely necessary that you curtail all nonessential consumption*. People have a tendency to pay off one thing and then turn around and buy something else with the extra cash, or believe that they can now afford the payments if they buy something else on credit. If you do this, you will perpetually remain in debt.

The Fold-Up Plan

As an added bonus, after your last debt is paid off, you would be wise to continue making payments as if you were following the original payment schedule. Now, however, put the payments into your savings account, where they will be *earning* interest rather than costing you interest. Using the monthly payment amount from Table 7.2 ($1,075), in six months you would have over $6,500 in the bank (including some earned interest). The family in this example went from being almost $10,000 in debt to having more than $6,500 in the bank in just 14 months. They rose from the bewildering stress of financial crisis to financial solvency and peace of mind.

Financial Crises and Stress

Both medical doctors and financial planners complain that many of those who need their professional help seldom contact them until their problems have become all but insurmountable. When people finally do seek professional help, they expect the professional to "make things right again," regardless of the severity of the condition. In most cases, it is much easier to prevent a crisis than to cure one. But some financial crises cannot be avoided, no matter what you do.

The word crisis is derived from the Greek word *krisis,* which means decision. A financial crisis is a situation in which you are obliged to make a financial decision. Financial crises often occur because of death, divorce, problems with employment, major medical costs, or overwhelming consumer debt. Whatever the cause, an inevitable by-product of a financial crisis is *stress.*

Reactions to Stress

The way people react to stress is related to their ability to see things in perspective, resolve conflicts, and make decisions. This ability correlates with the degree of maturity a person has achieved, and reactions are therefore classified as *infantile, immature,* or *mature.*

Infantile reactions. An infantile reaction to stress is a "total" reaction, in which emotions—often previously pent-up—are expressed in the extreme without regard for the consequences. This can result in a state of panic or rage—an overreaction that is disproportionately severe compared to the cause.

Such an extreme emotional reaction to even mild stress often indicates that certain external cues have been linked to an internal danger. For example, Greg's wife fails to enter the amount of a check in the record portion of the checkbook (external event). Greg comes unglued. Much to his wife's surprise, he rants and raves about how he will never trust her again, and he confiscates her checkbook. What Greg's wife may not know is that his first wife had cleaned out their checking account just before she filed for divorce. Greg was emotionally linking this incident with his second wife to the feelings of anger and helplessness (internal danger) stirred up by his first wife.

When the cumulative effect of stress threatens to overwhelm coping abilities, anything can become "the last straw." At this point, people often become virtually incapable of exercising proper self-control, and they "blow up."

Immature reactions. An immature reaction involves a tendency to take things personally, distorting happenstance so as to perceive it as a personal affront. One of the most memorable spiritual events I have ever experienced occurred as a direct result of my immature reaction toward a situation over which I seemed to have little or no control.

I had been a member of the LDS church for about a year when I felt strongly prompted to resign my teaching position at a college in California, sell our home, and move my family to Utah. After prayerful consideration, we obeyed these promptings. However, soon after our arrival in

Utah, our financial situation started to rapidly deteriorate. To begin with, the person who had bought our home in California lost his job. He was unable to make the mortgage payments, and foreclosure proceedings were imminent. We were carrying a large second mortgage that was also in jeopardy, and trying to recover from heavy moving expenses.

My reaction to all of this was extremely immature. I began to blame everyone else for my circumstances—the buyer, the real estate people, and even God. After I calmed down a little, I decided to go to the temple and pray for a resolution to my problems. While sitting in the celestial room, I petitioned the Lord with a barrage of silent questions: "Why does everything have to be so complicated? Why can't things go smoothly just once? Wasn't it your prompting that led me to make the move in the first place? Why would you do this to me and my family?"

Then, with my head buried in my hands, I "heard" some of the most meaningful words ever given to me. *"If you knew me, you would know that I would do nothing that was not an act of love in your behalf."* At first, I was stunned, but slowly the full meaning of the message began to sink in. In my mind, I repeated the words: "If you knew me, you would know that I would do nothing that was not an act of love in your behalf." I realized then that I *didn't* know him. My worry, doubt, and frustration was due to ignorance. I really didn't *know* Jesus Christ.

Upon leaving the temple, I acquired a copy of *Jesus the Christ*, and after reading it, I felt a little more familiar with who my Savior is. But it was from the incredible message he had left with me in the temple that my trust in him emerged. I no longer worried about the outcome of my financial situation, or what others might think of what I had done.

Fear of losing the esteem of others is a common component of an immature stress reaction. This fear often leads to "faking it" in order to maintain or enhance an image, rather than coping with the source of the stress.

Individuals who demonstrate an immature reaction to stress often show signs of depression. They can be very ego-oriented and have little concern for how the consequences of their behavior might affect others. "Why do these things happen to me?" they say. Or "Jack just told me that he wrecked his car. Now how am I going to get to work?" Immature individuals often cling to habitual ways of seeing things, agonize over conflicts, and put off making decisions.

Mature reactions. Individuals showing a mature reaction to stress usually have a high tolerance for frustration. They accept responsibility for their decisions and confront the inevitable with the necessary courage. They give considerable thought to the possible consequences of any action that they might take, but are also willing to try new things.

Mature decision makers attack the source of the stress. They see this merely as a task to be completed, something to be taken care of as effectively and efficiently as possible. They know they may lose this time, but things will improve in the future. Such individuals understand that the good and bad experiences of life tend to balance each other out over time, and so are not overwhelmed by fears about what might happen next.

Anticipatory Fear and Stress

Stress is usually a consequence of worrying about the future—what you fear *might* happen. Suppose you were notified that foreclosure proceedings would begin in 30 days unless you caught up on all back payments by a certain date. This kind of ultimatum can cause a great deal of anxiety. Anxiety about the future is called *anticipatory fear.* Social scientist Irving Jarvis classified the patterns of anticipatory fear into three general categories: *high, low,* and *moderate.*[2]

High anticipatory fear. Individuals experiencing high anticipatory fear may undergo extreme feelings of vulnerability before the threatening event occurs and are more likely than others to be anxiety-ridden afterward. For example, if a person with high anticipatory fear is informed that the bank in which his life savings are deposited has failed, he expects a worst-case scenario: He will never get any of his money back and will be destitute after he retires.

Sometimes the intensity of high anticipatory fear can increase to a state of *panic,* becoming overwhelmed by fear and incapable of rational thought. Three conditions are most likely to induce a state of panic: (1) being threatened by an impending danger that cannot be avoided, (2) lacking time or opportunity to act effectively during a crisis, and (3) losing emotional ties, support, or reassurance from loved ones or professionals.

To avoid panic, establish contingency plans *before* something happens. You could avoid a crisis arising from a drop in the stock market, for example, if you were to develop a diversified stock portfolio or to place a "stop order" with your stockbroker directing him or her to sell should the stock drop to a certain level. Another way to avoid panic is to act quickly in order to gain more time. You can get a great deal of relief by having an additional 30 days to resolve a crisis.

Low anticipatory fear. In contrast, individuals demonstrating low anticipatory fear before a crisis often perceive themselves as being nearly invulnerable. They tend to overextend their credit and leverage far beyond their means. Believing that their day of reckoning will never come, they think that somehow everything will get paid off, their luck will continue to hold out, some kind of miracle will happen, or at the last moment someone (such as a friend, a relative, or their financial planner) will come to their rescue.

However, after the financial crisis does occur—and it usually does—these same individuals have a propensity to blame and find fault, and they often make statements such as "You'll be hearing from my lawyer."

Moderate anticipatory fear. Fortunately, some people operate at neither extreme. They exhibit moderate anticipatory fear, and require less support than do those with high levels of fear. These individuals see themselves as being somewhat vulnerable but are usually confident in their ability to cope with an impending threat and optimistic about the outcome. They are much less likely to display emotional disturbances following a traumatic event. If they have had to file for bankruptcy, for example, they may feel some remorse; but once their debt situation has been resolved, their thoughts turn to plans for the future.

One of the most outstanding characteristics of these individuals is that they are task-oriented: they formulate a plan of action and then implement the plan as quickly as possible.

Steps to Take to Resolve a Financial Crisis

One of the most distressing emotions experienced in a crisis is a feeling of helplessness. During the initial stages of a crisis, most of us feel both helpless and hopeless—we believe there is nothing we can do to change the situation. To counter these feelings, we must immediately— at the very beginning of a financial crisis—implement a plan to cope with the possible consequences. Here are ten recommendations for developing and implementing such a plan.[3]

1. Reframe the situation. Since you cannot change what has happened in the real world (stock market fluctuations, swings in the real estate markets, changes in employment, etc.), the best alternative is to reframe, or change your perception of those events, as discussed in chapter 5. Reframing is the process of reinterpreting the meaning or significance of an event; it means seeing things from a different perspective. For example, you might realize that a loss in the value of your stock will have a major financial impact only if you sell your stock. Otherwise, it is only a loss on paper; and if you hold on to the stock until it regains its value, then you will not experience any real financial loss.

2. Avoid procrastination. Since most financial crises involve both time and money, it is essential that you not procrastinate. Immediately establish dates and deadlines by which to take certain actions. Develop contingency plans in the event your first plan of action is blocked. Establish *priorities* wherein you deal first with the most pressing tasks (legal action about to be taken or foreclosure about to be filed) and the most unpleasant tasks (contacting a creditor who has been particularly insistent).

3. Distance yourself. Putting a crisis behind you as quickly as possible can be very beneficial. Try to focus on the future rather than on the past. This is easiest if you can distance yourself— remove or reduce factors in the present that keep reminding you of the past.

CASE ILLUSTRATION

Brian and Joan divorced each other, and their divorce decree stipulated that Joan was to receive custody of their two children and Brian was to be assessed $200 per month for each child until the children reached 18 years of age. Shortly after the divorce, Joan remarried. Joan and her new husband wanted to establish their own family unit and raise Joan and Brian's children as their own, without the hassle of Brian's visits and of contending with two fathers. They made a verbal agreement that if Brian would not bother them about visits, they would not bother him about child support. After the agreement was made, Joan and Brian went their separate ways.

Twenty years later, Joan sued Brian for tens of thousands of dollars in unpaid child support. The court decided in Joan's favor, and Brian, who had remarried and had begun to raise a second family, was faced with writing a check for hundreds of dollars every month for the next 15 to 20 years. Brian was upset about the court's decision, and agonized over having to be reminded of the "injustice" by writing a check each month.

To put some distance between himself and this unpleasant task, Brian deposited a lump sum in a special account that would draw a reasonable amount of interest. He gave instructions to the bank to make an electronic transfer each month from this account to Joan's account until both the money he deposited and the interest it earned had been consumed. He would then deposit another lump sum, and the process would continue.

4. Appraise the alternatives available. If your stress comes from feeling trapped, you should attempt to generate at least *three* alternative courses of action. Try to remain receptive to suggestions from others. Don't disqualify a suggestion too quickly. For example, if your financial crisis has resulted from the death of your spouse, who was the wage-earner, you might consider the following:

A. Is employment an option?
B. Can you make your current assets work harder for you?
   1. Could some of your savings be transferred to income-producing investments?
   2. Could your spouse's life insurance policy be invested to compensate for pension reduction?
   3. Could assets such as the house be sold to take advantage of the one-time capital gains exemption for the elderly?
   4. Would either an equity loan or a reverse annuity be an option?
C. Can you identify areas where you can cut back on expenses?

5. *Take one thing at a time.* Set priorities, incorporate time buffers, and concentrate on one thing at a time. Your *first* priority should be to separate the people from the problem. Make it clear to your spouse or creditors that you are meeting for the purpose of attacking the problem and not each other.

Each of you should make a list of your top three priorities. What are your greatest concerns? What are your greatest sources of stress? Consideration of your feelings about a particular factor is essential to your development of a crisis-management plan. For example, some of the amounts you owe to creditors will be larger than others, but the feelings associated with a certain debt can be completely independent of the amount. "A hundred fifty dollars might not seem like much, considering what I owe everybody else," you might say. "But if I can't get this mechanic off my back, I'm going to end up in some kind of institution."

6. *Delegate tasks and authority.* Draw on the expertise of others; don't try to solve the entire crisis by yourself. Contact a credit counseling service, a lawyer who specializes in bankruptcies, or a tax expert to help you resolve your financial situation. Their experience can save you time and resources that could be better used in dealing with the stresses in your relationships.

Allow others to give you emotional support. The loss of employment, as with factory closures, can be both financially and emotionally devastating to a family and a community. During those times, mutual support and a willingness to pull together can make all the difference in how effectively the crisis is met.

7. *Act responsibly.* Make yourself available to your creditors. Always open the mail and answer

the telephone. Focus on negotiating rather than on winning. Negotiating means conferring with each other so as to arrive at a mutually beneficial settlement (see chapter 5).

8. Cooperate with creditors. When dealing with creditors, it is helpful to remember when you were first taking out the loan and you looked upon them as "friends in a time of need"—or, if not friends, at least members of a cooperative team. Even though you may have fallen on rough times, the "cooperative team" perspective is still one of the most effective tools in dealing with creditors.

In your initial contractual arrangement, you and your creditor both agreed to fulfill your obligations and to act honorably and responsibly. In most cases, regardless of what has transpired since the signing of the original agreement, the moral obligation to treat the other as you would want to be treated still holds (see **Moral Reasoning and Relationships,** chapter 4). This attitude is essential to negotiating a mutually satisfying arrangement.

9. Select alternative means of achieving goals. The principle of *equifinality* means that you can start from different places, take different routes and, in the end, arrive at the same destination. Be imaginative and courageous. For instance, suppose you had previously planned to maintain long-term savings to finance your children's college educations, but because of an unforeseen financial setback, your savings have been depleted. To still achieve your original goal of financing college educations, you might (1) transfer some of your children's inheritance prior to the time of your death, (2) establish a recyclable college fund, wherein each user pays back into the fund after graduating, (3) help your children apply for scholarships, grants, and loans, (4) sell some assets, (5) borrow on the cash value of your life insurance, or (6) decide not to take a particular trip or make a major purchase. Perhaps there are other possibilities as well.

10. Adjust levels of aspiration. We often use past experiences to establish future expectations, which can lead to upwardly mobile desires. In other words, yesterday's luxuries become today's necessities.[4] When families experience a prolonged period of prosperity, expectations of an ever-increasing ability to consume become an integral part of the family financial management process. "The more the family members feel they must have, the smaller the chance of gratifying their wants and the greater the possibility of these expectations creating financial problems," write social science researchers Hogan and Bauer.[5]

Adjusting your level of aspiration often involves compromise or accommodation. Those involved must be willing to settle for only part of what they had originally wanted. Sometimes, though, only the time or sequence needs to be adjusted, while the expected amount remains the same. For example, you may decide to buy a new car next summer instead of this summer; or you may decide to fix up the family room first and remodel the kitchen at a later date, instead of the other way around.

During such negotiations, it is essential that everyone try to express what their goals and aspirations really represent to them. Often, by adjusting levels of aspiration, everyone will be able to realize a portion of their demands and not only satisfy their financial needs but also maintain feelings of personal integrity and self-worth.

Summary

Contrary to what some believe, debt is not a natural state of being. Debt can rob you of your money, and also of your time and your peace of mind. Skills to help you with debt management and debt elimination, as well as how to cope with the accompanying fear and stress, will help you meet and surmount this challenge.

Are you tired of being an "indentured servant"? Begin now to develop and implement a plan to settle with your creditors, to get out of debt—and stay out!

Important Terms

Accelerated repayment: Paying off a debt quickly to save as much as possible on interest charges.
Distancing: Removing or reducing factors in the present that remind you of the past.
Equifinality: The principle that you can arrive at the same destination by taking a number of different routes.
Fold-down method: Debt elimination by paying off one debt and then adding that debt's monthly payment to the payment of another debt.
Fold-up method: Continuing to make payments into your savings account after you have paid off debts.
High anticipatory fear: Extreme feelings of vulnerability before a threatening event occurs, and high anxiety afterward.
Immature reaction: A reaction to stress that includes a tendency to take things personally, maintain an ego-oriented point of view, and have little concern for the consequences.

Indebtedness: The sum of your charge account balances, bank loans, and informal obligations. Although you may not list the latter on a loan application, they are real debts and should be acknowledged as such.

Indentured servant: Anyone who has contracted to pay off a debt by working for the creditor for a specified period of time.

Infantile reaction: A "total" reaction to stress in which emotions are expressed in the extreme without regard for the consequences; an overreaction that is disproportionately severe when compared to the cause.

Low anticipatory fear: Feeling nearly invulnerable before a crisis, tending to overextend credit and leverage; expecting to be rescued, and having a propensity to blame and find fault.

Mature reaction: A reaction to stress that includes a high tolerance for frustration, acceptance of responsibility for decisions, and consideration of the possible consequences of any action that might be taken.

Moderate anticipatory fear: Feeling somewhat vulnerable but also confident in your ability to cope with an impending threat, and optimistic about the outcome.

Reframing: Changing one's perception of an event.

Notes

1. Smith, 1977, p. 259.

2. Jarvis, 1971.

3. Poduska, 1989.

4. Ludwig and Myers, 1979.

5. Hogan and Bauer, 1988.

CHAPTER 8

Planning for the Future

One of the most common complaints about family budgets is "They don't work!" Many say in discouragement, "Budgets look great on paper, but as soon as you think you're getting on top of things, an eight ball ruins everything." Eight balls—the things that sabotage budgets—are usually unexpected and often come at the worst possible time. The car battery goes dead, the washing machine breaks down, someone chips a tooth, a daughter decides to get married and wants a big wedding, a son wins the debate competition, requiring a trip to the capital and two nights in a hotel—all these are examples of eight balls, and they just keep rolling in.

Since traditional budgets are not designed to handle these unexpected events, most families try to cope by consolidating old loans, taking out new loans, or using credit cards. "Robbing Peter to pay Paul" becomes a way of life; budget allocations are juggled so much that the original categories and amounts are no longer recognizable—the budget doesn't work.

Future events, both expected and unexpected, affect the budget. To be able to cope more effectively with those inevitable "eight balls," you need to become more future-oriented. Careful financial planning and goal setting are skills essential to successful living.

Setting Goals

Because wants usually exceed resources, it is vital to establish priorities and set financial goals. In most financial situations, we can't afford to satisfy all of our wants at the same time. More

153

often than not, we fail to achieve a particular goal because we had other conflicting goals that seemed, at the time, more important. We sometimes fail to meet long-range goals because funds keep getting diverted to short-range goals. Setting goals and reaching them involves strict maintenance of a step-by-step process of achieving one goal before taking on another.

Goals and Behavior

Goals are objectives worth working toward, such as saving for a down payment on a home, paying off a debt, buying a new car, or paying for an education. A goal is long-range if it will take more than one year to achieve, short-range if it takes less than a year. In either case, you must establish some goal-seeking behavior before you will ever reach any goal.

Actions that bring people closer to their goals—the steps needed to achieve an objective—are called *compatible* behaviors. *Incompatible* behaviors will postpone, or even prevent, the reaching of a goal. To reach a goal of saving $15,000 for college tuition, for example, a compatible behavior is to save $100 each month for the next 10 years. Spending that $100 on stereo equipment, computer payments, and Visa payments is incompatible behavior.

What Are Your Goals and How Will You Achieve Them?

Most goals, unless actively planned for, will not be achieved. Worksheets 8.1 and 8.2 will help you identify specific long- and short-range goals and steps you can take to achieve them. They can serve as a starting point for a family discussion.

Because many goals are in some way related to finances (feelings of security, buying a home, paying for college), allocating money to fund these goals is a prime consideration. Stabilizing both your income and your spending, and establishing a dependable, consistent savings program is essential to goal achievement.

Stabilizing Your Income

The financial ideal is for both income and spending to be as constant and steady as possible. In most cases, monthly income is regular and predictable, but for many occupations, such as those that are seasonal or dependent on commissions or successful project bids, it is not. When the size and frequency of income is unpredictable, an *income-draw system* can help stabilize income/expenditure difficulties.

An income-draw system is based on a predetermined monthly withdrawal from a particular account. First, set up two separate bank accounts. Deposit all of your income into Account A, as you receive it. Then decide how large your "salary," or monthly draw, will be. For instance, if you decide you need $2,000 a month for all your expenses, that amount would be drawn from Account A once a month on a specific date. This withdrawal becomes your "salary." The salary amount should be constant and not change from month to month. It is deposited in Account B, from which you pay all monthly financial obligations.

The amount you deposit in the first account will vary from month to month, but it should accumulate enough of a reserve to ensure continuous availability of funds in excess of the monthly "salary." This is how it works: Suppose it is January. After you've set aside the funds necessary to meet tax obligations, your January income is $2,500 and you withdraw your $2,000 salary. The reserve in Account A will be $500. February's income is $3,500. The $2,000 salary is withdrawn, leaving $2,000 in the reserve. March's income is only $1,500, but you can still withdraw your salary, and leave a reserve of $1,500. April's income turns out to be only $1,000; nevertheless, you are able to withdraw $2,000, leaving $500 in the reserve.

Unless you happen to be having an especially good month at the time you start your income-draw system, you may have to take a reduced "salary" until your reserves build up. Put aside small amounts each month for several months until you accumulate enough to cover normal monthly draws. At the end of the year, if you have money left over in your Account A reserves, you can consider increasing your "salary" for the upcoming year. If you find your reserves frequently being depleted, you may consider decreasing your draw during the next year. To easily facilitate this kind of system, most banks will arrange for an automatic transfer of funds from one account to another.

The income-draw system enables you to enjoy a steady income and get off the financial yo-yo that people with irregular incomes often experience—having money to burn one month and buying food on credit the next.

Stabilizing Your Spending

Once you've stabilized your income, you're in a better position to project amounts to budget for various expenditures. To stabilize your spending, you must consider both current and future expenditures. One way to stabilize current expenses is to, whenever possible, opt for *equal payment programs,* such as those offered with fuel, utility, and city services.

To stabilize future expenditures, learn to think of certain categories as *spent but not collected,* and create an *amortization reserve.*

Spent but Not Collected

Most budgets are set up to pay monthly bills. But what about money you owe that's not collected during the current month? You probably spend it on something else, and when the bill does arrive you decide to pay it with the food money—and from there your budget goes out the window.

This kind of financial mistake comes from thinking that because you do not have to pay a particular bill during the current month, you are free to spend the money on something else. In reality, however, you have already spent the money—it just hasn't been collected by the creditor yet.

To illustrate, take a look at last month's long-distance telephone bill, utility bill, or credit card statement. When a long-distance phone call is made, money has been spent; it's just not collected at that moment. When the lights are on, water is heated, or the air conditioner is running, money is being spent but not yet collected. As your house just stands there, taxes are being assessed and money is being spent, but again, nothing is collected at the moment.

Think of a vacation in a nice hotel. Your linen is changed daily, your meals are brought to the room, you eat dinners at the fine rooftop restaurant and enjoy cold sodas by the pool. All you have to do is write down your room number and sign your name. No one collects any money from you until the day you check out (or even later if you put it on a credit card).

Now think: Was there any doubt in your mind that the room was costing you $120 a day, that it cost over $45 to have meals brought to your room and $63 for the dinner on the rooftop? But even though you were *spending* the money, the hotel was not *collecting* it—until the day you checked out. The same thing happens at home. When this concept is not considered, the eight balls will keep rolling in and budgets will continue to self-destruct.

So what's the answer? How can a person who wants to develop a viable budget incorporate the idea that money is continuously being spent but not collected? The answer lies in amortization.

Amortization of Expenses

Amortization means spreading payments over a period of time, as when you pay for something in installments rather than in one lump sum. This is not a recommendation to take out a loan, but rather a recommendation to *pay as you go,* by making average monthly payments on bills that come due semiannually and annually.

Obviously, your income will not suddenly go up when these periodic financial obligations come due, so to have money available, you will need to set aside the cost of these services and items on a regular basis. Calculating and making average monthly payments—amortizing—will keep your expenditures constant. Rather than pay a lump sum of $1,200 for property taxes in January, for example, you can amortize your annual tax assessment by depositing in a bank account $100 per month throughout the year. Similarly, you may need to deposit $28 per month to pay for the annual car registration fee, and $12 to cover the costs of professional dues when membership renewal comes around. When you follow this principle, things like taxes, car registration, and dues are no longer eight balls, but normal *budgeted* obligations instead.

If you're paid weekly or twice a month, amortizing your monthly bills can also be beneficial. Most people pay each monthly bill from the paycheck that arrives nearest to the bill's due date. This process usually results in "feast or famine." Suppose, for example, you pay rent out of the first $700 check of the month and the car payment out of the second. Rent is $500, so you have only $200 left to live on during the first two weeks of the month. But the car payment is only $200, which leaves $500 to live on the second two weeks of the month. To smooth out this roller-coaster existence, amortize the bills by taking $250 for rent and $100 for the car payment out of *each* paycheck. In this way, you will have the same amount of money ($350) to live on during both two-week periods of the month.

Most people have a pretty good idea of their monthly income, but monthly expenditures are less predictable. One month might have few expenditures; the next might be very expensive. Most budgets are unable to adapt to such fluctuations and soon become inoperative. The purpose of amortization is to make the outgo as steady and predictable as the income.

There are four categories of expenditures to account for when amortizing: *scheduled fixed, scheduled variable, unscheduled variable,* and *savings/investments.* On Worksheet 8.3, Monthly Expense Amortization, record your expenses in each of these categories. Then divide the total amount by 12 so that the necessary funds can be set aside on a monthly basis until the time comes to make the actual payments.

Scheduled fixed expenses are usually either legal agreements such as car insurance and registration, life insurance, property taxes, or large annual or semi-annual expenses such as tuition and school fees. All debts that come due according to a predetermined schedule and for a fixed amount fall into this category.

Even though we know when these things are coming and how much they will cost, we often fail to plan for them. As a result, when we can least afford it, we get a nasty surprise when we open the envelope. To incorporate fixed obligations into a budget, you must remember that the car registration does not cost $84 for the month it comes due; it costs $7 every month of the year, *collected once a year.* Each month you should include $7 for car registration in your budget, and that money should be set aside as if it were already spent (because it is). Then, when the $84 comes due, the money is sitting in a bank account ready to be used, and your budget remains intact. All scheduled fixed expenditures should be divided into monthly payments and this amount set aside.

On Worksheet 8.3, record the due date and dollar amounts of your scheduled fixed expenses. Add each row and enter the total at the end of the row. Add these totals to obtain the *scheduled fixed subtotal.*

Scheduled variable expenses are those that come due on a predetermined schedule but for variable amounts. Examples are birthdays, anniversaries, Christmas, and family vacations. We know exactly when these events will occur, but the amount we spend on them is somewhat flexible. Costs of these special occasions are often far more than anticipated, as mentioned in chapter 6. For instance, the cost of a birthday is not always just the cost of a gift; it may also include the cost of invitations, food, and decorations for a party, wrapping paper, and perhaps long-distance phone calls. The cost of Easter could include new clothes and Easter baskets for each child. If on Mother's Day you spend $10 to $12 per mother, the event could cost at least $30 if you include your own mother, your mother-in-law, and your wife if she also happens to be a mother. If you make no plans for these events and make no payment toward them each month, you could end up using your credit cards excessively. Of course, it's up to you just how much you decide is an appropriate amount to spend per year on these events, but it helps to predetermine the amounts so they can be amortized over the entire year.

Once you have decided on amounts for each occasion, record them in the appropriate spaces on Worksheet 8.3. Enter the totals of these amounts at the end of each row. Then add up these totals to obtain the *scheduled variable subtotal.*

Unscheduled variable expenses are costs of events that may or may not happen during the year. Chances are, though, some of them will happen. These are sometimes unhappy events, such as unemployment, a death in the family, a car accident, or a prolonged illness. They may be happy events like weddings or births.

Emergency funds and insurance are ways to manage these expenses. Use Worksheet 8.4, Emergency Fund Estimate, to calculate your *unscheduled variable subtotal*. Then enter this subtotal on Worksheet 8.3. Worksheet 8.4 will help you become aware of how much money you need in order to be prepared for any eventuality. The *ideal* emergency fund would be large enough to cover (1) the deductibles on items covered by insurance, (2) the costs of services and property not covered by insurance, and (3) minimal living expenses for three months. Enter these amounts on the worksheet and total them on line A.

On line B, enter the value of resources that could be applied toward the emergency fund, such as the cash value of your life insurance policy and any savings you have already accumulated (keeping in mind the difference between amortized expenses and savings). The total amount you still need to deposit in order to complete your emergency fund (line C) is calculated by subtracting the resources on hand from the ideal fund amount. This savings goal can then be transferred to Worksheet 8.3 as the *unscheduled variable subtotal*.

Savings and investments is the final category to consider for amortization—and it is a vital one. Because of its importance, many people include savings in their scheduled fixed category. This reminds them to make a "payment" to savings on a regular basis in the same way that they pay their debts. In this way, future goals—dreams that give meaning to life—become not just feasible but probable. For most people, stopping the foreclosure, getting out of debt, and having enough food on the table are not enough. They want a financial management plan that goes beyond keeping them alive. They want one that helps give meaning to life.

"Meaningfulness" plays a vital role in goal setting (see **Personal Values,** chapter 1). When you spend your time in what seems to be meaningless pursuits, you're left with the question "What difference does it make?" For instance, people without meaningful goals might think to themselves, "What difference does it make whether I work overtime or not? It all seems to go for taxes anyway." Or "We used to barely make it on one salary. Now both of us are working and we're still just barely making it. No matter what we do, we never seem to get anywhere."

Savings have a way of letting you know that you are getting somewhere, that you are closer

YOUR FINANCIAL PAST, PRESENT, AND FUTURE

to achieving your goals, and that you are doing more than just getting by. The earlier you begin a savings program, the more you will benefit from the effects of time and interest.

Table 8.1 shows how much needs to be saved each month at a certain interest rate in order to accumulate a specified amount in a period of time. For example, if you wanted to save $20,000 in ten years at a 5 percent rate of interest, you would need to save $129 per month; at a 10 percent rate of interest you would need to save $98 per month. If you wanted to save $20,000 in five years at a 5 percent rate of interest you must save $294 per month; at 10 percent interest you would need to save $258 per month. If the exact amount of time or interest rate you need are not shown in the table, either use the next higher number or make an estimate based on the given numbers above and below the one you need.

TABLE 8.1—THE EFFECTS OF TIME AND INTEREST

AMOUNT NEEDED	INTEREST*	YEARS UNTIL NEEDED							
		1	2	3	4	5	10	15	20
$50,000	10%	$3,944	$1,873	$1,185	$843	$639	$241	$119	$65
	7%	4,010	1,935	1,244	900	694	287	156	95
	5%	4,055	1,977	1,284	939	732	320	186	121
$20,000	10%	$1,578	$749	$474	$337	$256	$96	$47	$26
	7%	1,604	774	498	360	277	115	63	38
	5%	1,622	791	514	376	293	128	74	48
$10,000	10%	$789	$375	$237	$169	$128	$48	$24	$13
	7%	802	387	249	180	139	57	31	19
	5%	811	395	257	188	146	64	37	24
$5,000	10%	$394	$187	$119	$84	$64	$24	$12	$6
	7%	401	193	124	90	69	29	16	9
	5%	405	198	128	94	73	32	19	12
$1,000	10%	$79	$37	$24	$17	$13	$5	$2	$1
	7%	80	39	25	18	14	6	3	2
	5%	81	40	26	19	15	6	4	2

*Compounded monthly

Note that the money set aside for amortized expenses is *not* savings, for in a very real sense that money has already been spent. Savings refers to money set aside *in excess of* amortized expenses; it is *not* intended to be spent during the current year.

The amount allocated for savings and investments will vary according to the circumstances and goals of each family. Enter the yearly amount you wish to allocate for *savings* as the *savings program subtotal* on Worksheet 8.3.

To complete Worksheet 8.3, add together the scheduled fixed, scheduled variable, unscheduled variable, and savings program subtotals. Then divide this total of all four categories by 12 to obtain the total amount you need to set aside each month. The total will probably shock you. But keep in mind that you are probably already paying this amount—plus interest—for these various expenses. Once your debt load has been reduced by the fold-down method (see chapter 6), those payments can go into your amortization reserves.

Keeping Track of Your Amortization Reserves

Keeping track of your amortization reserves is easier than you might think. The first step involves recording deposits in your checking account. Normally, when you make a deposit you add that amount to the balance as recorded in your checkbook register. For example, if your checkbook balance is $100, and you deposit $1,200, you add the two together, reaching a total of $1,300 in available funds. This we will refer to as the *active account* portion of your checking account.

The next step is to "transfer" money from the active account portion of your checking account to what we will call the *amortization reserve account* portion. The money is not really moved to any other account; it is simply recorded differently. The amount of the "transfer" is deducted from your check register just as if you were writing a check. For example, if you have $1,300 in the active account and want to put $200 into your amortization reserves, you subtract $200 from the $1,300, leaving $1,100 available in the active account. But instead of recording a check number adjacent to the $200 "withdrawal" (the amount being transferred to your reserve account), place a capital *R* in the check number space (see Figure 8.1).

You can record the amount you transfer to your reserve account in the back of the check register or in a separate accounting system. Record the date of the reserve account "deposit," and then distribute the deposit among the various amortized categories. Arrange the categories in columns so you can easily keep a running total for each one. To record and distribute the $200

CHECK #	DATE	PAYEE	AMOUNT OF PAYMENT	AMOUNT OF DEPOSIT	BALANCE
					100.00
	2/28			1200.00	1200.00
					1300.00
R	2/28		200.00		–200.00
					1100.00
238	2/30	City Utilities	89.50		–89.50
					1010.50

Figure 8.1. Recording a reserve account "withdrawal" in your check register.

from the above example, place $30 under the category labeled *Taxes*, $20 under *Car registration*, $100 under *College tuition*, and $50 under *Auto insurance*.

After distributing the "deposit," add up the amounts in each amortized category to determine the total accumulated to date. For example, if you had accumulated $120 in your reserve account for taxes and just "deposited" an additional $30, your new total in the *Taxes* column would be $150 (see Figure 8.2).

	DATE ACCOUNTS ARE TO BE PAID			
	4/15	3/25	9/2	2/31
DEPOSIT/WITHDRAWAL DATE AND AMOUNT	TAXES	CAR REGISTRATION	COLLEGE TUITION	AUTO INSURANCE
Balance	105.00	70.00	600.00	175.00
1/25/91 ($100)	15.00	10.00	50.00	25.00
Balance	120.00	80.00	650.00	200.00
2/28/91 ($200)	30.00	20.00	100.00	50.00
Balance	150.00	100.00	750.00	250.00

Figure 8.2. Recording a reserve account "deposit."

It is imperative that you continue to perceive these amounts as money *spent but not collected!* You should never view the money in the reserve account as available for uses outside of the categories for which it has been designated. The only money available for current expenses appears in the active account portion of your check register.

When you write a check for an item covered by one of the reserve account categories, you record the check normally, but instead of subtracting the amount of the check from the active account portion of your checking account, you place an *R* in the balance column of the active account and then subtract the amount of the check from the appropriate reserve account column in the back of the checkbook (see figures 8.3 and 8.4).

| DEPOSIT/WITHDRAWAL DATE AND AMOUNT | DATE ACCOUNTS ARE TO BE PAID | | | |
| | 4/15 | 3/25 | 9/2 | 3/1 |
	TAXES	CAR REGISTRATION	COLLEGE TUITION	AUTO INSURANCE
Balance	105.00	70.00	600.00	175.00
1/25/91 ($100)	105.00	10.00	50.00	25.00
Balance	120.00	80.00	650.00	200.00
2/28/91 ($200)	30.00	20.00	100.00	50.00
Balance	150.00	100.00	750.00	250.00
3/1/91				−240.00
Balance	150.00	100.00	750.00	10.00

Figure 8.3. Recording a withdrawal from the reserve account.

CHECK #	DATE	PAYEE	AMOUNT OF PAYMENT	AMOUNT OF DEPOSIT	BALANCE
					100.00
	2/28			1200.00	1200.00
					1300.00
R	2/28		200.00		–200.00
					1100.00
238	3/1	City Utilities	89.50		–89.50
					1010.50
239	3/1	Auto Insurance	240.00		R
					1010.50

Figure 8.4. Recording a check drawn on your reserve account.

Risk Management

During the course of a lifetime, some bad things will happen to us, as well as some good things. Risk management seeks to minimize the financial impact of the bad things.

The principles of risk management focus primarily on two variables: (1) the frequency at which a loss can be expected to occur, and (2) the severity of the loss that can be expected when one does occur. "Risk management" usually consists of one or more of the following approaches: *risk avoidance, risk reduction, risk retention,* and *risk transfer* (see Figure 8.5).

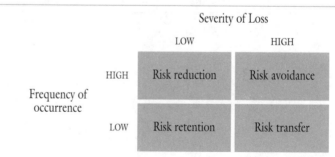

Figure 8.5. Approaches to risk management, based on expected frequency of occurrence and severity of loss.

Risk Avoidance

Avoiding risks is the preferred approach if you face risks that are very likely to occur and that can result in severe financial loss. An example of a risk to avoid is keeping an attack dog when you live next to a preschool. The chances are fairly high that the dog will bite a child, and resulting liability suits could bankrupt you. To avoid this risk, you would be wise to sell or give the dog to someone else, move the dog to a kennel, or move both yourself and the dog.

Similarly, if you do not own a swimming pool, you avoid the risk of someone drowning, as well as a possible lawsuit; if you do not skydive, you avoid the risk of being killed because of a faulty parachute; if you do not walk through a high-crime district at night, you avoid the risk of being mugged there, and so on.

Risk Reduction

The objective of risk reduction is to reduce both the probability and the severity of losses from events that occur with a fairly high frequency. Examples of reducing the probability of a loss include prevention measures such as conducting regular safety inspections around the home and workplace, exercising, losing weight, and having annual health checkups.

Unfortunately, despite even the most diligent attempts at prevention, accidents and injury still occur. But the severity of the loss can still be reduced if risk reduction programs are in place. For example, losses can be reduced by installing fire sprinkling systems, by having fire extinguishers readily available, or by wearing seat belts.

Risk Retention

Some events happen with low frequency and low severity of loss. An example would be the potential theft of a hose from your front yard. The chances are low that it will occur, and even if it were to occur, the cost would be minimal. It would be wasteful for you to pay for insurance against the loss of a $10 hose—the premiums would cost more than the theft. Instead, risk retention is your best option: you "retain," or keep, the risk rather than taking any great measures to do anything about it. These potential losses are small enough that you can just pay for them out of your own pocket. The deductible portion of your insurance policies is really a form of risk retention.

Risk Transfer

Risk transfer is the best approach to risks that have a low frequency but that can result in high financial loss. Examples of this type of risk are fires, medical emergencies, and liability suits. If these risks are retained and the event occurs, the individual or family faces financial catastrophe. Therefore, these risks should be covered by (transferred to) an insurance company. Risk transfer is the recommended approach because the cost of insurance premiums is far less than the cost of such a catastrophe.

Your Life Insurance Needs

The primary reason for buying life insurance is to provide financial security for your dependents. Although some individuals may use life insurance as a supplemental savings program, arguing that this provides greater assurance that the saving will actually take place, most savings alternatives (certificates of deposit, employee tax-deferred matching funds, savings bonds, and so on) provide a higher rate of return.

However, for the financial protection life insurance provides, there is no substitute. You may be tempted to use your life insurance for savings, but the primary reason you *need* life insurance is to guarantee financial resources for your dependents.

A couple with young children has a greater need for life insurance than does a well-established couple on the brink of retirement. Life insurance is used to help survivors meet their financial needs after the premature death of a breadwinner. Most people either under- or over-estimate the amount of protection they need. Those who have dependents are more likely to underestimate their needs, while those who do not have dependents, and therefore do not need as much protection, tend to have too much insurance.

To avoid this paradox, it is advisable to review your life insurance needs on a regular basis—at least once every three years—and also whenever there is a major family change, such as a birth, wedding, death, or remodeling of your home.

Two of the most common techniques used to determine the amount of life insurance you need are called the *human life value approach* and the *need approach*.[1] The human life value approach projects the future income that would be lost due to a person's premature death. This lump sum is then replaced by life insurance. To calculate this amount, it is necessary to (1) estimate the average annual income that would be earned through age 65, (2) deduct the amount that would be paid for all federal and state taxes, insurance premiums, and costs for self-maintenance, and (3) multiply this amount by the number of years left before retirement.

The need approach to life insurance analysis focuses on the projected cost of meeting the needs of the survivors rather than merely replacing the income that would be lost. The amount of life insurance needed is determined by adding up the estimated costs of such factors as income needs of the survivors, educational needs of the children, and medical needs of the chronically ill. Consideration should also be given to such items as the need to pay off mortgages and debts, funeral and probate expenses, and special needs such as providing for children's weddings and travel.

The money to cover all of these expenses must come from selling off assets, earnings provided by the survivors, or from life insurance proceeds. After you calculate how much your survivors can earn on their own or receive from the liquidation of your assets, you can subtract that amount from what will be needed. The rest must be covered by life insurance.

Worksheet 8.5, the Life Insurance Needs Analysis, based on the need approach described above, will help you better understand the purpose of and need for life insurance, and decide how much insurance you need.

The first section of the worksheet, labeled "Survivor Immediate Expenses," helps you determine the assets available and the amount of money survivors would need to eliminate existing debt and pay funeral expenses, estate taxes, and other costs. Calculate these amounts separately for each spouse. If the difference between assets and expenses is a deficit (negative), then additional life insurance is needed to correct the deficit.

In the worksheet's next section, "Survivor Income Needs," you identify sources of income and the amount of money needed to provide for your family in your absence. This does not mean you must provide for a life of luxury, but there should be enough for the family to survive. Other income needed until the surviving spouse's retirement, including money for education, also falls in this category. The difference between resources and needs, if negative, represents the amount of additional life insurance needed. Add this to the amount of life insurance needed to meet immediate expenses in order to determine the total amount of additional life insurance you need.

Summary

The process of drawing up a budget is incomplete if you focus only on present income and needs. Learning how to include future obligations in your financial planning begins with goal-setting—keeping in mind that your financial behavior must be compatible with your goals. The next step is to stabilize your income, through the income-draw system if necessary, and then your expenses. Employing the concept of *spent but not collected*, amortizing periodic bills over several pay periods, and understanding the various budget categories will help you see where your money is being spent.

Proper consideration of risk management issues can help you decide whether to avoid, reduce, retain, or transfer certain risks to an insurance company. It is very important that you determine the size of your emergency fund and life insurance needs.

With these perspectives and skills in place, the "eight balls" of life will not catch you off guard, and the misguided practice of "robbing Peter to pay Paul" will be a thing of the past.

Important Terms

Active account: The portion of your checking account that is available for immediate use after the reserve amounts have been transferred.

Amortization: Spreading payments over a period of time, as when you pay for something in installments rather than in one lump sum; making average monthly payments on bills that come due semiannually and annually.

Emergency fund: A savings account large enough to cover (1) the deductibles on insured items, (2) the costs of services and property not covered by insurance, and (3) minimal living expenses for three months.

Goals: Objectives worth working toward, such as saving for a down payment on a home, paying off a debt, buying a new car, or paying for an education. A goal is long-range if it will take more than one year to achieve, short-range if it will take less.

Income-draw system: A way to stabilize income by setting up two separate bank accounts, depositing all income into Account A, from which is drawn a "salary" once a month for deposit into Account B, from which all monthly financial obligations are paid.

Reserve account: The amount you have deducted from your check register in order to accumulate funds for paying bills that come due annually or semiannually.

Risk avoidance: Eliminating risks that are very likely to occur and that can result in very high financial loss.

Risk reduction: Finding ways of lowering financial losses from events that occur with a fairly high frequency; involves activities designed to reduce both the frequency and the severity of losses.

Risk retention: Absorbing the cost of events that are characterized by low frequency and low severity of loss.

Risk transfer: Handling risks of low frequency but high financial loss by transferring the risk to an insurance company.

Savings program: Funding for goals that require long-term planning.

Scheduled fixed expenses: Legal agreements; debts with payment amounts that are fixed and due on a regular schedule.

Scheduled variable expenses: Debts that are due on a regular schedule but that can vary in amount.

Spent but not collected: The concept that certain debts are incurred (money is being spent) even though there may be a delay before payment is requested.

Unscheduled variable expenses: Expenses that are not scheduled, that may or may not happen, but that are likely to occur.

Note

1. Rejda, 1982, pp. 315–16.

WHAT ARE YOUR GOALS?

Answer the following questions as imaginatively as possible. Consider your hopes, dreams, and wishful aspirations.

1. What are five of your most important goals for your lifetime?

_____

_____

_____

_____

_____

2. What are five of your most important goals for the next year of your life?

_____

_____

_____

_____

_____

3. What would be five of your most important goals if you had only six months to live?

_____

_____

_____

_____

_____

GOAL ACHIEVEMENT

Select one of the goals listed on Worksheet 8.1 and complete the following exercise. Be as specific as possible in your answers.

Goal

_____

_____

Time within which goal is to be achieved

_____

_____

Method of measuring progress

_____

_____

Obstacles to be overcome

_____

_____

What will be required

_____

_____

Resources

_____

_____

Action now being taken

_____

_____

Additional action that could be taken

_____

_____

Costs (time, energy, resources, emotional)

_____

_____

MONTHLY EXPENSE AMORTIZATION

SCHEDULED-FIXED EXPENSES	JAN	FEB	MAR	APR	MAY	JUN	JUL	AUG	SEP	OCT	NOV	DEC	TOTALS
Contributions													
Taxes													
Vehicle registration													
Educational expenses													
License renewals													
Insurance premiums													

SCHEDULED-FIXED SUBTOTALS _____

SCHEDULED-VARIABLE EXPENSES	JAN	FEB	MAR	APR	MAY	JUN	JUL	AUG	SEP	OCT	NOV	DEC	TOTALS
Birthdays													
Holidays													
Anniversary													
Weddings													
Births													
Scouting/camping													
Home/garden maintenance													
Back to school													
Vacation													
Other													

SCHEDULED-VARIABLE SUBTOTALS _____

UNSCHEDULED-VARIABLE SUBTOTALS _____

SAVINGS PROGRAM SUBTOTALS _____

TOTAL OF ALL FOUR CATEGORIES _____

MONTHLY AMORTIZED AMOUNT (TOTAL OF ALL FOUR CATEGORIES, DIVIDED BY 12) _____

EMERGENCY FUND ESTIMATE

Amounts deductible before losses are covered by insurance
(for example, car insurance with $100 deductible)

        Automobile   _____

        Other property   _____

        Medical   _____

        Other   _____

Loss for which individual or family is responsible under co-insurance
provisions (for example, insurance may pay 80 percent and you pay
20 percent) for:

        Property   _____

        Medical   _____

Other expenses not covered by insurance   _____

Minimal family living expenses for three months

        Contractual obligations:

                Rent or mortgage payments   _____

                Insurance premiums (on a monthly basis)   _____

        Debt payments:

                Installment credit   _____

                Charge accounts   _____

                Outstanding bills   _____

                Other   _____

        Variable obligations:

                Food   _____

                Utilities   _____

                Transportation   _____

                Other   _____

        Other obligations (specify)   _____

Unexpected replacement or major repair of equipment

        Automobile   _____

        Major appliance   _____

Legal expenses   _____

Veterinary bills   _____

    [A] TOTAL   _____

    [B] Current cash value of life insurance and demand deposits   _____

    [C] EMERGENCY FUND SAVINGS GOAL ([C] = [A] − [B])   _____

LIFE INSURANCE NEEDS ANALYSIS

Survivor Immediate Expense Analysis

ASSETS

	Husband	Wife
Life insurance		
Cash (savings/checking)		
Securities		
Property		
Other assets		
[A] TOTAL ASSETS		

IMMEDIATE EXPENSES AND DEBTS

	Husband	Wife
Mortgages		
Outstanding debts		
Uninsured medical expenses		
Estate taxes		
Probate		
Funeral		
Additional expenses		
[B] TOTAL IMMEDIATE EXPENSES		
[C] SURPLUS / DEFICIT = [A] – [B]		

If this figure is a deficit, it represents the amount of additional life insurance required to meet this need.

Survivor Income Needs Analysis

SOURCES OF INCOME

	Husband	Wife
Liquid assets		
Spouse earnings		
Pensions		
Social Security		
Other assets		
[D] TOTAL RESOURCES		

INCOME NEEDS

	Husband	Wife
Family income until retirement		
Education for children		
Education for spouse		
[E] TOTAL INCOME NEEDS		
[F] SURPLUS / DEFICIT = [D] – [E]		

If this figure is a deficit, it represents the amount of additional life insurance required to meet this need.

Total Additional Life Insurance Needed

[C] + [F]		

CHAPTER 9

Getting through the Month

oday's family often complains, "There always seems to be more month than money." In "the good old days," when money ran out before the end of the month, most families simply tightened their belts, stopped spending, and waited for the next payday. Those, of course, were the days when the primary medium of exchange was cash. Unfortunately, today's families usually do not stop spending when money runs out. Instead, they use credit cards as a life jacket to keep them afloat until the next payday arrives.

One of the primary reasons for using credit cards is that it enables us to obtain immediate gratification. In former times, when people wanted what another person had, they bartered. But nowadays, instead of exchanging goods, we offer our promise-to-pay in exchange for goods. In essence, credit cards enable us to receive what we want *prior* to working for it.

But in research laboratories, rats must always press the bar *before* they are given a reward. It is contrary to the rules of motivation to first reward subjects and then ask them to labor. This would be called *reverse conditioning*, and it rarely works with rats. Apparently, it does not work that well with people either: almost one million personal bankruptcies were filed in 1992,[1] and an untold amount of personal property was repossessed.

In today's credit world, our primary concern is usually the size of the monthly payments. We then make payments on an outstanding balance for so long that we forget what exactly it was that we bought. We also lose sight of the actual cost of individual items, including taxes and interest charges, in the homogeneity of minimal payments. Then, as most of today's families simply add the newly acquired credit card payments (including interest) to their other monthly expenditures, the next month's money runs out even sooner than the last month's—and the credit cards get used even earlier in the month. Too often, this insidious progression continues until families see bankruptcy as the only way out.

Until that day of reckoning does arrive, many families will go on believing they are living within their income. And in a sense they are—but they are not living within their budget.

Living within Your Income versus Living within Your Budget

Families who *live within their income* are usually able to pay all the monthly bills, but they have nothing left for amortization reserves or savings. In most of these families, the amount needed to get through the month increases at about the same rate their income increases. Often these families look back 10 or 15 years and marvel at how they used to get by on so little (even adjusting for inflation): "I used to bring home $1,500 a month and we still had a few dollars left over to play around with. Now, with both of us working, we're bringing home over $4,000 a month and we have to charge a pizza dinner."

In contrast, families who *live within their budget* keep monthly expenditures relatively constant as income increases. They then have money for amortization reserves and savings; and the amount of money left over at the end of each month gradually increases as their income increases.

Such a surplus is possible because these families have determined what is sufficient for them to live on (see chapter 6). They have already determined what is enough house, car, and vacation. Even if they might qualify for more, they know their values and are satisfied with what they have. Should some aspect of their lives become unsatisfactory, they *choose by budgeting* how much to spend, rather than just spending to the limit of their resources.

For example, if family members "outgrow" a house, they can either add to the existing home or buy a new one. Their decision will be based on how much they feel they *need* to spend (how much "new house" will be enough to satisfy their values), and not on how much they *could* spend (determined by the size of the loan they could qualify for with their current income). In other words, they make a budgeting choice of how much they want to spend, rather than letting the bank tell them how much they can borrow—and then spending all of it.

To become a family that lives within its budget, you must learn how to cut expenses, distinguish between needs and wants, and, as discussed in chapters 6, 7, and 8, incorporate into your budget the financial obligations associated with the past and the future.

Cutting Expenses

The time to cut expenses is *before* you start spending. The moment you make the decision not to spend, or at least not to spend as much as you had originally planned, you've started the process of cutting expenses. This happens, for example, when you decide to limit the purchase price of a new car to $10,000 instead of $15,000. It happens when you decide to rent an item rather than buy it, or repair rather than replace. It also begins when you borrow something from a friend or neighbor (unless this is contrary to your value system), or when you cut costs by being creative.

Sharing

Sharing can be an effective means of reducing your spending. For example, neighbors on one cul-de-sac went in together to purchase a snowblower. Friends and relatives sometimes go in on the purchase of cabins and boats. Although such arrangements are not without drawbacks, in most cases cooperation and imagination can solve the logistical problems. Whatever the stresses of sharing might be, they seldom compare to the stresses of heavy indebtedness.

Plugging the Holes

The next step in cutting expenses is to "plug the holes"—the places where money seems to disappear without much to show where it went. "Holes" are the *little things* in your spending patterns that tend to consume a *large portion* of your income.

They can appear in the form of "extras" added on to necessities: special phone services (call waiting and forwarding, extra phones) and excessive long-distance calls, extra cable channels, eating lunches out, subscribing to too many magazines and newspapers, grocery shopping without a list, or running the kids back and forth to the mall.

Nonessential food and drink

Consider, for example, one woman who worked for a company that made canvas awnings.

The work was hard and the factory was hot. On her morning break she would get a can of pop from one of the machines in the snack room, then another on her afternoon break. Each can cost 75 cents, for a total of $1.50 per day, $9 per week, or $35 per month. In addition, she was often tired when she got home from work, and sometimes she didn't feel like cooking a meal. So at least twice a week she would pick up fried chicken, hamburgers, or pizza. The take-home meals usually ran about $15 each, totaling $30 per week, or $120 per month. This woman was unknowingly spending more than $155 a month on pop and pizza. She had to earn about $250 a month to clear the $155 (after taxes, etc.) that then went into the "pop and pizza hole."

Between-meal snacks and desserts can also be a hidden hole in the budget. Imagine saying to your spouse, "I think we should set aside $22,000 for family snacks." This suggestion may seem ridiculous and irresponsible, but you might be surprised at how money for snack food can add up. If your child were to have, for example, half a Popsicle in the morning (a cost of 10 cents), a glass of Kool-Aid and a homemade cookie with lunch (8 cents plus 7 cents), the other half of the Popsicle in the afternoon (10 cents), and a bowl of ice cream that evening while watching TV (15 cents), the total cost for that day's snacks would be 50 cents. But what if Mom, Dad, and three or four other kids joined in? Then the daily total would come to $3, or almost $100 per month. And that translates into $1,200 per year, or almost $22,000 over an 18-year period!

These numbers are probably too conservative. Many parents who read this example may respond in mock surprise, "*One* Popsicle? *One* glass of Kool-Aid? *One* cookie? Surely you jest. That wouldn't even make *one* snack break." The example also does not include trips to the convenience store, candy bars, big mugs of soda pop, store-bought cookies, or Slurpees, which all help dig the "snack hole."

This is not to suggest that you should cut out all snacks; they can be an important part of family life. But a clear understanding of the monthly cost of treats is essential to maintaining a well-managed food budget. These examples are merely intended to help you review your values and make a conscious decision about how much you really want to spend in this category. Consider the alternative of having an extra $50 to $100 per month to help pay bills, pay for the car, or go on a vacation.

In a similar fashion, alcohol and tobacco can consume enormous portions of the family income. Sometimes the costs of these items are hidden in grocery bills or the entertainment category, so that no one is fully aware of the exact amounts. This "hole" can be much bigger and deeper than you would expect. Again we see the inspiration of the Word of Wisdom—and recognize that the advantages of obeying God's commandments reach into our temporal lives as well. If a chunk of your money is going into this hole, you need to discuss the problem together with openness and honesty.

Thirty-Day Menus

Using a shopping list when buying groceries can help stabilize your food budget, discourage impulse purchases, and enhance feelings of self-reliance.

For more efficient and less expensive grocery shopping, try a 30-day menu. Ask family members to make a list of their favorite meals. Taking into account how much you wish to spend on food each month, draw from their lists to develop menus for the next 30 days. You are now able to calculate exactly how many cans of peas you will need, how many pounds of hamburger, how many potatoes, and so on.

Once you compile this shopping list, you can use it again and again. Most family members will not remember that one month ago they had meatloaf, or that it's been four weeks since the last tuna casserole. By using this method, your food budget is almost the same every month, so you can take advantage of sales on food items without worrying about over- or understocking your pantry. If your menu calls for 8 cans of corn per month, for instance, you can take advantage of a case sale (24 cans) and acquire a three months' supply of corn.

Automobile extras

Extra mileage in the car can create a large hole in the budget—one you can easily reduce. The cost of driving 1,200 miles per month at 15 to 20 miles per gallon, with gas costing $1.30 per gallon, is about $80 to $100 per month, $160 to $200 per month if two cars are driven that much.

The first step in filling this "hole" is to monitor your driving habits for a month. Record the mileage to frequently visited locations such as malls, parks, movie theaters, supermarkets, and friends' homes. Then convert the mileage into cost-per-trip figures: Divide the miles to your destination by the miles per gallon your car gets, and multiply this answer by the price of a gallon of gas (miles *divided by* miles per gallon *times* cost per gallon). You can now begin thinking consciously about how much it costs you to drop the kids off at Ralph's, dash down to the store, go for a drive, or visit those friends you drive 15 miles to see because you have no money for entertainment! There are literally no free trips in life.

After you have monitored your driving habits for a month, begin cutting out unnecessary trips. A reduction of around 15 miles a day per car could save $25 to $40 per month in a single-car family, and $50 to $80 in a two-car family. In addition, consider having children take public transportation or pay from their allowance for the "taxi service" you provide. Most children do not realize what it costs for you to take them places.

Imagine the following conversation between a parent and a child: "Mom, could you take us down to the mall so we can hang out for a while?" Mom replies, "Well, things are a little tight this month. I'll take you if you contribute a dollar toward the cost of the trip." In shocked disbelief, the child wails, "A dollar! Why should we have to pay you a dollar? It doesn't cost you anything to take us!" With a patient smile, Mom explains, "Actually, it does. Running you down to the mall would take about a dollar and a half's worth of gas. Sounds like you're getting a good deal to me!"

Try mentally adding the cost of driving to some of your own destinations. For example, if you are going to a sporting event, the cost may be $5 for the ticket, $3 for refreshments—and $2 for the gas to drive there: a total of $10, not $8. If you *don't* attend the event, you aren't as likely to have to fill up on the way to work because you used so much gas for the sporting event—added to what it took to get to your child's Little League game earlier in the day.

To further cut expenses, check into increasing the amount of the insurance deductible on your car and home. You may save quite a bit on your yearly premiums by increasing your deductible from $50 to $100 or $250. If your car is older, you might also look into whether you really need collision coverage (the part of the insurance that covers the cost of repairing damage to your car).

For example, if you own an older car worth $1,000 and you are carrying a $200 deductible on collision insurance, the most you would receive from the insurance company if the car were totaled is $800. If you're paying $300 every six months for collision insurance for that car, in a year and a half you will have paid more in insurance than the car is worth. In this example, canceling the collision portion of your car insurance is a more practical way to manage the risk (see chapter 8). *You should always, however, maintain the liability portion of your car insurance.*

Spending Limits

Spending limits are pre-established checkpoints designed to prevent impulsive or careless purchases. A spending limit may be as simple as limiting the amount of cash you carry with you—

if you carry $10, you're likely to spend $10, but if you carry a dollar, you'll probably spend no more than that.

Other spending limits involve negotiating with others. You and your spouse might each agree to never make a purchase greater than an agreed-upon limit without first consulting the other. You may set a spending limit of $25, $50, $100, or even higher. By establishing spending limits, you are likely to have fewer surprises like these: "Well, what do you think of our new Saab?" Or "But we needed new drapes, and they were on sale. Don't you like them?"

You can also set ultimate spending limits in certain categories. A family may decide that they will spend no more than $300 for skiing in one season. They can choose to spend the $300 in one weekend or spread it out over the entire season, but when it is gone they will not use any additional funds for skiing.

Similar agreements can be made for entertainment, treats, or eating out, with set amounts allocated for a given week or month. Setting limits helps you live within your budget.

Distinguishing between Needs and Wants

A fundamental skill for living within your budget is being able to distinguish between needs and wants. A *need* is something required for survival. It provides a means to go on living, accomplishing, or contributing. A *want*, on the other hand, is something that provides greater convenience, enrichment, or pleasure. It provides motivation to continue living, accomplishing, or contributing.

Centuries ago, in A.D. 1272, St. Thomas Aquinas wrestled with the challenge of distinguishing between wants and needs and came to the conclusion that goods could be divided into two categories—*natural wealth* and *artificial wealth*.

> Natural wealth is that which serves man as a remedy for his natural wants, such as food, drink, clothing, conveyances, dwellings, and things of this kind; while artificial wealth is that which is not a direct help to nature, as money, but is invented by the art of man for the convenience of exchange and as a measure of things saleable.[2]

Worksheet 9.1, the Needs and Wants Exercise, will help you distinguish between your needs and your wants, an important first step in creating a survival budget that will show just how little you need to satisfy the basic necessities. The first section lists alternatives that satisfy the need for transportation. Some examples of how to meet this need are listed (walk, bike, public transportation). Write any additional alternative of your own choosing in the blank at the end of the list. Next to the listed alternatives, record the estimated cost of each. For example, it might cost $30 for a pair of walking shoes for the "Walk" alternative, $40 for bike repairs for the "Bike" alternative, and so on.

In the "Alternative chosen" blank, write the mode of transportation you prefer and its cost. Interestingly, you have just made a "need versus want" decision: You *need* transportation, but the way you have chosen to meet this need usually reflects what you *want*.

Compare the cost of the alternative you have chosen with the estimated costs of the other alternatives listed to arrive at the "Want cost/need cost difference" for each alternative. For example, if you choose to own a car that costs $400 a month in payments, insurance, and gasoline, subtract $30 (estimated cost for the "Walk" alternative) from $400 ("Owning one car" alternative) to produce a $370 "Want cost/need cost difference." Record the amount in the blank. This indicates that your "want" is costing you an additional $370 per month over what it would cost you to walk. Compared to a $100-per-month public transportation cost, the car alternative has a want cost/need cost difference of $300.

Now ask yourself, Is having a car worth an extra $300 to $350 a month in expenses? Is it really necessary? Do another cost comparison with car expenses and the costs of public transportation. The amount of money you save by using public transportation or carpooling can be substantial; you may be able to save hundreds or even thousands of dollars per year.

Of course, when it comes to transportation, the difference between a want and a need is determined by your actual circumstances. If you work at or near your home, you may be able to walk to the store or church, catch a ride with helpful neighbors, or occasionally take a cab—and not have the expense of a car at all. But if your work is farther away and not accessible to public transportation, you may have no choice but to carpool or, if that isn't feasible, drive your own car all the time. The key is to honestly determine what is needed for your *survival*. Once you know that, you can decide whether or not it's worth it to spend more for the thing you *want*. (Remember Principle 4.)

Use the above procedure to evaluate shelter, food, clothing, and other needs. Table 9.1, which highlights long-distance communications, indicates the financial difference between writing letters, sending audiotapes, and making long-distance phone calls. By phoning instead of writing you pay an extra $15.40; by phoning instead of sending audiotapes you pay an extra $14. Here again, your circumstances help you determine whether or not your choice is a "need" or a "want." If you simply desire to *send* communications, news, and so on, writing letters may be sufficient for you. For some, talking on the phone may fulfill an emotional need for *receiving* feedback that writing letters does not. Perhaps this need can be met in a less expensive manner. Evaluate your needs and options thoroughly, and then choose accordingly. But you must always be aware of the cost differences of choosing one alternative over another.

TABLE 9.1—THE COST DIFFERENCES OF LONG-DISTANCE COMMUNICATION ALTERNATIVES

ALTERNATIVES	FREQUENCY	ESTIMATED COST	WANT COST/NEED COST DIFFERENCE
Phone	2/month	$16.00	$ 0
Audio tapes	2/month	2.00	14.00
Write letters	2/month	.64	15.36

Preparing a Budget

According to financial experts, an effective financial management plan is the most important factor in the amount of satisfaction couples receive from their resources.[3] Yet only about 50 percent of families in America use some kind of budget—and only about 12 percent have one that is written down.[4] A budget is *a systematic plan for meeting expenses during a given period*. It should not be seen as something that restricts your financial behavior, but as something that can provide you with greater financial freedom. A budget is a road map showing you how to get where you want to go financially. Remember, your overall goal should be to spend your money on things you value, things that will last.

The budget you will develop using the principles and skills outlined in this book has a much better chance of working than your past budgets did because (1) you will include both *past* and *future obligations* to help you avoid the "eight balls" that often sabotage budgets, (2) you will consciously decide where to *cut expenses* and *plug the holes* so that your money can be applied to what you value, and (3) you will take a good hard look at what is *sufficient* to satisfy your *needs* and your *wants*.

These are the steps to developing a workable budget:

1. Evaluate how much money you *think* is coming in and from what sources, as well as how much you think is going out and for what purposes.
2. Compile an accurate account of what is *actually* happening financially.
3. Develop a survival budget to show just how little money would be required to take care of your basic needs, rather than satisfying your wants.
4. Develop a projected budget, making a relatively accurate guess about how much money you expect to bring in and how much you expect to spend in each budget category.
5. In order to fine-tune your budget, compare the projected budget to your actual income and expenditures.

Budget Categories

Following are suggested budget categories and items. The list is not exhaustive. Rather, it is designed to give you an idea of what items are typically included in each category—the same categories listed in this chapter's budget worksheets.

Income

Salary/wages: All earned income.

Other income: Includes interest, dividends, child support, welfare payments, rent subsidies, food stamps, education grants, garage sale proceeds, and inheritance.

Fixed Expenses

Taxes: Federal, state, local income taxes. (Do not include property taxes if they are included in the mortgage payment.)

Retirement programs: All contributions to retirement plans, including FICA (Social Security), company-sponsored plans, IRA, and Keogh plans.

Rent/mortgage: Rent or mortgage payments (include principal, interest, and property taxes).

Insurance premiums: Total insurance premiums paid—life, medical, auto, homeowner's, and any other premiums.

Vehicle license/registration: All car, boat, trailer, and airplane licensing and registration fees.

Debt repayment: Record one debt per line. The figure should reflect the total monthly payment (principal plus interest).

Other: Any other fixed expense your family has that is not included in a previous category, such as care for elderly parents or chronic medical costs.

Variable Expenses

Food: All money spent on food, both at home and away from home (groceries, school meals, restaurant meals, meals delivered).

Utilities: Gas, electricity, water, sanitation, cable TV, garbage pickup, and sewer.

Telephone: Local and long-distance service, leasing, and access fees.

Household operations: Maintaining the home and its operations (household repairs, cleaning supplies, and gardening supplies).

Furnishings/appliances: Household furnishings and both large and small appliances.

Transportation/vehicle maintenance: All bus fares, gasoline, and automobile and/or bicycle maintenance and repair.

Apparel: Purchases of clothing and accessories, as well as laundry and dry cleaning expenses.

Personal care: Permanents, haircuts, and styling; makeup, weight-loss and fitness programs.

Child care: Babysitting, day-care centers, and other forms of child care.

Education: Tuition, books, and all other costs of formal or informal education for parents or children; subscriptions to magazines and newspapers.

Recreation/entertainment: Theater and sporting events, club memberships, hobbies, and sporting goods.

Holidays/birthdays: All special events, such as Christmas, Easter, birthdays, graduations, and anniversaries.

Medical expenses: Any medical expenses not covered by health insurance.

Vocational dues/expenses: All expenses associated with work, including union and professional dues.

Donations: All contributions made to religious or charitable organizations.

Personal allowance: Miscellaneous category—"mad money" for parents and allowances for children.

Savings: Any amount put into either savings or investments and not spent during the year.

Vacation: All expenses associated with family vacations, weekend getaways, and day trips.

Other: Any other variable expense not included in a previous category.

Your Perceived Budget

Worksheet 9.2, Your Perceived Budget, will help partners express the amounts they perceive they are earning and spending each month. Each partner should fill out a worksheet and then compare it with the other's. Fill in the amounts you *think* you are earning and spending monthly in each category. This exercise familiarizes you with the budget categories and sets the stage for recording your *actual* budget.

Your Actual Budget

Worksheet 9.3, Your Actual Budget, is completed after you have finished Worksheet 9.2. The same categories are included, but in this case you list the *actual* income received and the price of each item. This means digging out loan contracts, mortgages, sales receipts, W-2 forms, pay stubs, and income tax filings, and noting the exact figures. This exercise tells where your money has actually been going—and how you got into your current financial situation.

After you fill out Worksheet 9.3, compare it with Worksheet 9.2 to see how close your estimates were to the actual numbers. You will probably find some minor discrepancies between partners' responses, but major differences are a sign that you need more communication in those areas (see chapter 5).

This activity can be combined with a discussion among family members about where their money is really going: Is the money being spent on things you value? What changes would you like to make?

Your Survival Budget

Putting together a survival budget demonstrates how little your family actually requires to meet *minimum* needs. This budget could be used in emergencies, when income is low, or when expenses become exceptionally high (because of unexpected medical costs, for example). Worksheet 9.4 is for recording *basic needs only*. You may be surprised at just how little your family really *needs* to survive; it is the *wants* that really cost you. Few people ever have to declare bankruptcy trying to satisfy their *needs*. It is trying to satisfy their wants that most often brings financial ruin.

Your Projected Budget

Worksheet 9.5, Your Projected Budget, will help you begin an accurate, effective budget. On the projected budget worksheet plan, list the amounts your family *expects* to earn and spend in each category. Try to be as accurate as possible in your estimations, but understand that even carefully considered projected budget amounts do not always reflect actual needs. After you have lived on the projected budget for a month, you will compare it with actual figures for that month.

Your Projected Budget versus Your New Actual Budget

You may need to monitor your spending over a three-month period, making appropriate adjustments each month. Worksheet 9.6, Your Projected Budget versus Your New Actual Budget, compares the projected amounts with what was actually spent in each budget category for an entire month. This will highlight discrepancies and enable you to gradually adjust either your projected budget or your spending (or both), so that projected costs become fairly accurate approximations of the actual amounts spent. Create a file of the adjusted actual monthly budgets, so they are available for reference when you develop next year's monthly budgets.

You will need to develop a projected/actual comparison sheet for each month of the year. Use an income-draw system, if necessary, to even out your income, and try to keep the expenses for each month as consistent as possible by amortizing. This will help both income and expenses to remain relatively stable, regardless of fluctuations in income or the arrival of a particular holiday or special event.

Summary

There is a difference between living within your income (just spending all that you have) and living within your budget (deciding what to spend so that there is some to save). One of the primary prerequisites for living within your budget is cutting expenses—by "plugging holes," setting spending limits, and making a distinction between needs and wants.

The steps to preparing an effective budget include: recording a perceived budget (providing insight into how you *think* you're doing financially), an actual budget (providing a view of what your financial situation *really* looks like), a survival budget (providing a picture of just how little you could get by on if you consider only your needs, and not your wants), a projected budget (providing an estimation of what you think things will cost per month), and your new actual (adjusted) budget (providing a view of what things really did cost).

These steps will produce a family budget you can really use, one that reflects real figures and that will give you a true perspective on what you can accomplish.

Important Terms

Actual budget: The amount of income that is actually available and the exact amounts being spent in various budget categories, based on actual records and documents.

Budget: Spending plan or allocation guideline.

Living within your budget: Keeping monthly expenditures relatively constant as income increases. Money is available for amortization reserves and savings; as income increases, the amount of money left over at the end of each month gradually increases.

Living within your income: Being able to pay all the monthly bills, but afterward having nothing left for amortization reserves or savings. The amount needed to get through the month increases at the same rate that income increases.

Needs: Requirements for survival; provide a means to go on living, accomplishing, or contributing.

Perceived budget: Estimate of how much income is available and how much is spent in various budget categories.

Plugging the holes: Eliminating spending for the "little things that add up" in a budget, such as snacks and other extras added on to necessities.

Projected budget: The best guess as to how much should be allocated to each budget category.

Spending limits: Pre-established checkpoints designed to prevent impulsive or careless purchases.

Survival budget: Budget based on the barest minimum amount require to take care of basic needs (wants and luxuries are not included).

Thirty-day menu: List of meals for the 30 days, repeated each month to stabilize the monthly food bill.

Wants: Elements that provide greater convenience, enrichment, or pleasure, and motivation to continue living, accomplishing, or contributing.

Notes

1. U.S. Department of Commerce, 1994, p. 548.

2. Aquinas, 1952, p. 616.

3. Williams, 1985.

4. Yankelovich, Skelly and White, 1975.

NEEDS AND WANTS EXERCISE

POSSIBLE ALTERNATIVES	ESTIMATED COST	WANT COST/NEED COST DIFFERENCE

Transportation

1. Walk
2. Bike
3. Public transportation
4. Car pool
5. Owning one car
6. Owning two cars
7. _____

Alternative chosen _____

Shelter

1. Live with relatives
2. Rent apartment (one room)
3. Rent apartment (two room)
4. Buy a trailer
5. Buy a condominium
6. Buy a house
7. _____

Alternative chosen _____

Food

1. Staples only
2. Home-prepared
3. Processed (frozen, etc.)
4. Fast foods
5. Restaurants
6. _____

Alternative chosen _____

Clothing

1. Hand-made
2. Second-hand
3. Chain stores
4. Designer

5. _____   _____   _____

Alternative chosen

_____   _____

Long-distance communication

    1. Write letters   _____   _____

    2. Phone   _____   _____

    3. Audiotapes   _____   _____

    4. _____   _____   _____

Alternative chosen

_____   _____

YOUR PERCEIVED BUDGET

Estimate the amounts spent monthly in each category. Those paid other than monthly are indicated by an asterisk (*). Divide annual amounts by twelve, semiannual amounts by six, and so forth, to provide the monthly equivalent.

INCOME

Husband's salary/wages	_____
Less: Withholding taxes	_____
FICA taxes	_____
Retirement programs	_____
Subtotal of deductions	
NET INCOME	_____
Wife's salary/wages	_____
Less: Withholding taxes	_____
FICA taxes	_____
Retirement programs	_____
Subtotal of deductions	
NET INCOME	_____
Other income	_____
TOTAL NET INCOME	_____

EXPENSES

Fixed Expenses

Rent/mortgage		_____
Retirement savings		_____
*Property taxes		_____
*Insurance premiums		_____
*Car license/registration		_____
Debt repayment	_____	_____
Debt repayment	_____	_____
Debt repayment	_____	_____
Debt repayment	_____	_____
Debt repayment	_____	_____
Other	_____	_____
TOTAL FIXED EXPENSES		_____

Variable Expenses
    Food   _____
    Utilities   _____
    Phone   _____
    Household operations   _____
    Furnishings/equipment   _____
    *Transportation/vehicle maintenance   _____
    Apparel   _____
    Personal care   _____
    Child care   _____
    *Education   _____
    Recreation/entertainment   _____
    *Christmas/birthday/special occasions   _____
    *Medical   _____
    *Professional dues/expenses   _____
    Donations   _____
    Personal allowances   _____
    Savings   _____
    *Vacation   _____
    Other _____   _____

                   TOTAL VARIABLE EXPENSES   _____   _____

TOTAL FIXED EXPENSES (from preceding page)   _____

                               TOTAL EXPENSES   _____

          TOTAL INCOME LESS TOTAL EXPENSES   _____

YOUR PERCEIVED BUDGET

Estimate the amounts spent monthly in each category. Those paid other than monthly are indicated by an asterisk (*). Divide annual amounts by twelve, semiannual amounts by six, and so forth, to provide the monthly equivalent.

INCOME

Husband's salary/wages	_____
Less: Withholding taxes	_____
FICA taxes	_____
Retirement programs	_____
Subtotal of deductions	
NET INCOME	_____
Wife's salary/wages	_____
Less: Withholding taxes	_____
FICA taxes	_____
Retirement programs	_____
Subtotal of deductions	
NET INCOME	_____
Other income	_____
TOTAL NET INCOME	_____

EXPENSES

Fixed Expenses

Rent/mortgage	_____
Retirement savings	_____
*Property taxes	_____
*Insurance premiums	_____
*Car license/registration	_____
Debt repayment _____	_____
Debt repayment _____	_____
Debt repayment _____	_____
Debt repayment _____	_____
Debt repayment _____	_____
Other _____	_____
TOTAL FIXED EXPENSES	_____

Variable Expenses
- Food _____
- Utilities _____
- Phone _____
- Household operations _____
- Furnishings/equipment _____
- *Transportation/vehicle maintenance _____
- Apparel _____
- Personal care _____
- Child care _____
- *Education _____
- Recreation/entertainment _____
- *Christmas/birthday/special occasions _____
- *Medical _____
- *Professional dues/expenses _____
- Donations _____
- Personal allowances _____
- Savings _____
- *Vacation _____
- Other _____ _____

TOTAL VARIABLE EXPENSES _____ _____

TOTAL FIXED EXPENSES (from preceding page) _____

TOTAL EXPENSES _____

TOTAL INCOME LESS TOTAL EXPENSES _____

YOUR ACTUAL BUDGET

Calculate the actual monthly amounts spent in each category. Those paid other than monthly are indicated by an asterisk (*). Divide annual amounts by twelve, semiannual amounts by six, and so forth, to provide the monthly equivalent. Compare the actual amounts with the perceived amounts listed previously. Note any major differences.

INCOME

Husband's salary/wages _____
    Less: Withholding taxes _____
        FICA taxes _____
        Retirement programs _____
    Subtotal of deductions
    NET INCOME _____
Wife's salary/wages _____
    Less: Withholding taxes _____
        FICA taxes _____
        Retirement programs _____
    Subtotal of deductions
    NET INCOME _____
Other income _____

        TOTAL NET INCOME _____

EXPENSES

Fixed Expenses
    Rent/mortgage _____
    Retirement savings _____
    *Property taxes _____
    *Insurance premiums _____
    *Car license/registration _____
    Debt repayment _____ _____
    Debt repayment _____ _____
    Debt repayment _____ _____
    Debt repayment _____ _____
    Debt repayment _____ _____
    Other _____ _____

        TOTAL FIXED EXPENSES _____

Variable Expenses

     Food   _____

     Utilities   _____

     Phone   _____

     Household operations   _____

     Furnishings/equipment   _____

     *Transportation/vehicle maintenance _____

     Apparel   _____

     Personal care   _____

     Child care   _____

     *Education   _____

     Recreation/entertainment   _____

     *Christmas/birthday/special occasions _____

     *Medical   _____

     *Professional dues/expenses   _____

     Donations   _____

     Personal allowances   _____

     Savings   _____

     *Vacation   _____

     Other _____ _____

                   TOTAL VARIABLE EXPENSES _____ _____

TOTAL FIXED EXPENSES (from preceding page)   _____

                               TOTAL EXPENSES _____

          TOTAL INCOME LESS TOTAL EXPENSES _____

YOUR SURVIVAL BUDGET

Estimate the minimal monthly amounts needed for survival (needs only) in each category. Amounts paid other than monthly are indicated by an asterisk(*). Divide annual amounts by twelve, semiannual amounts by six, and so forth, to provide the monthly equivalent.

INCOME

Husband's salary/wages		_____
Less: Withholding taxes	_____	
FICA taxes	_____	
Retirement programs	_____	
Subtotal of deductions		
NET INCOME		_____
Wife's salary/wages		_____
Less: Withholding taxes	_____	
FICA taxes	_____	
Retirement programs	_____	
Subtotal of deductions		
NET INCOME		_____
Other income		_____
TOTAL NET INCOME		_____

EXPENSES

Fixed Expenses

Rent/mortgage	_____	
Retirement savings	_____	
*Property taxes	_____	
*Insurance premiums	_____	
Other _____	_____	
TOTAL FIXED EXPENSES		_____

Variable Expenses

Food	_____	
Utilities	_____	
Household operations	_____	
*Transportation/vehicle maintenance	_____	
Apparel	_____	
Personal care	_____	
*Medical	_____	
Other _____	_____	
TOTAL VARIABLE EXPENSES		_____
TOTAL EXPENSES		_____

YOUR PROJECTED BUDGET

Project the monthly amounts you will spend in each category. Use the monthly amortization amounts calculated in previous worksheets where appropriate.

INCOME

Husband's salary/wages _____

    Less: Withholding taxes _____

        FICA taxes _____

        Retirement programs _____

    Subtotal of deductions _____

    NET INCOME _____

Wife's salary/wages _____

    Less: Withholding taxes _____

        FICA taxes _____

        Retirement programs _____

    Subtotal of deductions _____

    NET INCOME _____

Other income _____

      TOTAL NET INCOME _____

EXPENSES

Fixed Expenses

    Rent/mortgage _____

    Retirement savings _____

    Scheduled fixed amortization _____

    Savings _____

    Debt repayment _____ _____

    Debt repayment _____ _____

    Debt repayment _____ _____

    Debt repayment _____ _____

    Debt repayment _____ _____

    Other _____ _____

      TOTAL FIXED EXPENSES _____

Variable Expenses

    Food _____

    Utilities _____

    Phone _____

    Household operations _____

Furnishings/equipment _____
*Transportation/vehicle maintenance _____
Apparel _____
Personal care _____
Child care _____
Recreation/entertainment _____
Special occasions _____
Personal allowances _____
Scheduled variable amortization _____
Unscheduled variable amortization _____
Savings _____
Other _____ _____

TOTAL VARIABLE EXPENSES _____

TOTAL EXPENSES _____

YOUR PROJECTED BUDGET VERSUS YOUR ACTUAL BUDGET

Compare the monthly amounts you spent in each category with the amounts you projected at the beginning of the month. Adjust either the budget or spending for next month so the projected and actual amounts will agree.

INCOME

	PROJECTED	ACTUAL	DIFFERENCE
Husband's salary/wages			
Less: Withholding taxes			
FICA taxes			
Retirement programs			
Subtotal of deductions			
NET INCOME			
Wife's salary/wages			
Less: Withholding taxes			
FICA taxes			
Retirement programs			
Subtotal of deductions			
NET INCOME			
Other income			
TOTAL NET INCOME			

EXPENSES

Fixed Expenses			
Rent/mortgage			
Retirement savings*			
Scheduled fixed amortization			
Savings			
Debt repayment			
Debt repayment			
Debt repayment			
Debt repayment			
Debt repayment			
Other			
TOTAL FIXED EXPENSES			
Variable Expenses			
Food			
Utilities			

	PROJECTED	ACTUAL	DIFFERENCE
Phone			
Household operations			
Furnishings/equipment			
*Transportation/vehicle maintenance			
Apparel			
Personal care			
Child care			
Recreation/entertainment			
Special occasions			
Personal allowances			
Scheduled variable amortization			
Unscheduled variable amortization			
Savings			
Other			
TOTAL VARIABLE EXPENSES			
TOTAL EXPENSES			

PART 3

Yours, Mine, and Ours

*D*uring the twentieth century, the main philosophical purpose for the family has shifted. In the turn-of-the-century agrarian society, the primary function of the family was survival through *production,* so the needs of the whole family took precedence over the needs of individuals. In contrast, today's industrial society family is *consumption*-oriented, so the needs of individuals often take precedence over the preservation of the family unit. Family members tend to think of belongings as "yours," "mine," or "ours."

Some of the factors that contribute to this financial and interpersonal perspective were explored in parts 1 and 2 of this book. Part 1 examined how our personalities and families of origin affect both our relationships and the way we manage our finances.

Part 2 discussed financial principles that can lead us into and out of financial problems, and emphasized principles of avoiding, managing, and reducing debt.

Part 3 combines this information and applies it in ways designed to enhance your financial and personal relationships and to address real-life situations typical of those faced by today's families.

Life by Design

f you were to think back on all of the unexpected challenges that have already occurred in your life, the very thought of "designing" your life may appear to be an effort in futility. Life sometimes seems an endless series of challenges, interrupted by an occasional crisis. In his book *A Wonderful Flood of Light*, Elder Neal A. Maxwell comments on the repetitive nature of life's challenges, and explains why this must be so:

> When illuminated by true doctrine, it is no wonder that life's process must be so relentless! There is so much to be done in so little time. Thus a blessing is often quickly succeeded by a soul-stretching. Spiritual exhilaration is soon followed by frustration or temptation. Reveries are followed by adversities, since, left too long in extended spiritual musings, we would quickly forget others in need. We must get on with the next challenge.[1]

Elder Maxwell's words seems to be especially true with regard to finances and relationships. It would seem that as soon as you have successfully coped with one financial or relational crisis, you "must get on with the next challenge."

After the struggle, after you have made it through the hard times, you may justifiably experience a feeling of inner pride—of self-confidence and independence that comes from being self-reliant. You may also experience a feeling of relief, a re-evaluation of your limitations and capacities, and in many cases a redirecting of your resources toward growing rather than merely maintaining. This rechanneled energy often allows you to become more creative, more courageous—life indeed becomes worth living.

Life by Design versus Life by Default

Some of this rechanneled energy can be directed toward a renewed harmony between establishing your values, setting your goals, and controlling your behavior—the essence of living your life by design rather than by default. You can now come closer to being, as William Henley suggested in his 1875 poem "Invictus," the master of your fate.

> . . . In the fell clutch of circumstance
> I have not winced or cried aloud.
> Under the bludgeonings of chance
> My head is bloody, but unbowed. . . .
> It matters not how strait the gate,
> How charged with punishments the scroll,
> I am the master of my fate:
> I am the captain of my soul.[2]

Living your life by design means careful planning and preparation to take advantage of opportunity rather than relying on luck or chance. In fact, one definition of "good luck" is "when *preparation* meets *opportunity*." For example, an office worker might comment, "Boy, was Carol lucky to get transferred to the Paris office." But if he were to look behind the scenes, he would find that Carol had studied French for five years. When the opportunity came to work in the Paris office, she was prepared. Carol was living a life by design. She knew where she wanted to go and what she needed to do to get there.

When you live your life by default, you allow your destiny to be determined by the fickleness of fate. Think how vague and unfocused such a life would be. Imagine asking someone you had just met, "How did you end up living here?" and hearing the reply, "About 12 years ago, I was traveling through this part of the country in my old station wagon. This is where the transmission went out—and I've been here ever since." Life by default often means standing still, waiting for the next roll of the dice.

Knowing where you are, however, is not as important as knowing where you are headed. In 1858, Oliver Wendell Holmes, the distinguished Supreme Court justice, said,

I find the great thing in this world is not so much where we stand, as in what direction we are moving; to reach the port of heaven, we must sail sometimes with the wind and sometimes against it—but we must sail, and not drift, nor lie at anchor.[3]

As you may have discovered, facing heavy debt can often seem like being stranded on a sandbar—it leaves you unable to respond to the winds of change, to take advantage of the opportunities that come your way. Being free of debt, on the other hand, leaves you free to choose, to save or spend, to buy or sell, to stay or move, to change jobs or keep the one you have. Financial freedom enhances a very important part of personal freedom—freedom of choice.

Financial Freedom

Chapter 1's financial principles are fundamental to basic thinking about financial management decisions. Principles 7 through 10, in particular, contain advice that underlies financial freedom. Much of this advice concerns reframing—changing your attitudes, your outlook, the way you see things—so that, by taking charge of your circumstances, you can become "the master of [your] fate, the captain of [your] soul."

Spend Less, Need Less

Principle 7 states, *Financial freedom is more often the result of decreased spending than of increased income.* As chapter 7 explained, it is very difficult to *earn* your way out of debt. You would have to increase your income by as much as $1,000 before deducting taxes to achieve the same result as reducing your debt load by only $600. Similarly, it is usually more difficult to earn your way to financial freedom than it is to gain financial freedom by reducing your expenditures.

CASE ILLUSTRATION

Although Alberto and Mendy were reasonably frugal, their money seemed to "just disappear" with not a lot to show for it. They were getting by, but they weren't getting ahead. One month, after paying the bills and again having almost nothing left to live on, the two decided to take drastic measures. Should Alberto get a second job? Or should they decrease their spending? They decided to cut back on just about everything in an attempt to increase their available finances.

They rode the bus to work and school instead of driving ($100 spent on gas - $40 bus fare = $60 savings); they went to $1.50 movie houses instead of $7 movies ($14 per movie twice a month would come to $28 - $3 for discount movies = $25 savings); they bought a couple of inexpensive steaks and had a candlelight dinner at home instead of going out to a restaurant ($25 savings); they wore sweaters at home instead of turning up the thermostat ($15 savings); Alberto brown-bagged lunch instead of eating out ($50 savings); Mendy wrote a few letters instead of making long-distance calls ($20 savings); and Alberto bought a secondhand tool instead of a brand-new one ($15 savings).

Their efforts resulted in a $205 reduction in expenditures, which money they now could use to save for a new home, go on a vacation, or do whatever else they desired. If Alberto had gotten the second job, it would have taken around $325 per month in new earnings to clear that $205—an additional $4,000 in earnings to obtain $2,460 per year to spend. For many of us, like Alberto and Mendy, it may be easier to save $2,460 by good home economies than to earn $4,000.

Admittedly, in some ways this may be an extreme example. Your own situation may call for solutions that are less severe. Or perhaps it simply isn't worth it to you to cut back in the ways Mendy and Alberto did. But as you consider your options, it is important to understand this principle: Financial freedom is more often the result of decreased spending than of increased income.

Spending Inflation

Unfortunately, most families practice the very opposite of what Principle 7 advocates: They try to achieve financial freedom by increasing their incomes.

In 1970 the nation's total consumer debt was $131.6 billion; by 1980, this amount had grown to $349.4 billion and to $728.9 billion by 1988. Credit card debt alone increased from $81.2 billion in 1980 to $180 billion in 1988. During this same period (1980–88), family income also increased, but the ratio of debt to disposable income rose from 18 percent to 21 percent, meaning that the amount families were spending was increasing faster than the amount they were earning.[4]

For many families, the ever-increasing debt load meant only one thing: "We just can't make it on one income any more." But was this really the case? Perhaps it would have been more accurate to say, *"We just can't continue to sustain our increased level of spending on one income."* This amended statement is supported by the connection between family income and spending patterns over the past few decades.

In 1955, the median family income was $17,693 (in 1986 dollars) with only the husband working. By 1986, the median family income (with only the husband working) had grown to $24,390—a 40 percent increase after adjusting for inflation. A comparison of per capita personal income to personal consumption costs during that same time period indicates very little real change; both approximately doubled—personal income rose from $6,439 to $12,695 and personal consumption cost from $5,287 to $10,123.[5]

It seems, then, that in spite of the fact that our earning power is growing at the same rate as our spending, more and more families are believing that they "just can't make it on one income." In an attempt to compensate for the perceived shortfall, and for a variety of personal reasons, an ever-increasing number of wives and mothers have entered the labor force, thereby creating the "dual-income family."

In 1986, the dual-income family's median income (with husband and wife working full-time) was $44,666. This combined income was over *two and a half times* the income (in 1986 dollars) their parents used to raise their families in 1955, and almost twice the 1986 median income for families in which only the husband was working. *Two to two and a half times as much income!* Yet the belief that "We just can't make it on one income" persisted. Based on an analysis of the spending and earning patterns of families during the past 30 years, researcher Robert Rector concluded, "We have experienced not a decline in earnings capacity but a profound upward 'revolution of expectations' in living standards; . . . we have largely forgotten the actual income levels and standards of living of the preceding generations."[6]

The Need for Extra Income: Is It Real, Perceived, or Preferred?

Certainly one of the reasons the belief that "We just can't make it on one income" persists is the extremely high cost of housing in certain parts of the United States. In these areas, the entire income of one of the family's earners is required just to make the house payments. For other families, high medical costs and the need for medical insurance demand a second income. For these and similar situations, "We just can't make it on one income" is an irrefutable fact. But these families may still need to distinguish between what is a *real* need for extra income, what is merely a *perceived* need for extra income, and what is a desire to maintain a *preferred* standard of living.

In a 1980 survey of working women, 90 percent reported they were working for economic reasons.[7] Similar results were reached in 1984,[8] when 94 percent of the women surveyed reported they were working because of economic need. But only 6 percent of those surveyed reported they would miss their income if they did not work. Interest in this paradox led researchers David Eggebeen and Alan Hawkins to analyze data gathered from more than 60,000 white families with at least one child under 18.[9] The families were divided into two economic groups: those in which the husband's income was twice the official poverty cutoff level were designated "adequate income" families; those in which the husband's income was less than twice the poverty level were considered "inadequate income" families.

Eggebeen and Hawkins found that in 1960, only 9 percent of the mothers from the adequate income families were employed (part- or full-time), while 18 percent of the mothers from the inadequate income families were employed. By 1980, the percentage of employed mothers from the adequate income group had more than tripled, to 31 percent, while the percentage of employed mothers from the inadequate income families had increased by only 2 percent. The researchers concluded that "when married mothers cite economic motives for their employment outside the home, they are referring to standard-of-living preferences rather than basic economic necessities."[10]

There are indications that married mothers entering the work force may have been a contributing factor in the rise of the American family's standard of living. In 1950, fewer than 5 percent of the families surveyed had clothes dryers; by 1984, ownership had risen to 62 percent. Only 7 percent of the families surveyed in 1950 owned two cars, while more than 52 percent were two-car families in 1984. Similarly, television sets were found in only 12 percent of U.S. homes in 1950, but in 97 percent of homes by 1974.[11]

How does this trend increase the need for income? As one researcher, Claire Vickery, points out, "The sophisticated and diverse goods that advanced technologies produce . . . cannot be produced at home. As a result, families need less household production and more income to purchase goods and services."[12]

There is no doubt that there are powerful social pressures in the United States encouraging women to seek "fulfillment" in the workplace. For decades, similar social forces have been telling men that their "success" depends on how much money they make. But of course, from an eternal perspective, neither man nor woman will enhance their possibilities for exaltation by earning more money in their earthly existence.

President Ezra Taft Benson repeatedly addressed the issue of mothers working outside the home. While there are circumstances such as being single, divorced, widowed, or having a husband who is unable to work that make it necessary for some women to work, President Benson made it very clear that these situations were to be the exception and not the rule. In a 1980 devotional speech to the students of Brigham Young University, he declared:

> It is divinely ordained what a woman should do, but a man must seek out his work. The divine work of women involves companionship, homemaking, and motherhood. It is well if skills in these three areas can first be learned in the parents' home and then be supplemented at school if the need or desire presents itself. The first priority for a woman is to prepare herself for her divine and eternal mission, whether she is married soon or late. It is folly to neglect that preparation for education in unrelated fields just to prepare temporarily to earn money. Women, when you are married it is the husband's role to provide, not yours. Do not sacrifice your preparation for an eternally ordained mission for the temporary expediency of money-making skills which you may or may not use.[13]

Do we really need extra income? Perhaps we need to take a better look at *wanting less*, rather than at *earning more*.

Gratitude Brings Perspective

Research has shown that we cannot perceive how financially satisfied a person is simply by knowing how much money he or she makes.[14] Regarding quality of life, the degree of satisfaction a person feels about *what he or she has* is more important than the amount of *real income being earned*.[15] Similarly, what a person *wants* is more important to financial satisfaction than what *needs have already been met*.

One study found that the more severe a family perceived its financial problems to be, the less adequate they perceived their income to be—independent of the actual level of income.[16] Another study indicated that the higher the aspirations of both husband and wife, the less satisfied they were with their current financial situation.[17] In other words, as long as the wants of family members exceed the family's income, the income will be perceived as inadequate—regardless of its level or how much it increases.

Perhaps, however, you have come to the conclusion that enough is enough, and you no longer wish to participate in "the quest." You have determined what is sufficient for your needs (see chapter 7) and want to devote your energy to something besides earning the almighty dollar.

If you do decide to pull out of the "rat race," you might find that your lot in life is not all that bad.

Be grateful for what you have, advises Principle 8. One instructor in a sociology course asked a class three questions:

1. Do you own more than one pair of shoes?
2. Do you expect to eat more than just one kind of food each day?
3. Do you have access to your own personal form of transportation?

The instructor then pointed out that if you could answer yes to these three questions, you would be—financially—among *the top 10 percent of all the people who have ever lived on Earth!* Comparing yourself to others on the planet and throughout history instead of the people across the street can place you in a pretty good light. After all, don't we all start off and end the same? "Naked came I out of my mother's womb, and naked shall I return thither: the Lord gave, and the Lord hath taken away; blessed be the name of the Lord" (Job 1:21).

Freebie Exercise

Remember Principle 9? *The best things in life are free.* Fortunately, there are a great number of pleasurable things you can do in life. The enjoyment you find depends a lot more on your attitude than on your wealth. The following exercise is designed to help you, and those you love, rediscover some of the inexpensive activities you enjoy doing.

List 20 activities that you consider fun or that have made you happy. There are no other restrictions. You may enjoy snowball fights, for example, or diving into piles of autumn leaves, walking by a stream, going to foreign films, talking to a friend, reading a good book, going to a sports event, attending a concert, traveling, gardening, fishing, taking guitar lessons, and so on. Complete your list before reading any farther.

Now place a heart next to those activities you prefer to do with others. Complete this part of the exercise before going on. Next, place a $ next to those activities that cost more than $10 per person to do. Complete this part of the exercise before proceeding.

Now review your list. If you are like most people, you will find you prefer to do about one-third to one-half of your favorite activities with another person. Even more important, you may discover that most of the things you associate with being truly happy cost less than $10 or are absolutely free. These you can call your *freebies*.

This exercise illustrates that you don't need a lot of money to be happy. You need enough money to take care of your basic needs, a little more to take care of some of your wants and to add a certain degree of quality to your life, and a bit more to give you a sense of security; but money beyond these requirements will not necessarily bring you more happiness.

It IS Better to Give than Receive

Principle 10 reminds us that *the value of an individual should never be equated with his or her net worth,* and that what we give, to others and to the world around us, is far more important—and brings more happiness—than what we get.

CASE ILLUSTRATION

Nicholas was a relatively successful building contractor. He could drive through just about any part of town and point to a house that he had built. Some were large and grand while others were more suitable for middle-class families. But the homes he felt the best about were often those that were the least conspicuous. These were the homes that were built through what he referred to as his "program."

The "program" had its origins back when Nicholas was a teenager and prone to getting into trouble. A neighbor hired him to help build a room addition. After the addition was completed, the neighbor paid him to help build a garage. In the beginning, Nicholas had little or no carpentry skills, but as one project followed another, his apprenticeship led to journeyman status. From this meager beginning, he went on to become a contractor.

As a way of passing on the gift he had received from his neighbor, Nicholas developed the "program" in which troubled teenagers were paid to learn how to become carpenters. When a house was complete it was sold to low-income families. He made no money from this endeavor. However, he did have a drawer full of letters from parents, spouses, and former apprentices saying, "Thanks. Your kindness made all the difference."

Satisfying Your Needs

Part of the reason we keep spending beyond our basic physical needs is to satisfy some emotional need within ourselves. But while money is designed to meet some of our needs, there are others it can never satisfy. As explained in Principle 6, money and things cannot satisfy our needs for love and self-worth.

An important part of living our lives by design is knowing—and learning how to meet—the true needs of ourselves and our loved ones. Erich Fromm, noted psychoanalyst, proposed that humans have four basic needs beyond the physical: the needs for *identity, rootedness, transcendence* (or creativity), and *relatedness*.[18] I would add a fifth need: the need for *forgiveness*. As you can see, these needs don't have much to do with accumulating more wealth. And satisfying these needs has a lot more to do with the quality of your relationships than with the size of your pocketbook.

The Need for Identity

The need for identity refers to our need for recognition, respect, and self-esteem. A spouse's *recognition of your efforts* is especially important during times of struggle and financial hardship, which often occur during the years you are concentrating more on learning than on doing. A show of appreciation for your efforts is called *encouragement*.

Encouragement is often what motivates you to want to keep trying, even after initial attempts have failed. Encouragement is necessary when you study for an exam but receive a grade lower than you had expected, or when you try out for a sport but don't make the team. Under such circumstances you hope to hear encouraging remarks: "Even though you were well behind the front runners, that extra burst of speed you put on as you came around the last turn gave me such a thrill! You have so much courage—you just don't give up, even when it's rough going!"

During those brief, amazed moments in life when we know we have "made it," most of us can recall with gratitude someone who encouraged us when the outcome was still in doubt.

Less fortunate people will always be reminded of their ineptness and shortcomings: "Can't you do anything right? Look at the mess you've made of the checkbook." "I know you can do better. You're just not trying." "I don't care how much you say you've cut back. You're not going to get a cent more until *I* think you can be trusted."

Since most of our lives are spent trying to achieve goals, and only a small fraction of that time is spent savoring our accomplishments, most of us can benefit from a support system that cheers us on during the hard times rather than one that discourages us or just shows up for the celebrations.

Besides encouraging each other during hard times, we need to express appreciation for a job well done. Most of us thrive on *praise:* "Hey! I hear you got accepted. That's fantastic!" "I know you worked hard for that promotion. Congratulations!"

Unfortunately, some people concentrate more on what's wrong with their loved ones than on what's right about them, denying them even the smallest sense of worth from their achievements. They may even make degrading remarks: "Things come too easy for you." "You just got a lucky break. Anyone could have done what you did." "Now will you start listening to me? I kept telling you you could get that position if you would only try harder."

The Need for Rootedness

The need for rootedness refers to our need to connect with our present world as well as with the past and the future. While our accomplishments help us form our identity, our contributions help us find our place in history and where we fit with others in the world.

When others recognize our contributions, our self-esteem is based not on what we can *get* out of life but on what we can *give* to others. Our self-worth comes not from what we can *consume* but from what we can *contribute*.

The way we choose to recognize our partner's contributions can be either positive or negative. For instance, a funny person could be described as "a real comedian—she has us in stitches most of the time." Or she could be told, "Stop being so silly. You'll end up making us the laughingstock of the neighborhood." One spouse might hear, "Well, I'll have to admit that you were being your usual inventive self, and it just might have gotten off the ground if the Hendersons' barn hadn't been in the way!" Another might hear instead, "You and your ideas are going to end up putting us in the poorhouse. Your foolishness is nothing but a waste of money."

Much of the quality of our relationships—and the quality of life itself—depends on how we choose to relate to each other. Life, like relationships, is more than just "enduring to the end."

The Need for Transcendence

The need for transcendence refers to the need to be creative and productive, and goes beyond merely sustaining life. It's the need to become more than we already are, to reach our own potential. Like the expert appraiser who can appreciate the potential of a diamond in the rough, you, as a partner in a relationship, will frequently be called upon to recognize potential that is as yet unrealized in the other.

In *Hamlet,* Shakespeare writes, "We know what we are, but know not what we may be."

Much of "what we may be" is influenced by how those we esteem respond to us as individuals. For example, those with farsighted partners will hear, "Someday, somebody is going to have the good fortune to hire you, and when they do they'll soon realize that they got the best." "I wouldn't be a bit surprised to see you head of sales someday." Or "Honey, I think the world had better get ready for another great designer, because we've got ourselves a real winner here."

This kind of statement really communicates, "I believe in you and in your potential to grow," and we tend to respond, "If *you* believe in me, then *I* believe in me." Such faith in others' capability to enhance their talents reflects an ability to see them as well as ourselves as unique individuals. Such a perspective enables us to recognize our own potentials.

Unfortunately, some partners appear to be either unable or unwilling to recognize another's possibilities. Their communications tend to tear down and dishearten. "You have got to be the laziest good-for-nothing I have ever known." "You'll never amount to anything." "If you had a brain, you'd be dangerous." Under a constant bombardment of such appraisals, it usually isn't long before the partner decides that to even *try* is a waste of time and effort. Some give up not only on themselves but on life as well.

The Need for Relatedness

The need for relatedness is the need to establish positive love relationships with others. It means commitment and a willingness to be vulnerable. When the outcome of a love relationship is marriage, it means even more. President Spencer W. Kimball expressed it well:

> Marriage is not a legal cover-all; but it means sacrifice, sharing, and even a reduction of some personal liberties. It means long, hard economizing. It means children who bring with them financial burdens, service burdens, care and worry burdens; but it also means the deepest and sweetest emotions of all.[19]

One of the emotions you hopefully will experience is *unconditional love*. When you are loved unconditionally, you know that your existence is sufficient reason to be loved. You know that you don't have to accomplish anything or earn a certain amount of money to be loved. All you have to do is be yourself. You also know that there is nothing you can do to lose this love. You may at times catch your partner just watching you while you go about your business, then commenting, "I'm sure glad I married you," or "You know, I really do love you."

Unfortunately, not everyone receives such spontaneous gifts of affection. Far too many hear hurtful statements instead: "You've been nothing but trouble since the day I met you." "I'm sorry we ever got married." Strangely enough, even though some individuals may not receive unconditional love, they may still choose to love their partner. Sometimes this is Christ-like love and sometimes it is not. (Those who have been physically, emotionally, or financially abused over a long period of time will sometimes continue to "love" their abuser, hoping that someday they will be loved in return. But this may grow out of dependence or a poor self-image, rather than a love than can be productive and uplifting.)

President Kimball cautions, "Love cannot be expected to last forever unless it is continually fed with portions of love, the manifestation of esteem and admiration, the expressions of gratitude, and the consideration of unselfishness."[20]

Even for those who love unconditionally at the beginning of their relationship, love that is *conditional* can enter in. This kind of love is expressed when certain standards are met, and is withheld when the standards are not met. For example, one spouse may tell the other, "It's not that I don't love you. I just don't feel like being sexually intimate when there is so much distance in the rest of our marriage."

The purpose of conditional love is to teach us to be responsible and that there are consequences for our behavior. It is imperative, however, that the standards be reachable, that the partners convey their confidence in each other's ability to meet them, and that *unconditional* love also be found abundantly in the relationship.

If you are exposed solely to conditional love, you may begin to believe that love must be earned and that to be lovable you must be productive. You may believe that only if you earn a lot of money, come in first place, or become a success will you be worthy of being loved. You may even become convinced that if you were to stop and rest for a moment you would automatically cease to be lovable. You may then become preoccupied with keeping busy—staying productive to remain "worthy" of being loved.

You may also begin to believe that unless you are perfect, you are not lovable. When you make a mistake, you may think you have "blown it," and that you are unlovable until you have either worked off your sentence, made full restitution, or are forgiven.

The Need for Forgiveness

In addition to these four human needs suggested by Erich Fromm, I believe a fifth need is essential to the attainment of happy, gratifying relationships: the need for forgiveness.

The gospel of Jesus Christ is a gospel of forgiveness. Its very foundation lies in the act of atonement performed by Jesus Christ. Because of his love, our sins may be forgiven. And we are taught in the New Testament that God will forgive our debts as we love and forgive our debtors (Luke 11:4). We are commanded to forgive in modern scripture as well. In D&C 64:10, the Lord tells us " . . . of you it is required to forgive all men."

Sometimes forgiving is not an easy thing to do, especially when it involves one's husband or wife. Yet, forgiveness is absolutely essential in the marriage relationship if there are to be feelings of love and intimacy. President Gordon B. Hinckley remarked:

> We are all prone to brood on the evil done us. That brooding becomes as a gnawing and destructive canker. Is there a virtue more in need of application in our time than the virtue of forgiving and forgetting? There are those who would look upon this as a sign of weakness. Is it? I submit that it takes neither strength nor intelligence to brood in anger over wrongs suffered, to go through life with a spirit of vindictiveness, to dissipate one's abilities in planning retribution. There is no peace in the nursing of a grudge. There is no happiness in living for the day when you can "get even."[21]

Usually when we think of forgiveness in marriage, we think of major transgressions, such as infidelity, dishonesty, or public humiliation. However, within the intimate relationship of marriage it is often the little things that have the greatest impact on the relationship. President Hinckley taught that unforgiving attitudes within relationships sow the seeds of destruction, and tells of his interview with one couple:

> Not long ago I listened at length to a couple who sat across the desk from me. There was bitterness between them. I know that at one time their love was deep and true. But each had developed a habit of speaking of the faults of the other. Unwilling to forgive the kind of mistakes we all make, and unwilling to forget them and live above them with forbearance, they had carped at one another until the love they once knew had been smothered. It had turned to ashes with the decree of a so-called no fault divorce. Now there is only loneliness and recrimination. I am satisfied that had there been even a small measure of repentance and forgiveness, they would still be together, enjoying the companionship that had so richly blessed their earlier years.[22]

In order to avoid this couple's fate, I recommend that each partner in a marriage ask forgiveness for some of the everyday "little things" that are, in reality, big things. Following are a few suggestions of some things for which a spouse could ask forgiveness.[23]

Forgive me for not always being your friend. Forgive me for the times I wasn't someone you could talk to when you just needed someone to listen. I'm sorry I wasn't there to listen without criticizing or judging you or what you had to say. Forgive me for the times I wasn't someone you could relax and laugh with. I remember that during our courtship we talked and laughed for hours. Sometimes it was on the phone, or while we were driving. Those were the times when we wanted to be with each other above all else. Sometimes we were very good friends. Forgive me for those times I have not made the effort to be your friend.

Forgive me for not placing you as my number one priority in life. I can remember times when I allowed my parents, friends, hobbies, job, sports, or even church responsibilities to become more important to me than your happiness and welfare. My intentions were honorable, but the hurt you felt was nonetheless real. I know your image of yourself must have suffered when you saw everything else in my life coming first. I do want you to know, however, that there have been times when I did make you my top priority—times when I considered your feelings first when making a decision. I may not have always decided in your favor, but at least I considered your feelings. Being as sensitive as you are, you were probably quite aware of those times and of the place you held in my life. Please forgive me for the times your place was not first.

Forgive me for not showing my appreciation. Forgive me for the times I've taken your countless contributions—your gifts of time, effort, and concern—for granted. I sometimes wonder how many times your service and acts of devotion have gone unnoticed. I suppose there have even been times when I thought they were merely your "duty," part of your marital responsibilities. It's true that there are obligations that go with marriage, but it still might have helped if I had expressed my appreciation more often. You might have felt more that you *wanted* to do these things, rather than that you *had* to do them. I apologize for the times you had hoped I would notice and were disappointed.

Forgive me for not being there when you needed me. I'm sorry for waiting until you told me to do something rather than seeing and doing what was needed on my own. Sometimes I even waited too long and you did it yourself. Forgive me for the times you needed your load lightened and I did nothing in your behalf. I was probably preoccupied, but that's no excuse for being inconsiderate. Maybe I saw you as being strong and capable, not really needing my help. But since none of us can be strong all the time, I would especially like to ask your forgiveness for the times I was not there when you needed comfort, support, and understanding.

Forgive me for not accepting a less-than-perfect you. I'm not sure why I expected you to be perfect when I have been willing to accept imperfection in others. Our parents were not perfect, nor are our children perfect. I accepted their imperfection as a fact of life, yet I insisted on holding you up against an ideal or fantasy of what a spouse should be. I repeatedly placed on you the responsibility for solving my problems. I gave you the job of maintaining my happiness. Apparently, I was more involved with wanting you to be perfect than I was with helping you seek improvement in your own way. Forgive me for not accepting you for who you are.

Forgive me for the times I have been selfish. I'm sorry for all the times I satisfied my needs in ways that interfered with the satisfaction of your needs. I apologize for needing to be right even when I knew I was wrong. How frustrated and discouraged you must have felt when you tried to express your opinions, feelings, and needs, and I didn't hear you. Even more important, forgive me for the times I believed I was superior—more intelligent, more courageous, or more sophisticated than you. When I put myself above you in my mind I disqualified your ideas and suggestions, and I acted as if you were not worthy of my love. I can now more fully understand that we are truly equals in the eyes of God, and that this is how we should see each other as well. Please forgive me for my pride and my self-interest at your expense.

Forgive me for the promises, implied or explicit, that I have broken. I'm sure that at the time I made those promises to you I fully believed that I could keep them. Some can still be kept, while the time for others has passed. When we first got married, I made a promise to both of us that you would never regret marrying me. Forgive me if I have given you even one momentary regret for having made that decision. I would like to renew that promise: I promise you tomorrows that will be filled with both joy and sadness, but never with regret for having married me.

Forgive me for neglecting your hopes and dreams. I probably will never fully appreciate the sacrifices you made to marry me. I know that you have had some of your dreams since childhood; there were places you wanted to see, things you wanted to do, and goals you wanted to achieve. Granted, some of them have been fulfilled, but some dreams still cause you to pause and think a moment before you dismiss them with a sigh and a shrug. Forgive me for the times when I have not considered your hopes and dreams to be as important as my own.

Forgive me for not helping you to reach a greater level of exaltation. I apologize for the times when I didn't enhance, or even encourage, greater spirituality in our home. I regret the times my anger, depression, or resentment detracted from your level of spirituality. Forgive me for having offended you—intentionally or otherwise. If there has been anything that I have said or done that has discouraged your faith or diminished your testimony, I ask for your forgiveness. What little profit would there be for me to arrive at the celestial kingdom without you?

Forgive me for not forgiving you. Forgive me for the times I harbored resentments and used those feelings as an excuse to distance myself from you. I'm sorry I sometimes wanted to and tried to get even. I realize now that forgiveness means letting go of all desire for revenge. The Lord admonished us to forgive one another, " . . . for he that forgiveth not his brethren his trespasses standeth condemned before the Lord; for there remaineth in him the greater sin. I, the Lord, will forgive whom I will forgive, but of you it is required to forgive all men" (D&C 64:9–10). I ask for your forgiveness as I forgive you.

We have all, at one time or another, offended or been offended by our spouses, and, as with all debt, we can collect it or forgive it. We can make either choice, and close the books and be done with it. If we are to truly live the teachings of the gospel, we will "Let all bitterness, and wrath, and anger, and clamor, and evil speaking, be put away from you, with all malice: and be ye kind one to another, tenderhearted, forgiving one another, even as God for Christ's sake hath forgiven you" (Ephesians 4:31–32).

Summary

There is a great difference between living by design and living by default. Our God-given free agency motivates us to make choices that will keep us self-governed and unshackled by unnecessary obligations. Financial freedom, as opposed to financial independence, is possible if we will make the proper choices. One of those choices is to reduce spending, which is often easier than increasing income. An examination of our earning and spending patterns will help us to know whether our need for a second income is real—or more perceived than real. Another choice we can make is to be grateful for what we have and stop perpetually wanting more. We can learn to satisfy each other's real needs—such as respect, encouragement, and unconditional love—rather than keep trying to accumulate more things. We can learn how to establish and maintain fulfilling relationships. We can believe and remember that "the best things in life are free."

Important Terms

Conditional love: Love extended to us only if we meet certain conditions.

Financial freedom: Having enough discretionary income to be able to select a number of alternatives on which to spend your money, rather than having to face financial ultimatums.

Financial independence: Having accumulated enough wealth to sustain a high standard of living without further effort on your part.

Freebies: Activities you associate with being happy that are absolutely free.

Life by default: Allowing your destiny to be determined by the fickleness of fate.

Life by design: Knowing where you want to go and what you need to do to get there.

Need for identity: Basic need to be recognized, respected, and capable of self-esteem.

Need for relatedness: Basic need to establish positive love relationships with others.

Need for rootedness: Basic need to fit in and contribute to our present world, as well as the past and the future.

Need for transcendence: Basic need to be creative and productive, and to grow to fulfill our potential.

Spending inflation: When spending increases faster than earning; a characteristic of many families in the past three decades.

Unconditional love: Love extended to us just because we exist.

Notes

1. Maxwell, 1990, p. 47.

2. Henley, 1978, p. 206.

3. Holmes, 1858, p. 228.

4. U.S. Department of Commerce, 1990a.

5. U.S. Department of Commerce, 1990b.

6. Rector, 1989, p. 522.

7. Fox and Hesse-Biber, 1984.

8. Shehan, 1984.

 9. Eggebeen and Hawkins, 1990.

10. Ibid., p. 54.

11. U.S. Department of Energy, 1986; Vickery, 1979.

12. Vickery, 1979, p. 171.

13. Benson, 1988, pp. 548–49.

14. Campbell, Converse, and Rodgers, 1976.

15. Hafstrom and Dunsing, 1983.

16. Williams, Nall and Deck, 1976.

17. Davis and Helmick, 1983.

18. Fromm, 1955.

19. Kimball, 1982, p. 306.

20. Kimball, 1980. p. 8.

21. Hinckley, 1980.

22. Ibid.

23. Poduska, 1991.

CHAPTER 11

Financial Issues and Family Types

*T*oday's world includes several different kinds of families—those that are "intact," those headed by single parents, those we call "blended." To understand the diverse needs of each group, we must examine them from a modern, as well as a traditional, perspective. Each type of relationship presents unique financial and interpersonal challenges that affect each person's well-being and call for specific coping skills. Financial needs are only part of the picture; we must also understand family members' spiritual and self-esteem needs.

Today's families need help balancing not only their financial ledgers but also their emotional "ledgers" that reflect the personal losses and gains associated with marriage, divorce, widowhood, single parenting, and remarriage. And we need to understand the anguish of those who wish to be self-reliant yet find themselves dependent on the supplemental income of a spouse, court-ordered child support, or religious- or government-sponsored welfare.

Measuring a Family's Economic Well-Being

It is important to keep in mind that a family's economic well-being alone does not provide a complete picture of overall well-being. A more complete perspective of how well a family is doing would include a view of their spiritual well-being as well as the quality of their interpersonal relationships. The spirituality and cordiality present among family members can, however, be strongly influenced by family economics—not necessarily by the size of the family income, but by the family's *attitude* toward this income. In fact, most children don't know the actual size of their family's income, and when they do find out, they are usually surprised.

In many cases, the size of the family income does not even become an issue unless the emotional needs of the children are not being met. For those who have been raised in a loving family, it is not uncommon for them to exclaim as adults, "I never knew we were as poor as we were until I grew up and left home." Or "I knew we never had to scrimp, but I thought we were just a middle-class family until we had a meeting to go over the particulars of Mom's and Dad's wills." They may even comment, "Oh, sure, I'd see kids at school that I considered rich—they wore more expensive clothes than I did, for example. But I didn't feel *poor*—just not as well off as they were."

But for children whose needs for love and attention are not being met—whether at home or in outside relationships—being able to *buy* things can become extremely important. Remember Principle 6: *You can never get enough of what you don't need because what you don't need can never satisfy you.* A supporting maxim might be, "Most children can survive poverty, but only a few can survive wealth."

Nevertheless, a family's economic well-being is important, and it is influenced by both the amount of income available and the size of the family. Financial counselors commonly use two methods to determine a family's economic well-being: total family income, and income-to-need ratios.

Total Family Income

The total family income method of determining a family's economic well-being compares a family's income to a national norm. In 1992, the median income for *all* families (including single-wage-earner, dual-wage-earner, and single-parent families) was $36,812: for white families, income was $38,909, for Hispanic families $23,901, and for black families $21,161. For all *married* families the median income in 1992 was $42,064, but for dual-income families it was almost $8,000 greater.

The median income for single-parent families (female head of household and no husband present) was only $27,821: incomes for Hispanic and black families were even lower (see Table 11.1). In 1992, the average poverty threshold for a family of four was $13,199.[1] Family income is considered to be adequate when it is twice the poverty level for a family of a given size.

TABLE 11.1—MEDIAN FAMILY INCOME, 1992

	ALL FAMILIES	WHITE	HISPANIC	AFRICAN AMERICAN
All configurations	$36,812	$38,909	$23,901	$21,161
Married	$42,064	$42,738	$28,515	$34,196
Dual-income	$49,984	$50,653	$37,335	$41,799
Single-parent (female)	$27,821	$29,671	$19,468	$20,678

Adapted from *Money Income of Families—Median Family Income in Constant (1992) Dollars* (p. 471), by U.S. Department of Commerce, Bureau of the Census, 1994, Washington, D.C.: U.S. Government Printing Office.

Income-to-Need Ratio

The income-to-need ratio for a family is determined by dividing a family's income by the poverty threshold for a family of that size (see Table 11.2). For example, the income-to-need ratio for a family of four with an income of $16,442 is 1.25. This is calculated by dividing $16,442 by the poverty threshold for a family of four, which is $13,190. The income-to-need ratio for a family of five with an income of $16,442 is 1.05; for a family of six with the same income it drops to .93—below the poverty threshold. Results from the above calculation that are less than 1.0 indicate a ratio below the poverty level; all results above 1.0 indicate a ratio above the poverty level. The higher the ratio, the better the family is doing financially. A dual-income family of six with a median income for that kind of family would have a income-to-need ratio of 2.7. In 1990, 10.7 percent of all families in the United States lived below the poverty level. Of families with a female head of household, 33.4 percent lived below the poverty level. Of white families, 8.1 percent were below the poverty level; of white single-parent, female-headed families, 26.8 percent were below. Nonwhite ethnic groups fared even worse: 25.1 percent of all Hispanic families and 48.3 percent of single-parent Hispanic families were below the poverty level; 29.3 percent of black families and 48.1 percent of those headed by a black single parent lived below the poverty threshold.[2]

Single-Wage-Earner Families

A single-wage-earner family is a *two-parent* family in which only one parent is earning an income. Interestingly, and perhaps as a sign of the times, only about 10 percent of families in the

YOURS, MINE, AND OURS

TABLE 11.2—POVERTY THRESHOLDS, 1992

Number of Persons in Family	Threshold in Dollars
1	$6,672
2	8,407
3	10,292
4	13,190
5	15,596
6	17,606
7	19,869
8	22,131
9	26,449

Adapted from *Poverty in the United States,* 1994 (p. 480), by U.S. Department of Commerce, Bureau of the Census, 1994, Washington, D.C.: U.S. Government Printing Office.

United States currently fit the definition of the "traditional family," with the husband the sole breadwinner and the wife at home with two or more children.[3]

Following are some issues confronting single-wage-earner families:

1. Who will allocate and control finances?
2. How will the needs and wants of the individual family members be met?
3. How will members communicate about finances?
4. Will members compete or cooperate to manage family consumer behavior?
5. How will the family deal with value conflicts?

In these families, family-of-origin rules and perceived preferential treatment of certain family members are common sources of conflict. The system they choose to manage their income is an important issue.

Family-of-Origin Rules

As chapter 2 pointed out, because each spouse is raised in a different family of origin, each brings to the marriage a different set of rules about how finances should be handled. Such differences, if not resolved, can become a constant source of contention.

To effectively cope with family-of-origin rule differences, both partners should share how finances were handled in their family. Using Worksheet 2.1, chapter 2, decide which rules are most important, which ones you want to include or exclude in your current family, and what compromises and accommodations you need to make.

CASE ILLUSTRATION

Filled with frustration, Martin tries again to point out what he thought was obvious to every rational human being but his wife: "Marina, we cannot spend money we don't have. That credit card is to be used only in an emergency, not to buy things just because they happen to be on sale."

Marina, also upset, responds defensively, "Well, I can't run the house on what little you give me each month. Isaac made the basketball team and needed a pair of shoes."

Martin pounds his fist on his knee and mutters loudly enough to be heard, "My dad warned me that if I didn't hold a firm grip on the finances, you'd put us in the poorhouse. Well, I'm not going to let that happen. Mom never used a credit card in her life. She managed on what Dad gave her and did a darned good job of it. If she did it, you can do it."

Marina stands for a moment in an absolute state of shock. When she recovers, she speaks slowly and deliberately. "I have no intention of being treated the way your father treated your mother. My mom and dad shared everything on an equal basis, including money. They had a joint checking account, and each one carried a checkbook. My mother *never* had to beg for money, and I'm not about to start either."

Martin, somewhat unnerved by Marina's counterattack, says in a much calmer voice, "Well, then, what *are* we going to do?"

Grasping the opportunity, Marina presents her recommendation. "For one thing, if I had my own checkbook I wouldn't even consider using a credit card. My parents didn't like credit cards any more than yours did."

Martin protests, "If we both had checkbooks, we'd end up bouncing checks all over the place."

But Marina shakes her head and replies, "Not if we communicate with each other."

Martin is still a little reluctant—after all, his father was always the one who wrote the checks. But what Marina has said makes sense, and it could resolve the credit card issue. "I'm not sure how both of us having checkbooks is going to work out, but I guess it's worth a try. My mom did tell me I was marrying a gal with a head on her shoulders, and if I didn't listen to you, she'd come over and talk some sense into me."

Anger never justifies demeaning a loved one. Appropriately expressing your concerns and trying to understand the challenges your partner faces can be a far more effective means of bringing about change.

Preferential Treatment

If some members of the family believe that others receive preferential treatment when it comes to finances, they can become jealous and argumentative. To reduce these feelings, analyze the current distribution of financial managerial tasks—shopping for groceries, buying clothing, purchasing new or used cars, preparing the monthly budget, paying the bills, cashing checks and making deposits, earning income, and so on (see Worksheet 2.6, chapter 2). Determine who is responsible for which tasks and whether each person is satisfied with the current arrangement. Be sure to discuss how each family member perceives the fairness of the task distribution.

In addition, find out if family members feel that different standards or rules apply to different family members according to age or ability to earn money. Do the older children get a larger allowance than the younger ones? Do the younger children get more help because they aren't old enough to work? Similarly, conflicts often appear when parents pay for dance lessons but not for karate lessons, or when they support those who want to go to college but not those who want to learn a trade.

Favoritism is mostly perceived rather than real; therefore, you have to determine what you can do not only to ensure fair treatment but also to help family members perceive that they are being treated equally (see **Reframing,** chapter 5). You may also need to negotiate a settlement (see **Negotiations,** chapter 5).

Income Management Systems Used by Single-Wage-Earner Families

Single-wage-earner (single-income, two-parent) families usually use either the *whole-wage system* or the *allowance system* to manage their income.[4]

With the whole-wage system, (1) the wage earner turns all earnings over to the other spouse, (2) the spouse who is responsible for managing the finances pays all the bills and household expenses, and (3) the manager spouse returns personal spending money to the wage earner. The whole-wage system is frequently used among lower-income families, with the wife designated as the spouse responsible for managing the finances.[5] In a slight variation on this income management system, the wage earner withholds personal spending money before turning the earnings over to the manager spouse. (In some instances, though, the wage earner may attempt to deceive the manager spouse by working overtime without turning over the extra money.)

With the allowance system, (1) the wage earner deposits earnings in one account, (2) the wage earner pays the larger bills, and (3) the non-wage-earner receives an allowance to meet regular housekeeping obligations. The allowance system is more common among middle- and higher-income families.[6] Under this system, the wage earner pays the mortgage and major loans and makes investments. After these obligations have been met, the wage earner usually determines the size of the household allowance—which the non-wage-earner frequently feels is insufficient. Additional frustration occurs when income increases without a corresponding increase in the household allowance, or when the allowance increases only after a substantial delay.

This system can also be used when the household managing spouse becomes employed part-time. The couple usually considers this secondary income supplemental—available for buying extras for the family, and often for supplementing the household allowance.

In another variation of the allowance system, the couple mutually manages the income, with individual allowances for each partner. (This is a variation on the shared management system described under "Dual-Income Families.") Under this system, the couple considers income, obligations, and management tasks *our* responsibilities rather than *yours* or *mine*. It is interesting to note that a survey conducted by General Mills reported that couples enjoyed a greater degree of marital satisfaction when both spouses were involved in making financial decisions.[7]

Dual-Income Families

Whether or not both husband and wife work outside of the home is a sensitive issue for many Latter-day Saint households. President Ezra Taft Benson strongly admonished priesthood brethren to remember their responsibility to provide for their families:

> In a home where there is an able-bodied husband, he is expected to be the breadwinner. Sometimes we hear of husbands who, because of economic conditions, have lost their jobs and expect the wives to go out of the home and work, even though the husband is capable of providing for his family. In these cases, we urge the husband to do all in his power to allow his wife to remain in the home caring for the children while he continues to provide

for his family the best he can, even though the job he is able to secure may not be ideal and family budgeting may have to be tighter.[8]

Unfortunately, during the last part of the twentieth century, many western industrial countries, including the United States, have tended to devalue the role a woman plays in the home, and have tried to convince her that her worth is to be measured by the size of her paycheck. Of course, from an eternal perspective, nothing could be further from the truth. President David O. McKay declared:

> Motherhood is the greatest potential influence either for good or ill in human life. The mother's image is the first that stamps itself on the unwritten page of the young child's mind. It is her caress that first awakens a sense of security; her kiss, the first realization of affection; her sympathy and tenderness, the first assurance that there is love in the world. . . .
>
> This . . . make[s] motherhood the noblest office or calling in the world. She who can paint a masterpiece or write a book that will influence millions deserves the admiration and the plaudits of mankind; but she who rears successfully a family of healthy, beautiful sons and daughters, whose influence will be felt through generations to come, . . . deserves the highest honor that man can give, and the choicest blessings of God.[9]

It is extremely difficult, however, for a mother to fulfill her mission unless the father also fulfills his mission. President Benson again urged the brethren to be mindful of their stewardship when he said:

> Early in the history of the restored Church, the Lord specifically charged men with the obligation to provide for their wives and family. In January of 1832 He said, "Verily I say unto you, that every man who is obliged to provide for his own family, let him provide, and he shall in nowise lose his crown" (D&C 75:28). Three months later the Lord said again, "Women have claim on their husbands for their maintenance, until their husbands are taken" (D&C 83:2). This is the divine right of a wife and mother. While she cares for and nourishes her children at home, her husband earns the living for the family, which makes this nourishing possible.[10]

In spite of the counsel given by the prophets, many Latter-day Saint households have found it necessary for both the husband and wife to work outside of the home, and have become dual-income families.

In a dual-income family, both spouses are present, and both are employed either part- or full-time. The number of families with two working parents has been increasing for some time. In 1890, only 4.5 percent of married women worked, and women made up only 17 percent of the work force.[11] By 1993, 58 percent of the U.S. labor force was female, up from 51.5 percent in 1980. In 1960, 28 percent of American married mothers were employed in income-producing jobs. By 1990, that figure had more than doubled, to 67 percent.[12]

Attitudes toward women entering the labor force have changed correspondingly during the twentieth century. In 1930, only 18 percent of the population approved of women working outside the home. Today that proportion has grown to more than 80 percent.[13]

Marital Stress in Dual-Income Families

The income management system to be used in the dual-income family is an important decision. Issues of allocation and control often loom large: Who has claim on which income? How will the incomes be allocated to meet expenditures? How will the personal needs of both partners be satisfied? How might differences in earnings between partners affect self-esteem, personal interaction, and sharing of homemaking responsibilities? Marital stress is often a result of both partners being employed outside the home.

The financial advantages of a secondary income may not be as great as they seem at first glance. Having a second income does not necessarily mean a great increase in funds. As a rule, because of the additional deductions and costs associated with earning a second income, *only about one-third* of the gross amount of this income actually comes home with you.[14] If your family's second income were $15,000, for example, you could expect only about a $5,000 increase in the amount of money available for family use. The amount actually realized will vary in accordance with family income levels (see **Credit Abuse,** chapter 6) but it is almost always less than you expected.

Use Worksheet 11.1 to calculate the *net income effects* of a second income for your family. But keep in mind that it will *not* measure for you the time that you could have spent with your spouse or children instead of working, nor will it measure the toll taken in fatigue, health, and emotional well-being. It may be worthwhile to evaluate exactly what is gained from the extra income when compared to what is lost.

Allocation and Control

Allocation and control conflicts—common in dual-income families—usually center more on the way resources are allocated, and who controls it, than on how much there is to allocate. For example, one spouse might exclaim, "I ought to be able to afford an exercise bike with the kind of money I make, let alone what the two of us are making! The bike only costs $184. I want someone to tell me where all my money's going. I'm tired of working and having nothing to show for it." Though items and amounts differ, this scenario is a fairly typical financial argument in a dual-income family (see **Love versus Power,** chapter 4).

This tendency to argue over things is futile. Imagine watching two children through the porthole of a ship. You can see the children fighting over what one has and the other wants. You realize that what they are doing is just a waste of time and energy and you want them to stop. So you open the door to their stateroom, and try to convince them that the things they are arguing over don't really matter because they won't be able to take anything off the ship. They remain unconvinced. What they don't realize is that you are a member of the ship's crew, and the ship, the *Titanic,* has already struck an iceberg.

I wonder if our Heavenly Father must sometimes feel like the captain of the *Titanic* as he watches us argue and fight over things here on the Good Ship Earth. Concerned about our welfare, he repeatedly tries to convince us that the things we fight over don't really matter, because we, too, will not be able to take any of them with us when we leave. Yet, in spite of his efforts to convince us to look to our treasures in heaven rather than on earth, many still feel jealous when somebody else (such as a spouse) gets something and the other doesn't.

Like most other families, dual-income families are affected by the principle of *scarcity:* any allocation of resources to one end implies that fewer resources will be available for other ends. Family members need to work together so that resource allocation generates (1) the greatest benefits (2) for the most people, (3) at the least cost. In order to achieve this, the fundamental principles of negotiating should be observed: First, remember that negotiations are designed to produce a mutually beneficial outcome, not a one-sided victory. Second, cooperate, don't compete. Third, communicate with each other in a way that safeguards one another's self-esteem.

Arguments often occur when couples have inaccurate or incomplete information. They may not know what their actual income is, what their actual costs are, how much credit they have used—or how much credit they can handle. Their arguments are based on what each *perceives* is happening with their finances (see **Your Perceived Budget,** chapter 9). They may criticize, blame, and find fault with each other until each decides to take care of his or her own money and his or her own expenses. They develop a "yours, mine, and ours" attitude toward income distribution,[15] which can create feelings of emotional distance between partners.[16]

Negative feelings toward income distribution is not the only cause of emotional distancing. Distribution of the responsibilities of earning an income and running a household can also affect the perceived quality of the marriage and the happiness of the individual partners.[17] Research indicates that wives who are employed outside the home contribute more to homemaking chores than do their husbands,[18] and that individual incomes strongly influence the division of labor in the home.[19] Studies conclude that "the more a husband earns and the less money a wife makes, the less the husband's share in domestic work."[20] This condition cannot be expected to change for the better in the near future, since women in the work force consistently earn lower wages than men.

Equitable distribution of financial and household responsibilities in marriage depends on effective communication and the ability to understand the difference between consenting to be useful, consenting to be charitable, and being exploited (see **Relationships and Financial Priorities,** chapter 4). Neither being useful nor charitable means being exploited. To exploit others is to use them without their complete emotional and intellectual consent or to use them without sufficient consideration for their welfare.

Divorce in Dual-Income Families

One of the more measurable outcomes of the increase in the number of dual-income families and the consequent increase in family stress is divorce. A survey of census reports for the 48 continental United States showed that in states where more married women worked full-time, the divorce rate was higher. In states where more married women worked part-time, the divorce rate was lower.[21] President Spencer W. Kimball strongly believed that there is a relationship between divorce and wives working outside the home.

> Numerous divorces can be traced directly to the day when the wife left the home and went out into the world into employment. Two incomes raise the standard of living beyond its norm. Two spouses working prevents the complete and proper home life, breaks into

the family prayers, creates an independence which is not cooperative, causes distortion, limits the family, and frustrates the children already born.[22]

The relationship between divorce rates and the number of hours married women work seems to be supported by other research findings as well.[23] The number of hours away from home had a greater impact on the probability of divorce than the size of the woman's earnings. This relationship was strongest among middle-income families and those in which the husband disapproved of the wife's employment. (However, these researchers did not consider the question of how a reduction in hours worked *by husbands* in dual-income families might reduce marital stress.)

It is interesting that divorce is no more likely in a dual-income couple than in a single-income couple (in which it is the husband who works) if the wife earns an above average income and the husband has a high degree of approval toward her career.[24] But in cases where the wife earns more than her husband, or the husband is periodically unemployed, the probability of divorce is higher.[25]

Marital success, like individual happiness, depends more on the degree of satisfaction derived from the money earned than on the actual amount. Also, it seems that marital stability increases with the number of assets accumulated rather than with increases in income[26]—there are few situations more frustrating than when both spouses work hard to earn high incomes over a period of years and then have "nothing to show for it."

Dual-Career Families

A special category of the dual-income family is the dual-career family. One of the distinctions between the two is that in the dual-income family, the wife views work as a source of economic security without an organized intellectual or promotional sequence in mind. The woman who is career-oriented, however, views work as a developmental job sequence, with clearly formulated goals and time frames for reaching certain milestones.[27]

In spite of early predictions that dual-career couples would become the social innovators of the post-industrial era,[28] married women in selected professional careers (law, medicine, and college teaching) made up less than 7.5 percent of the labor force in 1982.[29]

Dual-career families tend to experience greater financial stress than either single-wage-earner or dual-income families.[30] They also experience emotional stress associated with discrepancies between personal and social norm expectations, concerns about personal identity and self-esteem, and trying to maintain a balance among multiple role expectations.[31] Some of the primary problems facing dual-career families can be listed this way:

1. Gender-based segregation that results in differences in pay, job opportunities, and career advancement.
2. Persistent inequality between husband and wife with regard to sharing homemaking responsibilities.
3. Additional expenses for full- or part-time housekeeping, gardening, and child care.
4. Required relocation that is not compatible with the other spouse's career.
5. Potential for professional competition and jealousy.

Income Management Systems Used by Dual-Income and Dual-Career Families

The two income management systems most commonly used by dual-income/dual-career families are the *shared management system* and the *independent management system*.[32]

In the shared management system, (1) both incomes are deposited in a joint account, (2) both partners have equal access to this account, (3) both assume responsibility for managing the account, and (4) household expenditures are randomly ascribed to either spouse. Under this system, *both* partners share in the managerial tasks. Both discuss allocation issues and try to arrive at a consensus for distribution of funds.

Studies show that marriages with this kind of equal control over financial decisions (either making joint decisions or agreeing to each assume responsibility for different tasks) have the least amount of conflict.[33] (These findings support the recommendation in chapter 4 that dominance/submission issues be viewed from the perspective of reciprocal roles of responsibility between equals rather than from a position of superiority/inferiority.)

One of the benefits of the shared management system is that it confronts problems of trust. Trust issues arise when one spouse tries to keep the other from knowing exactly how much is being earned, or when one spouse suspects the other of juggling the books or keeping some of the income for personal use. The shared management system is, in fact, based on trust. Since either spouse can write checks on the single account—and wipe it out if he or she wants to—this system requires both partners' mutual trust and mature, responsible behavior.

A common modification of this system is as follows: (1) one spouse assumes responsibility for managing the joint account and family expenditures, and (2) specific incomes are assigned to specific expenditures. The manager can be either husband or wife, and incomes are usually assigned to expenses on the basis of convenience. For instance, if one spouse is paid weekly, those checks might be assigned to buying food, gas for the cars, entertainment, and other cash expenses. If the other spouse is paid on a monthly basis, that income would be assigned to utilities, and mortgage and loan payments.

In the *independent management system,* (1) the income of each spouse is deposited in a separate account, (2) neither spouse has access to all of the income, (3) specific financial obligations are assigned to each spouse, and (4) each spouse's income is treated as personal money. One spouse might be responsible for paying the mortgage, while the other might be responsible for the utilities. Each might be responsible for his or her own car payments, insurance payments, and car maintenance costs. However, should one of the spouses be unable to meet his or her obligations, funds are transferred, on a temporary or permanent basis, from one account to the other.

One of the advantages of this sytem is that it provides clear, uncluttered records for income tax purposes. It is also a convenient way of providing income/expenditure stability when one of the incomes is variable due to commissions, seasonal work, and so forth.

Single-Parent Families

In a single-parent family, one parent is absent because of divorce (42 percent), separation (25 percent), or death (7 percent)—or there was no marriage in the first place (27 percent).[34] Two-thirds of all children born after 1980 will live some portion of their childhood with a single parent. In 1960, only 9 percent of U.S. households were headed by single parents. By 1986, this figure had increased to 24 percent. Of these, 89 percent were headed by females.[35]

For the single parent, poverty is often unavoidable, with a disproportionate part of the financial and emotional responsibility for childrearing falling on the mother. Unfortunately, many fathers, once they are *legally* divorced, seem to think that they no longer have a financial obligation for the children they co-created through the power of God, and who in some cases have been sealed to them *for eternity.* The Apostle Paul's counsel to fathers is quite clear: "But if any provide not for his own, and specially for those of his own house, he hath denied the faith, and is worse than an infidel" (1 Timothy 5:8).

Following are some of the "facts of life" of single-parent families:

1. Divorce means almost certain poverty for more than 50 percent of women who head single-parent households, so becoming a single parent usually means adjusting to a lower standard of living.

2. Only about 50 percent of ex-husbands actually make full child-support payments as stipulated by the courts, while 25 percent make only partial payments; 31 percent of black women and 23 percent of white women entitled to receive child support receive *no* payments.[36]

3. A great many extra costs are associated with being a single-parent provider, such as additional child care, loss of wages due to time off to care for children, and so forth.

4. Being a single parent usually means dealing with feelings of anger, frustration, and resentment about the current situation, as well as dealing alone with the children's problems.

5. On the positive side, being a single parent provides opportunities for the development of a greater sense of self-reliance and independence.

Enmeshment

One of the most common problems associated with being a single parent is a reduction in the emotional differentiation between parent and child. After a divorce or death, the parent and child often look to each other to satisfy their emotional needs. As a result, they can become *enmeshed*. This can have a great effect on finances.

People are enmeshed when they become so dependent on each other that it is unclear where one person's identity ends and the other's begins. It is no longer clear whether a need or emotion belongs to one person or the other. For example, a single parent may believe that a child wants a new toy, when actually it is the *parent* who *wants to buy* the child a new toy. Similarly, single parents may suffer for what they perceive to be the child's loneliness and deprivation, when in fact these are their own feelings.

In an economically solvent family, when a child says, "I don't want hamburger for dinner," the parents will probably infer that the child does not feel like eating hamburger; and when they ask what he or she would like to eat, they are told, "Hot dogs," or "Spaghetti-Os." But to a single parent who is under emotional and financial stress and who is still trying to adjust to a lower standard of living, the child's statement might imply, "I don't like the way we eat any more. I want to eat stuff like we used to eat." The parent may then reply, "I know it's been hard on you kids since the divorce, but I'm doing the best I can."

To stop being enmeshed, each member of the family needs to assume personal responsibility for his or her own feelings, appropriately expressing them and trusting that the other family members will cope with them. They need to accept the fact that their family is not perfect, and recognize that mistakes will be made and feelings will be hurt even if family members do their best to be responsible and considerate. They need to acknowledge that each person can belong to the family and still develop some degree of independence.

Doing without for the Children's Sake

The financial strain that often accompanies single parenthood can exacerbate problems of enmeshment and make parents feel that they need to deprive themselves for the sake of the children. Continually subordinating your own needs to those of your children may cause feelings of resentment and jealousy. Set aside for yourself some percentage of the money you normally spend on the children. For example, if you are going to spend $100 for children's clothing, you should either spend $10, $25, or $50 of that money for your own clothing or, if you can afford it, spend the $100 on the children and an additional $10, $25, or $50 on yourself.

Most parents are often willing to sacrifice for the sake of the children, but this seems to be especially true for single parents. Since they have less money to go around, they often put their own needs last. A typical single parent buys the children new clothes for school each year, but when it comes to clothes for the parent, he or she wears the same things year after year. These parents may be sending a different message to their children than they think they are sending. Perhaps their child will think, "Golly, Mom, I can hardly wait until I grow up. Then I can wear rags like you, and eat the scraps off other people's plates."

This exaggerated example may seem strong, but the point is that, within reason, a parent has needs, too. And children need to understand that. If parents show respect for themselves, their children will be more likely to respect them, too. Giving children everything they want while you do without is not love; it is martyrdom. In *The Road Less Traveled,* M. Scott Peck reminds us that "Love is not simply giving; it is *judiciously* giving and judiciously withholding as well."[37]

Things and Relationships

As noted in chapter 6, feelings often influence purchases. For example, single parents might buy things for their children in an attempt to compensate for the loss of the other parent, the amount of time the single parent is at work, or their lower economic status. But in most cases, the family can substantially reduce the "need" to acquire material things by developing warm, loving relationships among themselves.

If your purpose in buying things for the children is to let them know that you care about them, you might try just telling them directly. Perhaps a child asks for a new bicycle. Her harried parent responds, "Do you think I'm made of money? I've barely got enough to pay for the rent, let alone pay for a bicycle!" The child will most likely go away feeling resentful, guilty for having upset the parent, who is obviously overburdened already, and convinced that nobody cares about her feelings.

Now picture the same scenario with a different parental response. This time the parent focuses on the child's feelings rather than on the cost of the bicycle and responds, "I've had a feeling that you might be wanting to get a new bicycle, and I've been trying to juggle our budget to see if there was any way we might be able to buy one. I've got a pretty good idea how much having a bicycle would mean to you, but it just doesn't look like we can afford one right now. But I want you to know that *I want* you to have a new bicycle and I will do everything I can to make it happen."

The parent still cannot afford to buy a new bicycle, but now the child does not question her importance or whether someone cares about her feelings. This approach also affords some excellent opportunities to teach family goal-setting policies, effective problem-solving techniques, and how to cope with feelings associated with delayed gratification. In other words, instead of selfishly focusing on stress and problems, this parent has created a "teaching moment."

Blended Families

A blended family, or stepfamily, results from a remarriage in which one or both partners bring children from a previous relationship. Of all households with children, 17.4 percent are blended families.[38] Half of all children born in the 1980s will live some portion of their childhood in a blended family.

The divorce rate in blended families is about 55 to 60 percent, slightly greater than the divorce rate for first marriages.[39] But the rate of divorce among remarried couples is even higher when children from a previous relationship are present.[40] In interviews with couples who had remarried, researchers asked, "What issues or concerns did you discuss before you married?"

The most frequent topic mentioned was children from a previous marriage, followed by finances.[41]

As in other two-spouse families, the income management system is an important consideration. Since the financial demands of a blended family are typically more complex than those of an original marriage, the problems of allocation of resources are correspondingly more stressful.[42] Questions can center around family boundaries, old debts and liabilities, and previously acquired assets.

1. How can the divorced husband remarry and meet the needs of two families unless his new wife also earns an income?

2. How will the health care and educational needs of the various children be met?

3. How will the child support that is received be spent, and on whom?

4. If one of the parents in the new marriage adopts the other's children, how will the adoption and the subsequent loss of child support be handled?

5. How will perceptions of favoritism and neglect be handled?

6. How will either partner's debts acquired in the previous marriage be paid, and by whom?

7. How will assets acquired before the current marriage be redistributed, disposed of, or supervised?

8. What steps should be taken with regard to estate planning to protect the interests of all family members?

Family Boundaries

In a blended family, members from one side almost always think that members from the other side play favorites or neglect them in relationships and with resources. One reason for this is that blended families find it difficult to define family boundaries.[43] Family boundaries distinguish between who is "family" and who is not. Those who are considered family have certain privileges and rights that others do not have. Determining the family boundaries in a blended family can become a very complex task. Do the family boundaries include:

Children from the previous marriages living *within* the current household?

Children from the previous marriages living *outside* of the current household?

Children resulting from the current marriage?

Only blood-related members (even if none of them are living with the current family)?

Only those with the same last name (natural or adopted)?

Everyone currently living in the same house?

It is important to be able to resolve these issues, because family boundaries can affect how financial support is allocated as strongly as court action can. The complexity of allocation problems often center around the issue of fairness—whose money goes to which child for what purpose, and will there be the appearance of favoritism?

CASE ILLUSTRATION

John and Sally have divorced. Sally takes custody of the children and marries a man (Raymond) who is also divorced and has custody of his children. Sally and Raymond thus create a new blended family. John also remarries; his new wife (Michelle) also has children and she also has custody.

If John were to buy his children new winter coats (even though he doesn't have custody), while the children from Michelle's previous marriage had to wear hand-me-downs, Michelle's children would naturally ask, "How come they get new coats and we don't?" Likewise, the children that Raymond brought to the new blended family could ask the same question. In either situation, any attempts at an explanation would undoubtedly draw cries of "That's not fair!"

Family boundaries initiate such finance-related questions as: Will the natural parent pay for insurance for a particular set of medical expenses, or will the stepparent? Who will pay for a particular child's college education? On which children will the child support actually be spent?

Old Debts and Liabilities

Unless debts that originated in a former marriage are paid off, they can be a source of perpetual marital discord. As constant reminders of unpleasant feelings associated with the previous marriage, old debts and liabilities can cause emotional turmoil and resentment in the new relationship. For example, a wife might be quite willing to help pay off her new husband's car (part of the assets he brings to the current marriage), yet be adamantly opposed to making payments on his ex-wife's car. "Every time I write out a check for her car, I get so upset. I have to ride the bus to work while she drives around in a fancy car. It's just not fair."

A significant reduction in tension levels could be reached by determining which debts generate the most resentment and contention, and paying them off as soon as possible. It is helpful to arrange an electronic transfer of payments from one bank to another so that it's not necessary to write checks and be repeatedly reminded of a sore spot (see **Steps to Take to Resolve a Financial Crisis,** chapter 7).

Previously Acquired Assets

When people remarry, they bring not only debts and liabilities, but assets as well. Differences in the perceived value of assets brought into a marriage can cause contention and mistrust in blended families.

Assets are often divided by legal judgments in divorce proceedings. Sometimes the property a partner brings into a new marriage may represent the only things worth salvaging from the previous marriage. As a consequence, the partner who contributes that property may be very possessive of it and worry about who can use it under what circumstances and with what restrictions. If one spouse does not appreciate the intrinsic value of the other's possessions, he or she may appear insensitive. For example, a spouse might suggest, "Since we need a new car anyway, why don't we just sell your old pickup and get something decent?" The other, offended, might respond, "Don't even think such a thing! That 'old pickup' is the only thing that kept me sane in my first marriage—and the only thing she didn't get in the settlement. It's my reward for valor under combat conditions." Similar outcries can result from the husband using his wife's antique chairs for sawhorses.

If assets are relatively liquid, such as cash, stocks, or bonds, then problems can center around the proposed uses of those assets: if and how they will be redistributed, whether or not they will be consumed, and if so, at what rate and under whose supervision.

Financial Agreements

Most people develop attitudes toward assets and financial planning based not only on experiences with their families of origin, but also on experiences in their previous marriages. In order to avoid being exploited or making the same mistakes as in the past, each spouse may push for marital agreements that safeguard the way finances will be handled. If one spouse vigorously defends such agreements, the other may resent proposed restraints, conditions, or limits and interpret them as a lack of love, trust, or commitment.

To encourage greater trust and commitment, each spouse in the new marriage should place at least *some* assets under joint supervision. This action should be taken in a gradual, progressive fashion. When a building's foundation is constructed out of concrete, the footings are poured first and then allowed to set for a while to gain strength before the floor is poured. In a similar fashion, each spouse might transfer a portion of his or her assets from the "mine" account to the "ours" account. The couple might then let the situation rest for a period of time while they build their feelings of trust. Of course, some assets may remain forever separate, designated only for inheritance or emergency purposes, or as a source of security.

Income Management Systems Used by Blended Families

Although there is no one right way to manage family finances, some are better than others, as we have noted. A survey of married couples in which 20 percent of the husbands and 17 percent of the wives were remarried showed that between two-thirds and three-fourths of the couples preferred the shared management, or pooling, system.[44]

Eight to 10 percent of those surveyed preferred independent, or separate, accounts. ("Husbands and wives who do not believe that marriage should be forever are less willing to pool."[45]) Among dual-income blended families at higher income levels, the *independent management system* is commonly used.[46] There are several reasons remarried couples often use the independent management system: each partner already has an established bank account; each is used to meeting certain financial obligations (most of which were assumed before the current marriage); and unfortunately, each is likely to have been hurt financially in the previous marriage and may not be willing to be that vulnerable again—at least for a while.

As with assets brought separately to the marriage, progressively blending incomes helps to overcome feelings of distance and the lack of commitment. Pooling resources tends to encourage family unity while keeping separate accounts promotes personal autonomy and interferes with the integration of the blended family.[47]

At first, you may wish to keep *all* of your income separate. But as time passes and you become more familiar as husband and wife, you may want to begin committing a portion of your income to a common account. Begin with about 10 percent of your earnings; then, as mutual feelings of trust increase, progressively devote a larger portion to the joint account. In this way, you can develop a sense of unity and commitment in your new family without the overwhelming fear of "losing everything" again.

Summary

While some financial problems are common to every family, others are unique to particular types of families. Special consideration needs to be given to the distinctive financial challenges faced by single-wage-earner, dual-income, single-parent, and blended families as they try to develop viable budgets. Careful evaluation of income management systems, needs and feelings of family members, and blending of values and priorities contribute greatly to any family's economic well-being.

Important Terms

Allowance system: Income management system in which (1) the primary wage earner deposits earnings in one account, (2) the primary wage earner pays the larger bills, and (3) the non-wage earner receives an allowance to meet regular housekeeping obligations.

Blended family: Stepfamily resulting from a remarriage in which one or both partners brings children from a previous relationship.

Dual-career family: Family in which both husband and wife have a career-oriented view of work—that is, they view work as a developmental job sequence with clearly formulated goals and time frames for reaching certain milestones.

Dual-income family: Family in which both spouses are present, and both are employed either part- or full-time.

Economic well-being: Health of a family's finances, influenced by both the amount of income available and the size of the family.

Income-to-need ratio: Method of determining a family's economic well-being by dividing a family's income by the poverty threshold for a family of that size; the larger the number, the greater the family's financial well-being.

Independent management system: Income management system in which (1) the income of each spouse is deposited in a separate account, (2) neither spouse has access to all of the income, (3) specific financial obligations are assigned to each spouse, and (4) each spouse's income is treated as personal money.

Shared management system: Income management system in which (1) both incomes are deposited in a joint account, (2) both partners have equal access to this account, (3) both partners assume responsibility for managing the account, and (4) household expenditures are randomly managed by either spouse.

Single-parent family: Family in which one parent is absent because of divorce, separation, or death, or there was no marriage in the first place.

Single-wage-earner family: Two-parent family in which only one is earning an income.

Total family income: Method of determining a family's economic well-being by comparing the family's income to a national norm.

Whole-wage system: Income management system in which (1) the primary wage earner turns all earnings over to the spouse, (2) the spouse, who is responsible for managing the finances, pays all the bills and household expenses, and (3) the spouse returns personal spending money to the primary earner.

Notes

1. U.S. Department of Commerce, 1994b.

2. U.S. Department of Commerce, 1991c.

3. U.S. Department of Commerce, 1980.

4. McCrae, 1987; Pahl, 1983.

5. Heath, 1986; Pahl, 1990.

6. Pahl, 1983.

7. Yankelovich, Skelly and White, 1975.

8. Benson, 1988, p. 506.

9. McKay, 1976, p. 452–54.

10. Benson, 1988, p. 506.

11. Smith, 1979.

12. U.S. Department of Commerce, 1994, p. 402.

13. U.S. Department of Commerce, 1991a.

14. Hefferan, 1978.

15. Jensen and Jensen, 1981.

16. Glickauf-Hughes, Hughes and Wells, 1986.

17. Yogev and Brett, 1985.

18. Abdel-Ghany and Nickols, 1983; Berardo, Sherhan and Leslie, 1987.

19. Hiller and Philliber, 1986.

20. Kamo, 1988.

21. Yeh and Lester, 1987, 1988.

22. Kimball, 1977, pp. 9–10.

23. South and Spitze, 1985.

24. Nye and Hoffman, 1974; Thomas, Albrecht and White, 1984.

25. D'Amico, 1983; Moore and Hofferth, 1979.

26. Galligan and Bahr, 1978.

27. Rapoport and Rapoport, 1971.

28. Ibid.

29. Benenson, 1984.

30. Rapoport and Rapoport, 1969, 1976.

31. Price-Bonham and Murphy, 1980.

32. Heath, 1986; McCrae, 1987; Pahl, 1983.

33. General Mills, 1975; Blumstein and Schwartz, 1983; Schaninger and Buss, 1986.

34. U.S. Department of Labor, 1989.

35. Lino, 1988; U.S. Department of Labor, 1989.

36. Taeber and Valdisera, 1986; U.S. Department of Commerce, 1990c.

37. Peck, 1978.

38. Glick, 1989.

39. Cherlin, 1981; U.S. Department of Commerce, 1990a.

40. White and Booth, 1985.

41. Ganong and Coleman, 1989.

42. Messinger, 1976.

43. Ihinger-Tallman and Pasley, 1981; Pasley, 1987.

44. Blumstein and Schwartz, 1983.

45. Ibid., p. 103.

46. Heath, 1986.

47. Fishman, 1983.

NET INCOME EFFECTS OF A SECOND INCOME

EXPENSES ASSOCIATED WITH A SECOND INCOME

Federal income taxes (Includes increases due to moving into higher tax bracket.) _____

Social Security (If self-employed, this amount is *double* what it would be if
employed by someone else.) _____

State income taxes _____

Redundant insurance (Many employers have a mandatory participation
group insurance plan that may duplicate the coverage you already
have under the other wage earner's plan.) _____

Additional transportation costs _____

Additional meals costs (Meals at work, lunches out, fast foods, frozen meals,
and so on.) _____

Child care expenses _____

Household cleaning costs _____

Additional wardrobe and grooming costs _____

Total additional expenses _____

Gross monthly income _____

Minus additional expenses _____

NET BENEFITS _____

CHAPTER 12

Financial Challenges and the Life Cycle

amilies are in a constant state of change; yet it is our inherent nature to resist change. Parents encourage their children to grow up, and simultaneously discourage them from growing up too fast. Families outgrow their homes and want to move to bigger places but are reluctant to leave their old familiar surroundings. Such dilemmas create internal conflict and strain as family members attempt to adjust to change. These dilemmas can be solved with knowledge, preparation, and skills adapted to each stage in our lives.

Family Life Cycle Stages

Many changes are predictable and identifiable, and are the results of transition from one stage in the life cycle to another. Psychologists and sociologists have proposed a number of theories concerning the stages we go through in life. Since our primary interest here is the dynamics between relationships and finances, we will divide the life cycle according to changes in age, marital status, and the presence of children in the home. (See Table 12.1, which also includes average income figures for each stage.)

Each stage in the life cycle has its own unique set of financial responsibilities or tasks. For example, during Stage 2, beginning families are primarily concerned with the costs of completing an education, creating a household, and establishing credit. A retired couple in Stage 6 is more likely to be concerned with adjusting to a lower income, obtaining adequate insurance protection, and transferring their estate.

TABLE 12.1—LIFE CYCLE STAGES

STAGE	AGE	MARITAL STATUS	INCOME
1	15–24	Single, with no children	$17,778
2	25–34	Married or single, with no children, or children ages 1–9	$31,434
3	35–44	Married or single, with children ages 10–19	$40,090
4	45–54	Married or single, launching children	$44,540
5	55–64	Married or single, with children launched	$36,062
6	65–over	Married or single, retired	$17,160

From *Statistical Abstract of the United States,* 1992 (p. 465), by U.S. Department of Commerce, Bureau of the Census, 1994, Washington, D.C.: U.S. Government Printing Office.

Fulfilling these financial responsibilities can be difficult, and there are ample opportunities to make mistakes. The following discussion includes lists of financial obligations and common pitfalls associated with each stage in the life cycle. These lists are based on information compiled by the American Council on Life Insurance (1970).[1]

Stage 1: Single, with No Children

You are in Stage 1 of the life cycle if you are just out of school, not currently married and have no children living with you. (If you are single and have children living with you, or if you are responsible for the support of children not living with you, you are classified in one of the stages that include children.)

Financial tasks associated with Stage 1 are:
1. Beginning to establish credit.
2. Making first major purchases (car, stereo, boat, furniture, and so on).
3. Establishing financial record-keeping procedures.
4. Establishing financial goals.
5. Providing for educational/vocational training expenses.
6. Establishing financial independence from family of origin.

Common financial mistakes associated with Stage 1 include:

1. Impulse buying.
2. Excessive indebtedness, overextended credit.
3. Failure to file income taxes.
4. Failure to provide for education and career training expenses.
5. Failure to establish an effective financial management plan or to adhere to sound financial principles.
6. Failure to establish long-range goals and objectives.
7. Remaining financially dependent on parents.
8. Becoming addicted to alcohol or drugs.

Living for Today, Preparing for Tomorrow

Remember that "free at last" feeling you had when you graduated from high school, and how impatient you were to get on with your life? Full-time employment, adult wages, and a big paycheck were your keys to freedom. You were finally going to buy the car of your dreams, rent your own apartment, and live a carefree life. All this seemed possible—unless, of course, you were able to find only part-time work for minimum wages in an unskilled, dead-end job. In that case, the only things you could afford were an old "junker" that didn't run half the time, a room with four weird roommates, and a box of saltine crackers to tide you over until payday.

Education is the answer to most problems of underemployment. In 1990, the average high school graduate earned $22,236 (male) or $11,439 (female) a year. The average college graduate earned $38,820 (male) or $20,376 (female), and someone with an advanced degree earned $58,980 (male) or $37,944 (female).[2]

If you keep school loans to a minimum, an education can really pay off. But if your educational loans become excessive, you can find yourself deeply in debt at the very time you're attempting to finance the needs of a new family and career. A $15,000 student loan with a 9 percent rate of interest over a ten-year payback period would cost you $7,800 in interest, and your monthly payments would be $190. You would have to earn around $325 additional each month to clear (after deductions) enough to make those payments. This is equivalent to an almost $4,000 reduction in your yearly wages. To make up this difference you might be tempted to use your newly acquired credit cards.

The Credit Card Trap

Financial institutions often automatically mail credit cards to college graduates, hoping to cash in on newly acquired high incomes. Many graduates, having existed in a state of material deprivation for the past four or five years, experience a great deal of pent-up desire for consumption. To resolve this tension, they use their credit cards to acquire material goods without delay.

Credit cards allow you to immediately enjoy things that may have taken your parents a lifetime to acquire. And credit cards are more convenient than checks and safer than cash—what could be wrong with using them? When used wisely, credit cards can actually help you manage your finances efficiently—provided your monthly bills are paid on time and in full, and provided you use them only for emergencies or to purchase items that last longer than the payments.

Young adults often lack the experience or discipline needed to properly manage an open-ended line of credit. *Open-ended credit,* or a revolving charge account, provides you with a pre-approved credit limit and flexible terms of repayment. The creditor allows you to settle the loan with one payment, pay interest plus a minimum portion of the principal, or pay interest plus a larger-than-minimum portion of the principal. *Installment credit,* on the other hand, involves a prearranged schedule of repayment that is determined when the credit is approved.

Another difference between open-ended and installment credit is that many credit card applications do not undergo the same scrutiny that most loan applications do. As a result, young people often acquire numerous credit cards, with a combined credit limit that far exceeds the amount they could qualify for through a bank installment loan (see **Stop Qualifying for Loans You Don't Really Qualify For,** chapter 7). You can accumulate a large amount of debt over a short period of time without fully realizing the magnitude of the financial problems you're generating.

As a young adult you may tend to purchase assets that *consume income* or *depreciate* rapidly (cars, stereo equipment, boats, poor-quality furniture, clothing, accessories) instead of assets that *produce income* or at least have a chance to *appreciate* (stocks, real estate, IRAs, savings bonds). You may also be more inclined to spend a larger portion of your income on entertainment and recreation.

Looking Ahead

Many young adults are extremely responsible during this stage of their lives, planning and preparing well for their futures. But those who have been "living for the moment" will inevitably begin to feel frustrated when they fail to progress financially. Many re-evaluate their spending habits, weighing how much they have earned over the past few years against how much they have to show for it.

Usually this re-evaluation takes place when the single person starts thinking about getting married. Unfortunately, whether marrying for the first time or remarrying, many singles fail to prepare adequately for the financial challenges they will face. An ever-increasing percentage of singles approach marriage already deeply in debt.

Stage 2: Married or Single, with No Children or Children Ages 1–9

Stage 2 in the life cycle also includes singles with no children, because these singles are now older and in a higher income bracket. Nevertheless, this stage is commonly referred to as the beginning family stage, because the majority of the people of this age are married.

Most couples during this period realign relationships with their extended family to accommodate their new spouses. They focus time and energy on getting to know their new partner's values and behavior patterns and make adjustments for the arrival of children. President Spencer W. Kimball, in an address to married students at Brigham Young University, clearly stated that deliberate postponement of children was not recommended:

> I have told tens of thousands of young folks that when they marry they should not wait for children until they have finished their schooling and financial desires . . . they should live together normally and let children come. . . . I know of no scripture where an authorization is given to young wives to withhold their families and go to work to put their husbands through school. There are thousands of husbands who have worked their own way through school and have reared families at the same time.[3]

For some, the term *beginning family* carries an implied message that a beginning family is somehow "under construction" and therefore incomplete. But for many couples, being married with no children constitutes a finished product. And for a growing number of people, being "single with no children" constitutes a finished product.

For those who do have children, this stage has two distinct parts—before and after the arrival of children. Financial responsibilities and common financial mistakes differ in these two parts.

Married or Single, with No Children

Financial tasks of Stage 2 are:

1. Establishing the household—highly mobile, few possessions.
2. Completing education, career training.
3. Purchasing medical insurance (taking into account future childbearing costs).
3. Beginning a savings program.
4. Establishing credit.
5. Establishing a mutually acceptable financial management program.
6. Clarifying values and resolving differences.

Common financial mistakes associated with Stage 2 include:

1. Continuing to be self-indulgent—income used to purchase expensive "toys" rather than to accumulate assets.
2. Failure to develop vocational/educational potential.
3. Failure to plan for the future.
4. Overextending credit.
5. Failure to prepare for the possibility of having to live on one income.

One of the most difficult transitions in life is the transition from single life to marriage. The ritual and wording of the marriage ceremony may vary, but the intent is always the same: to set the couple apart from all others, as an exclusive union entitled to special privileges and trusts not enjoyed by any other.

During this transition we realize that we must replace much of the autonomy we experienced as a single person with a sense of togetherness. Togetherness does not mean becoming inseparable, nor does it mean losing all personal identity. It does mean that both individuals must commit themselves to thoughtful consideration of the consequences of their actions on their partners. For example, as a single person, you are free to sell your house and move on impulse. But you cannot greet an unsuspecting partner with "Hi, dear! Guess what? I sold the house today." Most spouses would consider such behavior an act of betrayal and insensitivity.

But many newly married couples may feel betrayed and deceived even without having the house sold out from under them. "Before we got married," they might say, "we used to go to nice restaurants, compliment each other on our appearance, and promise that things would only get better. But they haven't . . . Maybe being single was better!"

Much of the so-called "deception" regarding people's behavior before and after marriage can be explained by the mere fact that a new set of rules has come into play. As we progress through stages in our life cycle, we are governed by different rules—rules that we learned from our families of origin. One set of rules governs how we should act while dating; a second set governs how we act after becoming engaged; a third describes how to treat each other as husband and wife; a fourth, what constitutes being a good father or a good mother; and a fifth, the way we should raise our children.

If a husband no longer takes his wife to nice restaurants as he did when they were courting, he may simply be adhering to his family rules. He might explain to his wife that while he was engaged to her he followed the rules for being a fiancé, and after he married her he began following the rules for being a husband. Since he learned the "husband" rules primarily from observing his father's treatment of his mother, he learned that husbands save money by eating at home. Had he been raised by a father who had continued to court his wife after marriage, he would probably recognize the value of romantic dinners at fine restaurants.

The intent of courtship is not merely to "land a partner," but to perpetuate feelings of affection. The most important issue is not that you and your partner *got married* but whether the two of you still *want to be married*. Failure to recognize the need for lifelong courtship often leads to divorce. President Kimball reminds us that love "cannot be expected to last forever unless it is continually fed with portions of love, the manifestation of esteem and admiration, the expressions of gratitude, and the consideration of unselfishness."[4]

Divorce usually represents a financial setback for both partners. In fact, for most divorced people, divorce is *the* most expensive event—both financially and emotionally—that will ever happen to them. As we grow up, we develop a timetable of when we believe certain events are supposed to take place and in what sequence; this "schedule" provides us a general guideline for where we should be in life at a given age. Traumatic events such as divorce tend to throw people off track and make them feel they are "behind schedule" in the life cycle.

But life operates on its own schedule, and anticipated timetables are disrupted when divorce unexpectedly returns the married people to single life. (In 1987, the median age for a first marriage was 23 for women and 25 for men. The median age for a first divorce was 30 for women and 32 for men.[5] The median number of years before a divorce in first marriages is about seven years, followed by about three years of single life before the ex-partners remarry. About 75 percent of divorced women remarry, and an even greater proportion of divorced men eventually remarry.[6])

Married or Single, with Children Ages 1–9

The financial tasks associated with this part of Stage 2 are:

1. Providing for child care, childrearing costs.
2. Providing for expanded housing costs, saving for house purchase.
3. Buying medical/life insurance.
4. Beginning education funds for children.
5. Making out a will and guardianship instructions.
6. Adjusting to the income of one wage-earner.

Common financial mistakes associated with this part of Stage 2 include:

1. Overextending credit.
2. Failure to provide adequate insurance coverage.
3. Failure to establish provisions for children's education.
4. Failure to save for home purchase.
5. Failure to accumulate emergency funds.
6. Failure to establish short- and long-term goals.

As all parents know, raising children is an expensive undertaking. The 1992 *Family Economics Review*, estimates that for a middle-income family, the average annual cost of a 6-year-old child in the United States is $6,760; $7,780 for a 16-year-old. Over an 18-year period it costs about $125,000 to raise one child. Adding the costs of education, totals jump to between $245,000 and $275,000 per child.[7]

Since children can share resources, each additional child does not represent an exact multiple of the cost of raising one child. For instance, the cost of raising one daughter is $250,000, but the cost of raising two is $400,000.[8] A family with *five* children can expect to devote 75 percent of its projected real income to the cost of raising children. (If a couple without children were to invest the amount of money it costs to raise and educate two children, they could retire and live for the rest of their lives on the $40,000 a year they would earn from just the *interest* on that investment!)

Many of us have heard the counsel, "Have fun while you can, because once the children come along, it's just hard work and debt." If we hear this kind of thing repeatedly while we're growing up, it can become part of the rules that govern how we think and act as adults. After we have children of our own we may become preoccupied with working to provide for the family and not have as much time for each other. We may feel ill-prepared for the job of being parents, and overwhelmed by the ever-increasing costs of raising children.

If you have received from your family of origin the message that mothers and fathers are supposed to sacrifice themselves for the sake of the children, you may feel guilty taking time or money for your own needs. But "men are that they might have joy" (2 Nephi 2:25). How would things change if you were to teach your children that parents are people too, and that they do not relinquish their right to the "pursuit of happiness" when they have children? What if you remembered more often that even though there are burdens associated with marriage and children, these burdens are made lighter because of the great accompanying joy. President Ezra Taft Benson gave us this observation: "Yes, blessed is the husband and wife who have a family of children. The deepest joys and blessings in life are associated with family, parenthood, and sacrifice."[9]

Stage 3: Married or Single, with Children Ages 10–19

Everyday lives and family finances are becoming more complex at this stage. As children continue to grow and change, family rules governing their behaviors must also change. The rules governing a 12-year-old are most likely different from those governing a 6-year-old. This applies to money matters as well. Parents begin to extend or restrict money limits as the child becomes able to handle the financial responsibilities of growing up.

Financial tasks of adults in Stage 3 are:
1. Maximizing insurance protection for wage earners.
2. Beginning to teach children how to manage finances.
3. Beginning retirement planning.
4. Increasing income to accommodate expanded household needs.
5. Modifying wills to adjust to changes in the family.
6. Maintaining educational funds.
7. Adjusting to possible dual income.

Common financial mistakes include:
1. Overextending credit.
2. Overindulging the children.
3. Failure to provide funds for replacement of major appliances.
4. Failure to plan for retirement.

YOURS, MINE, AND OURS

5. Lack of adequate insurance protection.

6. Failure to adequately increase income.

7. Lack of adequate disability insurance.

8. Failure to provide an adequate emergency fund in case of underemployment or loss of employment.

If your children seem to be getting caught up in wanting the latest fads and basing their self-esteem on how much money is spent on them, it would be well for you to review chapter 4's recommendations. Building bonds of love through spending time together and treating each other with respect and affection will be far easier on your budget than trying with money to satisfy insatiable desires for things.

When Children Become Teenagers

The transition from having elementary-school-age children to having teenage children is particularly difficult. One parent commented, "I wonder why they call them *teen*-agers when it would be more accurate to call them *parent*-agers." This kind of remark stems from the emotional and financial changes families undergo during this stage of the life cycle.

As children grow from pre-teens into teenagers, their parents' financial tasks in this stage grow as well:

1. Maximizing investment funding.

2. Increasing amount of income allocated to household expenses.

3. Establishing cost-sharing practices with children.

4. Increasing entertainment/recreation budget.

5. Discussing estate plans.

6. Discussing child-launching plans.

7. Providing for costs of weddings, missions, and higher education.

Common financial mistakes include:

1. Failure to adjust to changing lifestyles.

2. Failure to use professional expertise.

3. Failure to provide sufficient retirement funds.

4. Indulging the children's wants, competing with others.

Teenagers' transportation costs are eight times greater than those of third graders, and their food consumption costs three times as much.[10] Money previously budgeted for running the household often no longer stretches to the end of the month. Food budgets that had been sufficient for years become woefully inadequate. Sometimes the spouse who is responsible for household expenditures can be accused of mismanagement by an unsympathetic partner. Unfair comparisons are often made to other families of equal size with younger children.

Remember that each family is different, and each parent approaches teenage issues from a different perspective—usually based on rules that governed him or her as a teenager. These differences frequently can lead to conflicts over who is being "too soft" or "too hard" on the child. One way of resolving such differences is to implement a *fifty/fifty agreement*.

A fifty/fifty agreement can help to encourage mutual consideration for each other's feelings, increase the level of cooperation, and broaden a sense of appreciation for assets. A fifty/fifty agreement states that the parents will pay half the cost of an item if the child will pay for the other half—a dollar-for-dollar matching agreement. The benefits of such an agreement are that (1) the child is more able to accumulate enough money to buy the item, (2) the child must put forth some effort and sacrifice to obtain his or her half of the money, and (3) the child has an opportunity not only to learn the benefits of cooperating with others but also to appreciate the efforts and generosity of others.

Remember that people cooperate most effectively when each sees the other as an equal and when dominance and submission are *reciprocal roles of responsibility* rather than positions of superiority and inferiority (see chapter 4).

Stage 4: Married or Single, Launching Children

When a child leaves home it can be hard on everyone involved. Yet most parents know from the beginning that their primary purpose is to prepare their children to become independent and succeed on their own. A universal family rule is "Sooner or later, the child must go." The only question is when and under what circumstances the launch will take place.

Financial tasks associated with Stage 4 are:
1. Providing for future needs of the parents' parents.
2. Analyzing and adjusting estate plans.
3. Providing for future security.

4. Investigating part-time employment.

5. Investigating possible housing adjustments.

6. Developing and implementing a launching fund.

Common financial mistakes include:

1. Failure to provide supplemental retirement funds.

2. Failure to adjust to income changes.

3. Failure to make a will, or having an outdated will.

4. Subsidizing of adult children.

Launching Adult Children

Until recently, children were expected to leave home upon reaching adulthood or sooner. During the sixteenth century in pre-industrial England, many children left home for school or apprenticeships at the age of six or seven.[11] During that period, seven- and eight-year-old children in France left home to work as servants, and Swiss children of a similar age went to work for weavers.[12] During the seventeenth century, the age of departure from home was more frequently between 10 and 15.[13] Adolescent children in European families between the seventeenth and nineteenth centuries left home much sooner than those in today's families.[14]

Differences in the age of launching children exist between socioeconomic groups as well as between time periods. While social norms generally determine the appropriate launching age,[15] this can vary greatly. For example, one parent may believe that a child of 17 is too young to leave home but a 27-year-old child is way past due. Another parent's rules might dictate that age 22 is the appropriate time for a child to leave home if he or she is not attending college. A child may be considered too young to get married at one age and yet be pressured to get married after reaching another age.

A child's ethnic group and religion can also dictate appropriate ages for leaving home.[16] For example, Hispanics are less likely than non-Hispanics to live independently before marriage, and Asian Americans tend to leave home later than either Hispanics or African Americans. Similarly, children in the United States who regularly attend religious services of some kind are less likely to live independently before marriage.

Research data support the impression that a large portion of today's adult children live with their parents.[17] More than 60 percent of adult children living with their parents are between the ages of 18 and 22, and 25 percent are between 23 and 29. About 90 percent of the 18–22 age group are single (5 percent of these were previously married), while 84 percent of the males and 75 percent of the females in the 23–29 age group are single. The percentage in this category increases in the 23–29 age group to 10.5 percent for men and 17 percent for women. Those who are single but were formerly married represent 33 percent of adult children over age 30 living with their parents.

Similar findings are reported by the Bureau of the Census.[18] In 1970, 47 percent of all children between the ages of 18 and 24 lived in a parent's household. Ten years later (1980) this figure had increased by just one percent, but in only five more years (1985) it had increased to 54 percent, and remained relatively unchanged in 1987. In each of the years chosen for comparison, a greater percentage of males than females were living at home.

Failure to Launch

One reason that children of today leave home at an older age could be financial. The 1970s and 1980s offered extensive financial growth to the "baby boom" parents. Their success enabled them to provide a setting that is difficult for their children to duplicate. The children may be somewhat reluctant to leave the comfortable, parent-financed environment for a less comfortable, self-financed one. "I have it pretty good here at home," they may think. "Nice house, car, laundry service, good food—and I don't have to pay for it. Why in the world would I want to leave?" One of the problems with this perspective is that many parents look forward to life after their children leave home!

But sometimes the reasons adult children do not leave home may not lie entirely with the children. For one thing, when marriages fail, the children sometimes feel obligated to fulfill their parents' emotional needs. The parents develop an emotional dependence on their children while the children maintain their financial dependence on their parents. They each begin to believe they cannot make it on their own, so they fail to develop self-confidence and self-reliance.

Occasionally, families have an implicit rule that a child is *not* to leave home but is to stay with or near the parents. While they may not verbalize such a rule, the siblings seem to know which one of them has inherited the primary responsibility of taking care of the parents. The rest of the children are free to marry and move to whatever part of the country they wish—unless, of course, the family rules tell them not to live too far away.

Sometimes the designated caretaker is allowed to marry but not to move far away, or is allowed to marry but must keep the parents at the top of the priority list. Either of these rules can conflict with the family rules of the caretaker's spouse, which may admonish children to leave their father and mother, set up their own household, and have the spouse as the top priority.

This lack of launching, or delayed launching—whether because of parents' or children's reasons—can have rather far-reaching financial implications for the parents. In previous decades, married couples tended to have their children during their late teens or early twenties. Most of those children would leave home by the time they were 18 or 20 years old, when the parents were in their late thirties or early forties. This left the parents about 25 years to prepare for retirement.

Many of today's married couples—who do not even marry until their mid-twenties—do not have children until their *late* twenties or early thirties. If their children do not leave home until the children's late twenties, then the parents' time—and funds—to prepare for retirement can be cut to fewer than 10 years. In addition, the parents often sustain the rather substantial costs of maintaining or supplementing adult children (those who are still at home as well as those who have moved out) with money that could be diverted to retirement needs.

The Launching Fund

Some families' rules dictate that children should be provided for until they leave home at a certain age but that they should be able to make it on their own after that. Some parents allow their adult children to use an old car until they can afford to buy a new one, but the children's other living expenses are their own responsibility. Some parents provide a *launching fund* to assist their children in reaching a state of self-reliance as soon as possible.

A launching fund helps children leaving home make the transition from financial dependence on their parents to financial independence. For example, a launching fund might help pay for a child's rent over a five-month period. During the first month, the parents pay for all the rent. During the second month, they pay 75 percent of the rent, and their child pays 25 percent. The third month, the parents pay half the rent, the fourth month 25 percent, and by the fifth month, the child pays all of the rent. By providing a progressively less supportive fund, the parents help the child feel less abandoned or "kicked out," and the parents feel that they are helping to support their child as he or she moves into the adult world.

Launching funds can help pay for a college education, specialized vocational training, a new business, moving costs and rent, or the down payment on a new home. These funds can also be used to re-launch adult children who have returned home due to loss of employment, divorce, illness, or such. You can set whatever conditions, restrictions, and guidelines you feel comfortable with to govern the fund's use.

The launching fund can be paid into by the parents alone, by predetermined contributions from all family members, or through a payback agreement whereby each person who uses the fund agrees to reimburse it in a timely and responsible manner. If a child should break the rules, he or she forfeits privileges to use the fund. After the children are all launched, if any money remains, it will be available for the parents' use.

Stage 5: Married or Single, with Children Launched

As the number of people living in the home becomes smaller, income is divided among fewer individuals, and the economic well-being of the remaining family increases. Then, when all of the children have been successfully launched, the income is divided between only two people; and dreams and goals that have been put off "until the children are raised" can finally be realized. For many couples, this opportunity comes just in time, because their income typically starts to decrease in this stage of the life cycle.

Financial tasks associated with Stage 5 are:
1. Providing for future needs of the parents' parents.
2. Analyzing and adjusting estate plans.
3. Providing for future security.
4. Investigating part-time employment.
5. Investigating possible housing adjustments and plans for relocation after retirement.

Common financial mistakes at this stage include:
1. Failure to provide supplemental retirement funds.
2. Failure to adjust to income changes.
3. Failure to make a will, or having an outdated will.
4. Subsidizing adult children.

There was a time when the "empty nest syndrome" described parents who were depressed and devoid of meaning in their lives. This does not seem to be the case in today's families. An ever-increasing number of parents who have launched their children now launch themselves into meaningful and fulfilling endeavors. "Empty nest, full life" is a more accurate description of people in this situation.

Couples are likely to expand both as individuals and in their relationship during this period. Husbands and wives once again experience becoming top priorities in each other's lives. They can concentrate more on their own lives and outside interests than was possible while they were raising children.

Stage 6: Married or Single, Retired

In 1988, almost 13 percent of the population of the United States was over 65; by 2025, almost one in every five will be 65 or older,[19] and the vast majority of these people will be retired. For many of us, the dream of retirement includes being independent enough to do what we want, adventurous and healthy enough to go where we want, and financially secure enough to realize both. But such is not always the case.

Retirement has been defined as the "institutionalized separation of an individual from his or her occupational position, with entitlement to a continuation of income based on prior years of service."[20] To many, retirement is either a time to enjoy the "good life"—or a time to struggle on a fixed income.

Financial tasks associated with Stage 6 are:
1. Adjusting living standards and conditions to retirement income.
2. Adjusting insurance protection.
3. Finalizing estate-transfer plans and letter of last instructions.
4. Beginning to transfer the estate to avoid taxes and fees.
5. Utilizing community and governmental resources.

Common financial mistakes at this stage include:
1. Failure to finance leisure activities.
2. Failure to write letter of last instructions.
3. Failure to recognize interdependency with others.
4. Failure to develop an estate transfer plan.
5. Failure to identify and utilize community resources.
6. Failure to prepare for increased medical costs.
7. Victimization by financial scams.

How Long Will You Live?

One of the unique challenges associated with financial planning for retirement is estimating how long you will live. During the first half of this century, longevity was not a real issue because the average worker was not expected to reach the retirement age of 65. The life expectancy for females was 65.4 in 1940, but the life expectancy for males did not reach 65 until 1950. In 1990, the life expectancy for females had risen to 78 and for males to 72.

To estimate more accurately your life expectancy, you may wish to complete Worksheet 12.1, How Long Will You Live?

How Much Income Will You Need?

Although with the elderly, as with other age groups, income and personal satisfaction are related, a sense of well-being depends on other things as well.[21] Many people with low incomes are quite satisfied with their lives, while some with high incomes are dissatisfied—satisfaction being largely dependent on the concept of *relative deprivation*.[22] Relative deprivation is an interpretation of your well-being compared to that of your peers. You can have a low income but be better off than those around you and feel fairly satisfied. Conversely, if you have a fairly high income but the incomes of those around you are higher, you could feel dissatisfied.

The amount of income you will need in retirement is largely determined by the standard of living you wish to maintain. The U.S. Department of Labor estimates that a retired couple needs 65 to 80 percent of their pre-retirement income to maintain their current standard of living. Income is distributed differently depending on the standard of living (see Table 12.2).

Missions for Retired LDS Couples

Retirement from our obligation to earn money does not necessarily permit us to retire from our obligation to spread the gospel. Many couples heed the prophets' call and plan their retirement around being able to serve missions. President Ezra Taft Benson pointed out:

> There are three great and important obligations, possibly overshadowing all others, which rest upon this people and upon this great Church of Jesus Christ of Latter-day Saints. The first of these, at least in the order of emphasis in this dispensation, is that of missionary work—the responsibility which rests upon this people to carry the message of the restored

TABLE 12.2—ESTIMATED DISTRIBUTION OF RETIREMENT INCOME BY PERCENTAGE

	STANDARD OF LIVING		
ITEM	LOWER	INTERMEDIATE	HIGHER
Food	30.0%	28.0%	24.0%
Housing	33.0	33.0	35.0
Transportation	7.6	10.0	13.0
Clothing	3.3	3.9	4.2
Personal care	2.7	2.8	2.8
Medical care	15.0	10.6	7.2
Recreation, tobacco, and alcohol	3.8	4.4	5.9
Gifts, life insurance	0.3	6.0	7.4

From *Monthly Labor Review* (p. 37–41), by U.S. Department of Labor, Bureau of Labor Statistics, March 1989, Washington, D.C.: U.S. Government Printing Office.

gospel to the people of the world. We have been engaged in that work ever since the Church was organized, yea, even before. . . .

This grand mission of the Church is accomplished by proclaiming the gospel, perfecting the Saints, and redeeming the dead. In each of our homes, may we prayerfully consider specific ways we as families and individuals can accomplish this mission. . . .

As a mature couple, having raised your children, have you prayerfully considered serving a full-time mission? The Lord needs many more couples in the mission field who can love and fellowship and lead people to Christ.[23]

Wills and Estate Transfer

A will enables you to transfer your property to others after your death. A will should do the following:

1. Revoke previous wills.
2. Identify members of your family.
3. Appoint a personal representative.
4. Identify debts, taxes, estate taxes.

5. Provide instructions regarding the distribution of personal belongings.

6. Explain which responsibilities the spouse should assume.

7. Explain how all other responsibilities should be distributed.

8. Include a common disaster clause: what to do if both spouses die simultaneously.

9. Give authority to others to help the spouse deal with taxes and complicated business transactions.

10. Describe the scope of the will, the property it pertains to.

11. Define terms such as *children:* Do you mean all descendants, only natural children, adopted children?

12. Include a severability clause: If part of the will is unenforceable, the rest is still valid.

13. Specify whether inheritances are to be divided among grandchildren on a per capita basis or on the basis of their parent's share.

14. Appoint guardians for dependent children.

15. Provide living will instructions, answer life-support questions.

If you should die *intestate*—that is, without a will—your state's intestate laws will distribute the resources of your estate as prescribed in the state code. A will, however, does not avoid *probate*, the legal process in which the state transfers property; property referred to in a will is still subject to probate. You can avoid probate for your heirs, saving them time and money, if you make arrangements for your property to transfer automatically upon your death. Such a transfer can take place in three ways: *joint ownership, incomplete transfers,* and *revokable living trusts.*

Joint ownership. A couple own real estate jointly if they own the property as joint tenants. Cars are owned jointly if both names appear on the title, as are any bank accounts that have both names on them.

Incomplete transfers. In an incomplete transfer, you transfer property to a child, but you retain the right to revoke the transfer if you desire. For example, you might transfer ownership of your home to your child, with the understanding that you will live there rent-free until you die. It is a legal and literal transfer, and your child must pay the taxes. But the right to revoke the transfer provides protection against unscrupulous offspring who might decide they need the equity in your house more than you do and try to sell the property before you are finished using it. An incomplete transfer is revokable as long as you are alive; however, upon your death the property automatically transfers to whomever has been named on the deed.

Revokable living trust. A revokable living trust functions as an incomplete transfer does, except that it applies to non-real-estate assets. A revokable living trust is set up prior to your death. Details identifying specific assets and the trustee who will act as executor are included in your will. When you use a revokable living trust, you still have to pay taxes on the property while you are living, but upon your death the trust will automatically transfer.

Summary

Various financial challenges are associated with the different stages of the life cycle. The stages, differentiated by age, marital status, and average income, are characterized by certain behaviors, responsibilities, and errors. Realizing that we will face different issues at different points in our lives helps us prepare for and adapt to changes in our family structure and our financial obligations. The costs of raising and launching children, the impact of divorce, and providing for retirement need to be understood and carefully evaluated. The more information we have, and the better we prepare, the greater will be our peace of mind when life's changes come upon us.

Important Terms

Family life cycle: Series of stages through which a family passes during its lifetime.

Fifty/fifty agreement: Agreement that the parents will pay half the cost of an item if the child will pay for the other half; a dollar-for-dollar matching agreement.

Incomplete transfer: Property is transferred to a child, but the right to revoke the transfer is retained.

Installment credit: Credit that involves a schedule of repayment arranged when the credit is approved.

Joint ownership: When a couple own real estate as joint tenants; cars are owned jointly if both spouses' names appear on the title, as are any bank accounts that have both names on them.

Launching fund: Monies made available to help children leaving home make the transition from financial dependence on their parents to financial independence.

Open-ended credit: Credit subject to a pre-approved limit that gives the consumer flexible terms of repayments.

Probate: Legal process in which the state transfers property.

Revokable living trust: Trust that functions as an incomplete transfer does, except that it applies to non-real estate assets.

Notes

1. American Council on Life Insurance, 1970.

2. U.S. Department of Commerce, 1994c, p. 474.

3. Kimball, 1974, p. 263.

4. Kimball, 1980, p. 8.

5. U.S. Department of Commerce, 1990a.

6. Norton and Moorman, 1987.

7. U.S. Department of Agriculture, 1992.

8. Facing up to the high cost of kids, 1983.

9. Benson, 1988, p. 540.

10. Facing up to the high cost of kids, 1983.

11. Illick, 1974.

12. Shorter, 1975.

13. Illick, 1974; Wall, 1978.

14. Shorter, 1975.

15. Elder, 1974.

16. Goldscheider, 1988.

17. Grigsby and McGowan, 1986.

18. U.S. Department of Commerce, 1990a.

19. Euzeby, 1989.

20. Atchley, 1988.

21. Russell, 1990.

22. Liang and Doherty, 1980; Liang and Fairchild, 1979.

23. Benson, 1988, pp. 175, 178.

HOW LONG WILL YOU LIVE?

Start with the number 72.

Personal Facts:

If you are male, subtract 3.

If female, add 4.

If you live in an urban area with a population over 2 million, subtract 2.

If you live in a town under 10,000 or on a farm, add 2.

If any grandparent lived to 85, add 2.

If all four grandparents lived to 80, add 6.

If either parent died of a stroke or heart attack before the age of 50, subtract 4.

If any parent, brother, or sister under 50 has (or had) cancer or a heart condition, or has had diabetes since childhood, subtract 3.

If you earn at least $50,000 a year, subtract 2.

If you finished college, add 1. If you have a graduate or professional degree, add 2 more.

If you are 65 or over and are still working, add 3.

If you live with a spouse or friend, add 5. If not, subtract 1 for every ten years alone since age 25.

Lifestyle Status:

If you work behind a desk, subtract 3.

If your work requires regular, heavy physical labor, add 3.

If you exercise strenuously five times a week for at least half an hour, add 4. If two or three times a week, add 2.

If you sleep more than ten hours each night, subtract 4.

If you are intense, aggressive, or easily angered, subtract 3.

If you are easygoing and relaxed, add 3.

If you are happy, add 1. If unhappy, subtract 2.

If you have had a speeding ticket in the past year, subtract 1.

If you smoke more than two packs a day, subtract 8; if one to two packs, subtract 6; if half to one, subtract 3.

If you drink the equivalent of one and one-half ounces of liquor a day, subtract 1.

If you are overweight by 50 pounds or more, subtract 8; if by 30 to 50 pounds, subtract 4; if by 10 to 30 pounds, subtract 2.

If you are a man over 40 and have annual checkups, add 2.

If you are a woman and see a gynecologist once a year, add 2.

Running Total _____

Age Adjustment

If you are between 30 and 40, add 2.

If you are between 40 and 50, add 3.

If you are between 50 and 70, add 4.

If you are over 70, add 5.

Add up your score to arrive at your life expectancy.

Total (Your Life Expectancy) _____

From: Robert R. Allen with Shirley Linde, Lifegain, 1981, Englewood Cliffs, New Jersey: Appleton Books.

The Ten Financial Principles

Principle 1: Financial problems are usually behavior problems rather than money problems.

Principle 2: If you continue doing what you have been doing, you will continue getting what you have been getting.

Principle 3: Nothing (no thing) is worth risking the relationship for.

Principle 4: Money spent on things you value usually leads to a feeling of satisfaction and accomplishment. Money spent on things you do not value usually leads to a feeling of frustration and futility.

Principle 5: We know the price of everything and the value of nothing.

Principle 6: You can never get enough of what you don't need, because what you don't need can never satisfy you.

Principle 7: Financial freedom is more often the result of decreased spending than of increased income.

Principle 8: Be grateful for what you have.

Principle 9: The best things in life are free.

Principle 10: The value of an individual should never be equated with the individual's net worth.

References

Abdel-Ghany, M., and Nickols, S. (1983). Husband/wife differentials in household work time: The case of dual-earner families. *Home Economics Research Journal*, 12:159–67.

Adler, A. (1927). *The practice and theory of individual psychology*. New York: Harcourt, Brace and World.

Alamshah, W. (1963). *The pursuit of excellence*. Unpublished essay, University of California at Fullerton.

Albrecht, S. L. (1979). Correlates of marital happiness among the remarried. *Journal of Marriage and the Family*, 41:857–67.

Albrecht, S. L., Bahr, H. M., and Goodman, K. (1983). *Divorce and remarriage: Problems, adaptations, and adjustments*. Westport, CT: Greenwood Press.

Allen, R. R., and Linde, S. (1981). *Lifegain*. Englewood Cliffs, NJ: Appleton Books.

Altus, W. D. (1966). Birth order and achievement. *Science*, 152:1177–84.

American Council on Life Insurance. (1970). *Adult financial management matrix*. Poster, 1850 K Street, N.W., Washington, D.C.

Aquinas, T. (1952). Summa theologica. In *Saint Thomas Aquinas, Great Books of the Western World*. New York: Encyclopedia Britannica, Inc.

Aristotle (1952). Politics. In *Aristotle, Great Books of the Western World*. New York: Encyclopedia Britannica.

Ashton, M. J. (1975). One for the money. *Ensign*, July:72–73.

Atchley, R. (1988). *Social forces and aging: An introduction to social gerontology*. Belmont, CA: Wadsworth.

REFERENCES

Bader, E. (1981). Do marriage preparation programs really help? Paper presented at the annual conference of the National Council of Family Relations, Milwaukee, Wisconsin.

Benenson, H. (1984). Women's occupational and family achievement in the U.S. *British Journal of Sociology,* 35:19–41.

Benson, E. T. (1988). *Teachings of Ezra Taft Benson.* Salt Lake City: Bookcraft Publishing.

Berardo, D. H., Sherhan, C. L., and Leslie, G. R. (1987). A residue of tradition: Jobs, careers, and spouses' time in housework. *Journal of Marriage and the Family,* 49:381–90.

Berger, P. K., and Ivancevich, J. M. (1973). Birth order and managerial achievement. *Academy of Management Journal,* 16:515–19.

Bernard, H., and Huckins, W. (1975). *Dynamics of personal adjustment.* Boston: Holbrook Press.

Blood, R. O., and Wolfe, D. M. (1973). Husbands and wives. In R. E. Bell (Ed.), *Studies in marriage and family therapy.* New York: Thomas Y. Crowell.

Blumstein, P., and Schwartz, P. (1983). *American couples: Money, work, sex.* New York: William Morrow.

Bornemann, E. (1976). *The psychoanalysis of money.* New York: Urizen Books.

Campbell, A., Converse, P. E., and Rodgers, W. L. (1976). *The quality of American life.* New York: Russell Sage Foundation.

Canner, G., and Cyrnak, A. W. (1985). Recent developments in credit card holding and use patterns among U. S. families. *Journal of Retail Banking,* 3:63–73.

Cherlin, A. (1981). *Marriage, divorce, and remarriage.* Cambridge, MA: Harvard University Press.

Coleman, M., and Ganong, L. N. (1985). Remarriage myths: Implications for the helping professions. *Journal of Counseling and Development,* 64:116–20.

Corey, G., and Corey, M. S. (1990). *I never knew I had a choice* (4th ed.). Pacific Grove, CA: Brooks/Cole.

D'Amico, R. (1983). Status maintenance or status competition? Wife's relative wages as a determinant of labor supply and marital instability. *Social Forces,* 61:1186–1205.

Davis, E. P., and Helmick, S. A. (1983). Composite measures of financial satisfaction: An analysis of two indices. In M. M. Dunsing (Ed.), *Proceedings of the Midwest Symposium on Perceived Economic Well-Being* (27–39). Urbana, IL: Illinois Agricultural Experiment Station, University of Illinois.

Eckstein, D., Baruth, L., and Mahrer, D. (1978). *Life style: What it is and how to do it.* Dubuque, IA: Kendall/Hunt.

Edmondson, M. E., and Pasley, K. (1986). Financial counseling attitudes and interests: An exploratory study of remarried individuals. In K. Kitt (Ed.), *Quality control in an emerging profession: Proceedings of the Association for Financial Counseling and Planning Educators annual conference* (1–10). Austin, TX: University of Texas, University Press.

Eggebeen, D. J., and Hawkins, A. J. (1990). Economic need and wives' employment. *Journal of Family Issues,* 11:48–66.

Elder, G. H., Jr. (1974). Age differentiation and the life course. In A. Inkeles (Ed.), *Annual Review of Sociology, 1975,* 1:165–90.

Euzeby, C. (1989). Noncontributory old age pensions: A possible solution in OECD countries. *International Labor Review,* 128:11–28.

Facing up to the high cost of kids. (1983). *Changing Times,* Apr.: 28–31.

Fishman, B. (1983). The economic behavior of stepfamilies. *Family Relations,* 32:359–66.

Foa, U. (1971). Interpersonal and economic resources. *Science,* 29 Jan.:345–51.

Fox, M. F., and Hesse-Biber, S. (1984). *Women at Work.* Palo Alto, CA: Mayfield.

Fromm, E. (1955). *The sane society.* New York: Holt, Rinehart.

———. (1970). *The art of loving.* New York: Harper and Row.

Freud, S. (1913). On beginning the treatment. In J. Strachey (Ed. and Trans.), *The standard edition of the complete psychological works of Sigmund Freud.* (Vol. 1). London: Hogarth Press.

Galligan, R., and Bahr, S. (1978). Economic well-being and marital stability: Implications for income maintenance programs. *Journal of Marriage and the Family,* 40:283–90.

Ganong, L. H., and Coleman, M. (1989). Preparing for remarriage: Anticipating the issues, seeking solutions. *Family Relations,* 28:28–33.

General Mills. (1975). *The General Mills American family report, 1974–75; A study of the American family and money.* Minneapolis: General Mills.

Glick, P. (1989). Remarried families, stepfamilies, and stepchildren: A brief demographic profile. *Family Relations,* 38:24–27.

Glickauf-Hughes, C. L., Hughes, G. B., and Wells, M. C. (1986). A developmental approach to treating dual-career couples. *American Journal of Family Therapy,* 14:254–63.

Goldscheider, C., and Goldscheider, F. K. (1988). Ethnicity, religiosity, and cultural bases of traditional family values. *Sociological Forum,* 3:525–47.

REFERENCES

Grigsby, J. and McGowan, J. B. (1986). Still in the nest: Adult children living with their parents. *Sociology and Social Research,* 71: 146–48.

Hafstrom, J. L., and Dunsing, M. M. (1983). Level of living: Factors influencing homemakers' satisfaction. *Home Economics Research Journal,* 2:119–32.

Hanson, S. L. (1991). The economic costs and rewards of two-earner, two-parent families. *Journal of Marriage and the Family,* 53:622–34.

Heath, D. (1986). *America in perspective.* Boston: Houghton Mifflin.

Hefferan, C. (1978). Pros and cons of whether wives should work. *U. S. News & World Report,* 27 Nov.: 82–83.

Henley, W. E. (1978). Invictus. In S. Honor and T. Hunt, *Philosophy.* Belmont, CA: Wadsworth.

Hiller, D., and Philliber, W. (1986). The division of labor in contemporary marriage: Expectations, perceptions, and performance. *Social Problems,* 33:191–201.

Hinckley, G. B. (1980). Address. In *Conference Report,* Oct. Salt Lake City: The Church of Jesus Christ of Latter-day Saints.

Hogan, J., and Bauer, J. (1988). Problems in family financial management. In C. S. Chilman, F. M. Cox, and E. W. Nunnally (Eds.), *Employment and economic problems* (137–53). Beverly Hills, CA: Sage Publications.

Holmes, O. W. (1858). *The autocrat of the breakfast table.* Boston: Phillips, Sampson, and Company.

Hornung, C. A., and McCullough, B. C. (1981). Status relationships in dual-employment marriages: Consequences for psychological well-being. *Journal of Marriage and the Family,* 43:125–41.

Hudson, V. (1990). Birth order of world leaders: An exploratory analysis of effects on personality and behavior. *Political Psychology,* 11:583–601.

Ihinger-Tallman, M., and Pasley, K. (1981). *Factors influencing stability in remarriage.* Paper presented at the annual meetings of the International Sociological Association, Leuven, Belgium.

Ilfeld, F. W. (1982). Marital stressors, coping styles, and symptoms of depression. In L. Goldberger and S. Bregnitz (Eds.) *Handbook of Stress* (303–50). New York: Psychohistory Press.

Illick, J. E. (1974). Children in seventeenth century England and America. In L. de Mause (Ed.), *The history of childhood* (pp. 303–50). New York: Psychohistory Press.

James, W. (1890). *The principles of psychology.* (Vol. 1). New York: Holt.

———. (1956). *The will to believe*. New York: Dover.

Jarvis, I. (1971). *Stress and frustration*. New York: Harcourt Brace.

Jensen, L., and Jensen, J. (1981). *Stepping into stepparenting: A practical guide*. Palo Alto, CA: R & E Research Associates.

Jourard, S. (1971). *The transparent self*. Princeton, NJ: Van Nostrand.

Kamo, L. (1988). Determinants of household division of labor. *Journal of Family Issues*, 9:177–200.

Kant, I. (1982). *Critique of pure reason*. Aalen, Germany: Scientia.

Kimball, S. W. (1969). *The miracle of forgiveness*. Salt Lake City: Deseret Book Company.

———. (1972). *Faith precedes the miracle*. Salt Lake City: Deseret Book Company.

———. (1974). Marriage is honorable. In *1973 Speeches of the Year*. Provo, UT: Brigham Young University.

———. (1977). Address at LDS fireside. San Antonio, TX. In E. T. Benson (1988). *Teachings of Ezra Taft Benson*. Salt Lake City: Bookcraft Publishing, p. 514.

———. (1980). *Marriage*. Salt Lake City: Deseret Book Company.

———. (1982). *Teachings of Spencer W. Kimball*. Salt Lake City: Bookcraft Publishing.

Kohlberg, L. (1963). The development of children's orientations toward a moral order: Sequence in the development of moral thought. *Vita Humana*, 6:11–33.

———. (1969). Stages and sequence: The cognitive-developmental approach to socialization. In C. A. Goslin (Ed.), *Handbook of socialization theory and research* (374–80). Chicago: Rand McNally.

Krueger, D. (1986). *The last taboo*. New York: Brunner/Mazel.

Lewin, K. (1935). *A dynamic theory of personality*. New York: McGraw-Hill.

Liang, J., and Doherty, E. (1980). Financial well-being among the aged: A further elaboration. *Journal of Gerontology*, 35:409–20.

Liang, J., and Fairchild, T. J. (1979). Relative deprivation and perception of financial adequacy among the aged. *Journal of Gerontology*, 34:746–59.

Lino, M. (1988). Financial status of single-parent households. *Family Economics Review*, 2:2–7.

Ludwig, T. E., and Myers, D. G. (1979). How Christians can cope with inflation: Get off the hedonic treadmill. *Christian Century*, 96:609–13.

Maxwell, N. A. (1970). *For the power is in them*. Salt Lake City: Deseret Book Company.

———. (1979). *All these things shall give thee experience*. Salt Lake City: Deseret Book Company.

———. (1990). *A wonderful flood of light*. Salt Lake City: Bookcraft Publishing.

McConkie, B. R. (1966). *Mormon doctrine*, 2nd ed. Salt Lake City: Bookcraft Publishing.

McCrae, S. (1987). Allocation of money in cross-class families. *Sociological Review*, 35:97–122.

McKay, D. O. (1965). Unpublished manuscript sheet in author's personal file.

———. (1976). *Gospel ideals*. Salt Lake City: Deseret Book Company.

Messinger, L. (1976). Remarriage between divorced people with children from previous marriages: A proposal for preparation for remarriage. *Journal of Marriage and Family Counseling*, 2:193–200.

Moore, K., and Hofferth, S. (1979). Effects of women's employment on marriage: Formation, stability, and roles. In *Marriage and Family Review*, 2:27–36.

Mueller, M. J., and Hira, T. K. (1984). Impact of money management practices on household solvency status. In K. P. Goebel (Ed.), *Proceedings of the American Council on Consumer Interests annual conference* (76–79). Columbia, MO: University of Missouri Press.

Nibley, H. (1989). *Approaching Zion*. Salt Lake City: Deseret Book Company, and Provo, UT: Foundation for Ancient Research and Mormon Studies.

Norton, A. J., and Moorman, J. E. (1987). Current trends in marriage and divorce among American women. *Journal of Marriage and the Family*, 49:3–14.

Nye, F. I., and Hoffman, L. W. (1974). *Working mothers*. San Francisco: Jossey-Bass.

Orthner, D. (1990). Parental work and early adolescence: Issues for research and practice. *Journal of Early Adolescence*, 10:246–59.

Pahl, J. (1983). The allocation of money and the structuring of inequality within marriage. *Sociological Review*, 31:237–62.

———. (1990). Household spending, personal spending, and the control of money in marriage. *Sociology*, 24:119–38.

Pasley, K. (1987). Family boundary ambiguity: Perceptions of adult remarried family members. In K. Pasley and M. Ihinger-Tallman (Eds.), *Remarriage and stepparenting: Current research and theory* (206–24). New York: Guilford Press.

Pasley, K., and Ihinger-Tallman, M. (1982). Stress in remarried families. *Family Perspectives*, 16:181–90.

Peck, M. S. (1978). *The road less traveled*. New York: Touchstone Book.

Poduska, B. E. (1985). Financial counseling using principles of Adlerian psychology. *Individual Psychologist: The Journal of Adlerian Theory, Research, and Practice*, 41:136–46.

———. (1987). Negotiating skills for financial counselors and planners. Paper presented at the meeting of the Association of Financial Counseling and Planning Educators, Oct., Atlanta, Georgia.

———. (1989). Crisis counseling. *Journal of Financial Planning*, 2:114–19.

———. (1991). Forgiveness in marriage. *Ensign*, June: 26–27. Used by permission.

Poduska, B. E., and Allred, G. H. (1987). *Personal financial management and birth order.* Unpublished manuscript, Brigham Young University, Provo, Utah.

Price-Bonham, S., and Murphy, D. C. (1980). Dual-career marriages: Implications for the clinician. *Journal of Marital and Family Therapy*, 6:181–88.

Rapoport, R., and Rapoport, R. (1969). The dual-career family. *Human Relations*, 22:3–30.

———. (1971). The dual-career family: A variant pattern and social change. In C. Safilios-Rothschild (Ed.), *Toward a Sociology of Women* (128–47), Lexington, MA: Xerox.

———. (1976). *Dual-career families reexamined.* New York: Harper and Row.

Rector, R. (1989). Fourteen myths about families and child care. *Harvard Journal on Legislation*, 26:517–45.

Reeves, J. (1983). Financial counseling from a behavioral perspective. Paper presented at the conference of the International Association for Financial Counseling, Oct., Provo, Utah.

Rejda, G. (1982). *Principles of insurance.* London: Scott, Foresman and Company.

Russell, R. (1990). Recreation and quality of life in old age. *Journal of Applied Gerontology*, 9:77–90.

Schaninger, C. M., and Buss, W. C. (1986). A longitudinal comparison of consumption and finance handling between happily married and divorced couples. *Journal of Marriage and the Family*, 48:129–36.

Shehan, C. L. (1984). Wives' work and psychological well-being: An extension of Gove's social role theory of depression. *Sex Roles*, 11:881–89.

Shorter, E. (1975). *The making of the modern family.* New York: Basic Books.

Smith, J. F. (1977). *Gospel doctrine.* Salt Lake City: Deseret Book Company.

Smith, R. E. (1979). *The subtle revolution: Women at work.* Washington, D.C.: Urban Institute.

Snow, L. (1984). *Teachings of Lorenzo Snow.* Salt Lake City: Bookcraft Publishing.

South, S., and Spitze, G. (1986). Determinants of divorce over the marital life course. *American Sociological Review*, 51:583–90.

Spitze, G., and South, S. (1985). Women's employment, time expenditure, and divorce. *Journal of Family Issues*, 8:307–29.

Steggell, G. L., Allred, G. H., Harper, J. M., and Poduska, B. E. (1990). Influence of spouses' birth order on couple's income and expenditure patterns. Unpublished dissertation, Brigham Young University, Provo, Utah.

Taeber, C., and Valdisera, V. (1986). *Women in the American economy, current population reports.* Bureau of the Census Series P-23, No. 146, Washington, D.C.: U.S. Government Printing Office.

Thomas, S., Albrecht, K., and White, P. (1984). Determinants of marital quality in dual-career couples. *Family Relations*, 33:513–21.

Troelstrup, A. W. (1974). *The consumer in American society: Personal and family finance.* New York: McGraw-Hill.

U.S. Department of Agriculture. (1992). Updated estimates of the cost of raising a child. *Family Economics Review*, 5(1):54.

U.S. Department of Commerce, Bureau of the Census. (1980). *Household and family, by type: Advance Report.* Series P-20, No. 375. Washington, D.C.: U.S. Government Printing Office.

———. (1990a). *Statistical abstract of the United States, 1990.* Washington, D.C.: U.S. Government Printing Office.

———. (1990c). *Child support and alimony: 1987.* Series P-23, No. 167. Washington, D.C.: U.S. Government Printing Office.

———. (1991a). Employed civilians by occupation, sex, race, and Hispanic origin in 1983 and 1989. *Statistical abstract of the United States, 1991*, 652:395. Washington, D.C.: U.S. Government Printing Office.

———. (1991c). *Poverty in the United States, 1990.* Washington, D.C.: U.S. Government Printing Office.

———. (1994, 1994b, 1994c). *Statistical abstract of the United States, 1994.* Washington, D.C.: U.S. Government Printing Office.

U.S. Department of Commerce, Bureau of Economic Analysis. (1990b). *The national income and product accounts of the United States, 1929–82.* Washington, D.C.: U.S. Government Printing Office.

U.S. Department of Energy, Energy Information Administration. (1986). *Residential energy survey: Housing characteristics, 1984.* Washington, D.C.: U.S. Government Printing Office.

U.S. Department of Health and Human Services. (1990). *Alcohol and health. Special report to the U.S. Congress.* Washington, D.C.: U.S. Government Printing Office.

U.S. Department of Labor, Bureau of Labor Statistics. (1989). *Monthly Labor Review,* 112:37–41.

Vickery, C. (1979). Women's economic contribution to the family. In R. E. Smith (Ed.), *The subtle revolution: Women at work* (159–200). Washington, D.C.: Urban Institute.

Wall, R. (1978). The age at leaving home. *Journal of Family History,* 3:181–202.

Watzlawick, P., Weakland, J., and Fisch, R. (1974). *Change: Principles of problem formation and problem resolution.* New York: Norton.

White, L. (1990). Determinants of divorce: A review of research in the eighties. *Journal of Marriage and the Family,* 52:904–12.

White, L., and Booth, A. (1985). The quality and stability of remarriages: The role of stepchildren. *American Sociological Review,* 50:689–98.

Wilhelm, M. S., Iams, D. R., and Ridley, C. A. (1987). Unemployment and marital well-being: The impact of changes in financial management. In M. Edmondson and L. Perch (Eds.), *Accenting our focus on competing professional enrichment: Proceedings of the Association for Financial Counseling and Planning Educators annual conference.* Lexington, KY: University of Kentucky, University Press.

Williams, F. (1985). Family and personal resource management as affecting quality of life. *Thinking globally—Acting locally.* Washington, D.C.: American Home Economics Association.

Williams, F., Nall, M., and Deck, P. (1976). Financial problems of urban families. *Home Economics Research Journal,* 4:195–96.

Yankelovich, Skelly, and White, Inc. (1975). *The General Mills American family report, 1974–75.* Minneapolis: General Mills Consumer Center.

Yeh, B., and Lester, D. (1987). Statewide divorce rates and wives' participation in the labor market. *Journal of Divorce,* 11:107–14.

———. (1988). Wives who work full-time and part-time: Correlates over the states of the U.S.A. *Psychological Reports,* 62:545–46.

Yogev, S., and Brett, J. (1985). Perceptions of the division of housework and child care and marital satisfaction. *Journal of Marriage and the Family,* 47:609–18.

Young, B. (1864). Address. In *Journal of Discourses* 10:329.

———. (1954). *Discourses of Brigham Young.* Salt Lake City: Deseret Book Company.

Index